FRENCH ENTRÉE 13

PROVENCE

A Gatwick *Eat and Sleep* Guide

Peter King

Series Editor: Patricia Fenn

Quiller Press

G000024089

First published 1993 by Quiller Press Ltd
46 Lillie Road, London SW6 1TN

Copyright © 1993 Text: Peter King
Illustrations and maps © 1993 Quiller Press Ltd
Wine Section text: © 1993 John Doxat

Line Drawings: Emma Macleod-Johnstone
Area Maps: Helen Humphreys
Front cover: Sue Bailey

ISBN 1-870948 84 X

Photoset by Townsend Typesetter Ltd, Worcester

Printed and bound by Firmin-Didot (France)
Groupe Hérissey - N° d'impression 23447

Contents

Notes on using the book – and an appeal

1 The area maps are to help the reader to find the place he wishes to visit on his own map. Each place is given a reference on the relevant area map, but they are not designed to replace a good touring map.

2 A number in brackets at the beginning of a telephone number is the area dialling code, used when making calls from outside the area.

3 o.o.s. stands for 'out of season'. Other abbreviations such as f for francs, are standard.

4 L, M or S in the margin stand for 'L' = Luxury, 'S' = Simple and 'M' for those in between.

5 H stands for Hotel and R for Restaurant in combination with 4 above, ie (H)S, (R)L etc.

6 stc means service and taxes are included (service et taxes compris).

7 The ➤ symbol means the establishment fulfils exceptionally well at least one of the author's criteria of comfort, welcome and cuisine – see also page 41.

8 P. stands for parking, (T) for Tourist Office and (M) for market day.

9 Credit cards: A = Access, AE = American Express, V = Visa, DC = Diners Club, EC is Eurocard and CB = Carte Bleue.

10 Prices represent a room for two people, except for demi-pension, which is per head.

11 The numbers with the addresses, eg. 62000, are the postal codes, which should be used in all correspondence.

Author's appeal
In order to keep French Entrée up to date I need all the latest information I can get on establishments listed in the guide. If you have any comments on these or any other details that might supplement my own researching I should be most grateful if you would pass them on.

Please include the name and address of establishment, date and duration of visit. Also please state if you will allow your name to be used.

Patricia Fenn,
c/o Quiller Press
46 Lillie Road
London SW6 ITN

FOREWORD

The warm and relaxed region of Provence is fast becoming a holiday favourite. And here at London's Gatwick Airport we're pleased to help thousands on their way there every year.

London Gatwick has strong links with the region, offering flights to Marseilles, Montpellier and Lourdes. These are just three of the many destinations in France served by the airport.

Now we're strengthening our links further by supporting *Entrée to Provence,* an essential piece of holiday packing for those bound for this beautiful region.

Working with our airlines and airport-based companies, we aim to ensure travellers receive as warm a welcome at the airport as they find at their final destination.

These days air travel knows no bounds and, there's no doubt about it, flying remains the most exciting way to start a holiday. Our task here at London Gatwick and all our 'sister' BAA airports is to give our passengers the best possible service from check-in to take-off. And when it's time to fly home we aim to provide a smooth and efficient end to the journey.

At London Gatwick we have always been at the forefront of passenger aviation and have earned our place as one of the world's busiest international airports, handling around 20 million leisure and business travellers a year.

We aim to give passengers the best possible start to their trip to Provence and, aided by this Entrée guide, we're sure their holidays will go on to be an all-round success.

Allan Munds
Managing Director
Gatwick Airport Ltd.

INTRODUCTION

Provence is many lands. It is the snow-covered Alps of Haute Provence and it is the golden beaches of the Riviera coast. It is history from the Greeks and the Romans, the invasions of the North African barbarians, to the Knights Templars of the Middle Ages and the excesses of the religious wars and the Revolution. It is architecture from Roman cities, bridges, viaducts and amphitheatres to Crusaders' castles, Napoleonic fortifications and the Maginot Line. It is lavender, honey, truffles, garlic, olives, fennel, basil and thyme.

It is holiday country without comparison. Whether you want to ski, swim, dive, sail, fly, climb, fish, golf, hike or sightsee, you have a vast choice in Provence. You could even do all of them in one day.

You can wallow in luxury at 3,000 francs a day or you can stay in a home which is part of a centuries-old building and with modern comfort, for 200 francs. You can taste wines at a dozen vineyards before lunch if you have the stomach for it.

Provence is a land of art and letters. Matisse, Renoir, Cézanne and Van Gogh lived and painted here; you can see studios which are as they left them and visit their homes. You can see the village virtually established by Picasso.

Writers such as de Maupassant, Somerset Maugham, Scott Fitzgerald, Lord Tennyson, Chekhov, Aldous Huxley, Zola, Pagnol, Tolstoi, H. G. Wells, Alexandre Dumas and Robert Louis Stevenson have lived and worked here. Musicians from Berlioz, Offenbach and Gounod to Saint Saëns, Bizet, Massenet and Paganini have composed here.

You can follow the Rhône, river of history, overflowing with sorrow, joy and passion as it passes castles, vineyards and the place where Hannibal rafted his elephants across the waters. You can follow the coast, stopping to visit the castles which held prisoner the Man in the Iron Mask and the Count of Monte Cristo. You can see the spot where Napoleon came ashore to raise a new army after exile on Elba and not far from it the site where the first motion picture was shown. Nearby too is the church established where the three Marys came from Palestine after the Ascension.

In the marshy flatlands of the Camargue, you will have difficulty deciding where water begins and land ends and you will see pink flamingoes, black bulls and small white horses. In the streams and rivers of Provence, you can catch fat trout and you may see chamois, wild boar and mountain goats.

Provence is a land of perched villages – often communities of less than a thousand people, centuries-old houses and narrow crooked streets paved with cobblestones, all huddled around a thousand-year-old castle, with views as far as the sparkling blue Mediterranean.

Vaucluse is unsurpassed in the beauty of its landscape and its tourist sights are staged from sea level up to 2,000 metres altitude. Fontaine-de-Vaucluse is a source of mystery – and a source of 40,000 gallons of water a second, while Roussillon is famed for its blood-red cliffs, stained by 17 different shades of ochre deposits. Spectacular Mont Ventoux has views as far as the island of Corsica and still brings pilgrims just as it has brought barons and kings in the past. Avignon has its Palace of the Popes which defied the power of Rome for half a century.

For many years, Vaucluse was the crossroads between Spain and Italy and the land contains numerous reminders of this in

Val de Cuech: Abbaye de Sainte Croix

Roman remains, milestones, wells and places named after Caesar. Today, it offers many strange sights too – 'bories', beehive-shaped stone huts put up without mortar; the Dentelles de Montmirail, jagged-toothed white limestone peaks which claw into the intense blue sky; and the Lubéron, a national park region where eagles and vultures soar, where at night you can hear the cry of the great horned owl, where beavers build colonies in the rivers and where giant grasshoppers and the biggest lizards in Europe scamper through the scrubby grasslands.

Provence is a land of castles. The village which does not have at least one is impoverished indeed. The castles range from grim fortresses with arrow slits, battlements and deep dungeons such as that at Le Barroux, to châteaux, built (or re-built) as gracious homes designed for luxury living such as those at Lourmarin and Buoux. At Ansouis, the castle has been in the hands of the same family for almost a thousand years while on the Rhône, the magnificent castles of Tarascon and Beaucaire glare at each other across the river as they have for centuries.

There are few towns in Provence – but countless villages. Many are deserted, some laid waste by the Saracens, some devastated by the Black Plague and some which lost their livelihood so that all the young men moved away. Oppede was a deserted village but now it has been brought back to life. Crillon-le-Brave seems to exist mainly because of a famous hostellerie while Lacoste survives on the lurid memories of its one-time seigneur – the infamous Marquis de Sade.

But if one theme has to typify Provence more than any other then surely it is legend. Its mountains, its rivers, its plains and its villages – even its dreaded Mistral – all are wreathed in legend and wrapped in folklore. Strange beasts such as the Tarasque which crawled out of the Rhône to snatch children, and mysterious beings who live in the tunnel-ridden rock beneath Les Baux, one of the most haunted places in the world; the golden treasure of the alchemist-Pope John XXII, still hidden in the palace at Avignon and the Black Virgin, revered by gypsies; undecipherable rock drawings and the Barbarotto, like a gargantuan snail; miracles galore including that performed by St. Eloi, patron of many a village and the blacksmith who chopped the leg off a mule then put it back into place – all contribute to the magic. There are even legends about a soldier who came from Africa to march against Rome with an army of monster elephants … leaving several signs of his passage through Provence. Or so they say…

THE CUISINE OF PROVENCE

Provençal dishes are piquant, aromatic and colourful and reflect the joy of living in the Mediterranean region. Olive oil, tomatoes, onions, garlic and herbs (thyme, parsley, rosemary, sage, basil) are the main ingredients in almost all the specialities produced here.

An apéritif is usually accompanied by green or black olives à la pichouline or canapés of tapenade (a black paste of capers, black olives and anchovies). Aigo-boulido (garlic and cabbage soup), aigo-saou (fish, cabbage and tomato soup) and soupe au pistou (vegetable soup flavoured with basil) are all popular.

Salade niçoise, to be authentic, should contain tomatoes, eggs, anchovies, cucumber, green pepper, spring onions, broad beans, artichokes and olives. Today it usually contains tuna and even potatoes.

Meat is usually cooked in its own juices like daube (a rich beef stew), pieds et paquets marseillais (sheep's feet and stuffed tripe with garlic and parsley). Provençal chicken dishes are variants of chicken sautéed with tomatoes and onions. Vegetable dishes are tomatoes à la Provençale, fried aubergines, sea-kale beet au gratin, stuffed courgettes. The influence of neighbouring Italy is strong on Provençal cooking and pasta is very frequently seen – ravioli, canneloni, spaghetti and cappelletti.

Pizza reigns in the fast-food market. Pissaladière is onion flan garnished with olives and anchovies. Pan-bagnat is a special, flat round loaf, sliced across and rubbed with garlic, sprinkled with lots of olive oil and a little vinegar then filled with salade niçoise and the top replaced.

Ratatouille and anchoïade (anchovy paste) are popular in Provence while aïoli is an indispensable part of a village feast. It is like mayonnaise heavily flavoured with garlic and is eaten with cold white fish, new potatoes and salad.

It is fish from the Mediterranean though which is the principal feature of the food of Provence. Rouget (red mullet), merlan (hake), loup (sea-bass), pageot (sea bream) and perch may be grilled with fennel or flavoured with rosemary. Shellfish abound in the warm waters – palourdes (clams), pétoncles (small scallops), gambas (giant prawns), moules (mussels), oursins (sea urchins) as well as crabs, lobsters, cuttle fish, limpets and octopus. The famous bouillabaisse originated in Marseille but can be found all along the coast in various disguises. Bourride too is another kind of fish soup while few restaurants do not serve the traditional soupe de poissons. Trout are pulled out of every stream – often after you have placed your order.

Duck, pigeon and guinea-fowl are as popular as chicken. Pigeon is often accompanied by pine nuts. Rabbit and hare are cooked in red wine and wild boar (sanglier) is roasted.

The regional cheeses are goat's and ewe's cheese. The town of Banon is known for its goat cheese which is wrapped in chestnut leaves. Brousse du Rove is a creamy, fresh goat cheese while Tomme du Mont Ventoux is soft, sweet and creamy. Poivre d'âne is usually a mixture of goat and cow milk and is flavoured with savoury and rosemary.

The truffle, weight for weight, is more valuable than gold and the climate of the Var is ideal, truffles being found around the roots of the Provence white oak. (*French Entrée 10 – the South of France* deals with this subject in detail in the chapter entitled 'Black Diamonds of Provence'.)

Oranges and lemons grow in the streets in some towns. Besides limes, plums, cherries, grapes, apples, pomegranantes, persimmons, figs, peaches, pears and apricots, the melons from Cavaillon are shipped all over the world and the pasteque (water melon) is a summer favourite.

Confectionaries and pastries make use of fruit extensively nougat, crystallised fruit and flowers, caramelised figs, pralines, glacéed chestnuts while calissons from Aix are seen all over France (they are like marzipan).

Wine lovers adore Provence. Less than twenty years ago, most of the celebrated wines were denied AOC status. Today, a host of them have achieved it. Of course some of the great names in the wine world come from this region, notably Châteauneuf-du-Pape, but you have the opportunity to taste many others less well-known but vying closely in quality. Gigondas, Rasteau, Cairanne, Vacqueyras, Séguret, Visan and Roaix are some of these. Bandol is a coastal strip with fine wines and nearby Cassis produces fresh, aromatic white wines. Côteaux des Baux and Côteaux d'Aix get better every year and so do many of the VDQS wines from Côtes du Ventoux and Côtes du Luberon.

Pastis is the favourite apéritif of the Provençal with its unique flavouring of star anise, a strange spice from China. Sweet wines are drunk chilled as apéritifs or as a dessert wine. Beaumes-de-Venise and Rasteau are two of these, both made from the muscat grape.

Food and drink in Provence are like the region itself, earthy and full of sunshine but may lack the elegance and refinement of Paris and Lyon.

FREDERIC MISTRAL

The Poet Troubador of Provence

Everywhere you go in Provence, you will run into the name of Frédéric Mistral. Streets and museums are named after him, so are libraries and parks and bus-stops. Who was he? you may well ask and your enjoyment of a visit to Provence will be greatly enhanced by knowing something about him.

He was born in 1830 near Maillane, about five miles from Saint Rémy, the son of a farmer. His mother was the daughter of the Mayor of Maillane and spoke by choice and habit only the Provençal language. She was very religious but was also

Pavillon de la Reine Jeanne – Vallon de la Fontaine – LES BAUX

imbued with the legends and superstitions of the strange region which includes such haunted places as Les Baux and Tarascon.

Delaide, as his mother was called, handed on to her son all the stories of monsters and magic and miracles that are so much a part of Provence. Frédéric became convinced that the world was governed by mysterious laws and repeated (and sometimes originated) disturbing tales of coincidence and the influence of fate on his own life.

His parents were determined that Frédéric should have a better education than either of them had had and he attended two lycées in Avignon. When he found that he was expected to speak and write only French, he was furious. All that he loved most – the traditions, customs, language and legends of old Provence – meant nothing to people who talked only French and cared nothing for the region's past.

This made Mistral determine to devote his energies to restoring the Provençal language to wider usage and at one of the lycées he met others who were like-minded. Together, they formed the 'Felibrige', a loose-knit organisation to promulgate these ideas. (The word 'Felibrige' has no particular meaning and was chosen mainly for that reason.)

Mistral soon gathered around him more poets and romantics whose work consisted of lyric poetry and epic verse. They attracted attention and support from Lamartine and Gounod but it was Mistral's own work, *Mireio*, that was the most successful. It is a simple tale of the tragic love affair of a young girl in the Camargue. Another work, *Calendau*, tells of a young fisherman at La Ciotat who falls in love with a beautiful water-nymph but must carry out various acts of bravery before he can claim her.

Stories based on the chivalrous Middle Ages in Provence provided much of the material for Mistral and his fellow troubadors. In 1904, he won the Nobel Prize for Literature. Spreading of the Provençal language was not achieved to any great extent although an increased awareness of its existence could be said to be due to the Felibrige. They even introduced the first newspaper in the Provençal language – *Bouillabaisso*. They did not attempt any kind of autonomy for Provence (like, for instance, the Basques) but there is no question that they accomplished a national revival of interest in the traditions, folktales and legends of the region. That many of these are known today is due to the poet-troubador Frédéric Mistral and his gallant band of romantics known as the 'Felibrige'.

Les Baux: Hôtel Jean de Brion

SPECIAL RECOMMENDATIONS

The following establishments (marked by an arrow ➤) have been singled out for excellence in one, or preferably all, the criteria of good food, comfortable lodgings, good value, friendly welcome, outstanding site.

Aix-en-Provence. *Le Manoir* (H)S. Delightful historic building full of charm. Quiet, convenient and inexpensive.

Aix-en-Provence. *Saint Christophe* (HR)S. Convenient, modern, well-equipped, very good value hotel.

Ansouis. *Le Jardin d'Ansouis* (C)M. Excellent chambre d'hôte. Personalised service, cosy, reasonable.

Bonnieux. *Hôtel l'Aiguebrun* (HR)M-L. Elegant and efficient hotel in superb grounds. Very good food.

Cereste. *Hôtel Aiguebelle* (HR)S-M. Comfortable hotel with superb food.

Châteauneuf-du-Pape. *Hostellerie Château Fines Roches* (HR)M. Fine château, all comforts. Good food.

Crillon-le-Brave. *Hostellerie de Crillon le Brave* (HR)M-L. Luxurious hotel in an ancient building. Very good food.

Eygalières. *Le Mas de la Brune* (HR)M-L. Magnificent old residence with lovely surroundings. Excellent food.

Forcalquier. *Hostellerie des Deux Lions* (HR)M. Famous old post house, full of character. Excellent cooking with local fare.

Gemenos. *Le Relais de la Magdeleine* (HR)M-L. Old mansion, very welcoming.

Gordes. *Auberge de Carcarille* (HR)M. Delightful building, lots of atmosphere, very good value.

Glanum. *Villa Glanum* (HR)S-M. Unbeatable location, pleasant hotel, good food, excellent value.

Graveson. *Moulin d'Aure* (H)S. Charming setting, quiet surroundings, lovely building, unbeatable value.

Malaucène. *La Chevalerie* (HR)S. Unusual and charming. Reasonable meals.

Maussane-les-Alpilles. *Ou Ravi Provençau* (R)S-M. Cosy restaurant and great decor. Excellent food.

Oppède. *Mas des Capelans* (HR)M. Luxurious but reasonable, very good food.

Le Puy-Sainte-Réparade. *Domaine de la Cride* (HR)M. Luxurious but homey. Very attractive country setting. Excellent food.

Salon-de-Provence. *Mas du Soleil* (HR)M. Comfort and service, outstanding food.

Vaison-la-Romaine. *Les Auric* (H)S-M. Atmosphere in peaceful setting. Exceptional value.

Venasque. *La Maison des Volets Bleus* (C)L. Outstanding quality chambre d'hôte in village centre. Excellent value.

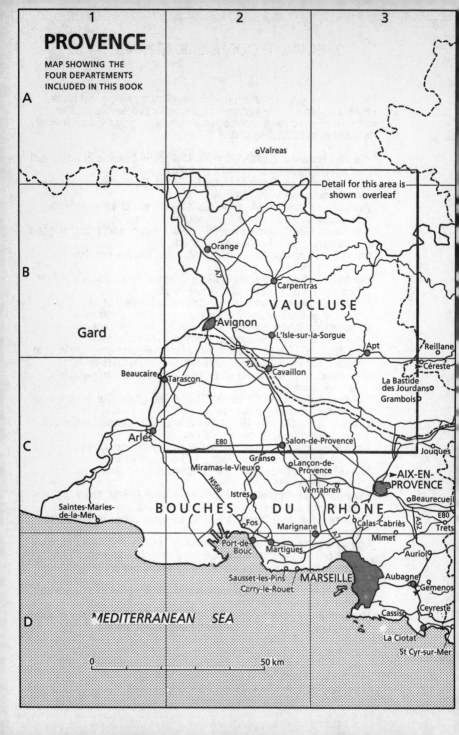

PROVENCE

MAP SHOWING THE
FOUR DEPARTEMENTS
INCLUDED IN THIS BOOK

Valreas

Detail for this area is
shown overleaf

Orange

Carpentras

VAUCLUSE

Avignon

L'Isle-sur-la-Sorgue

Apt

Reillane

Gard

Beaucaire

Tarascon

Cavaillon

Céreste

La Bastide
des Jourdans

Grambois

Arles

E80

Salon-de-Provence

Jouques

Grans

Miramas-le-Vieux

Lançon-de-
Provence

**AIX-EN-
PROVENCE**

Beaurecueil

Saintes-Maries-
de-la-Mer

BOUCHES

Istres

Ventabren

DU

Calas-Cabriès

RHÔNE

E80

Trets

Fos

Marignane

Mimet

Port-de-
Bouc

Martigues

Auriol

Sausset-les-Pins
Carry-le-Rouet

MARSEILLE

Aubagne

Gemenos

Ceyreste

Cassis

MEDITERRANEAN   SEA

La Ciotat

St Cyr-sur-Mer

0   50 km

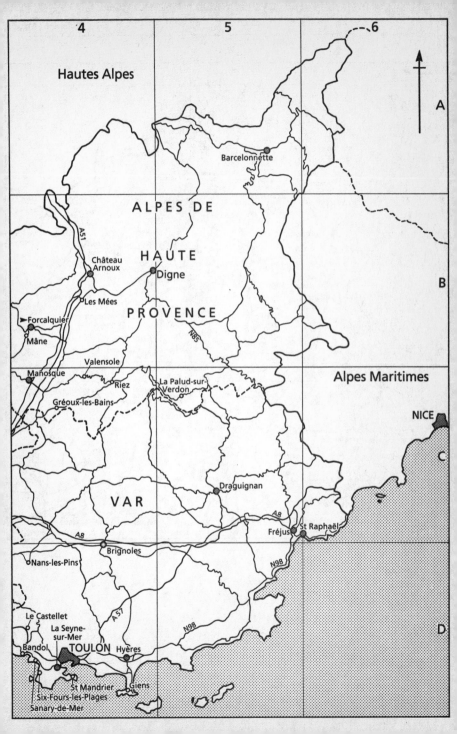

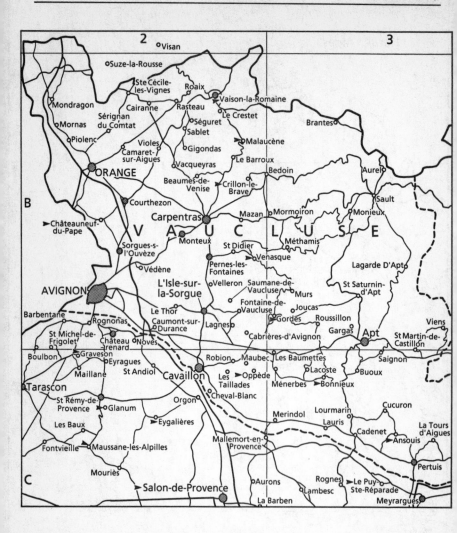

Map 3C   **AIX-EN-PROVENCE** 13100 (Bouches-du-Rhône). 31 km N of Marseille; 175 km W of Nice; 81 km NW of Toulon

Aquae Sextiae was the original name, 'The Waters of Sextius', named after the Roman Consul who subdued the local tribes in 125 BC. Sextius founded it as a thermal spa (possibly the first in Gaul) and suitable recuperation centre for legionaries. Its charm has persisted to the present. It is one of everybody's favourite Provençal cities and is frequently compared with Florence.

From the 12th to the 18th century, Aix was the political and religious capital of Provence and much of its power and prestige stemmed from its famous King René. Strictly speaking, he was a count in Provence but, exiled as King of Naples, he became a legend in the land of poets and troubadors. The romantic image of King René is that of a good-natured man, patron of the arts, friend of the people and booster of the Provence region. The truth seems to be that he did not understand the Provençal tongue and liked neither olive oil nor Provence wine. He spent vast sums of money on architecture and delighted in staging spectacular pageants and fairs.

Today, Aix is important for its university, founded in the 15th century, which attracts students from all over the world. Many literary celebrities have lived in Aix including Malherbe, Frédéric Mistral and Blaise Cendrars. The café Deux Garçons on Cours Mirabeau was the meeting place and even rivalled similar cafés in Paris.

The Cours Mirabeau which runs through the centre of Aix is one of the great boulevards of Europe. Its elegant 18th-century façades are now being superseded by more modern structures but the elms originally planted in 1657 have been replaced by four rows of magnificent plane trees. The four fountains along the Cours still bubble water from the same springs that Sextius tapped for his legions.

The old town sprawls around the area north of Cours Mirabeau and a stroll through the mediaeval streets must not be missed. Park behind the casino or along the Avenue Victor Hugo or around the tourist bureau. The old town is small and La Rotonde, the massive and impressive fountain in the centre of Place Général de Gaulle, is the best starting place. The Place des Augustins adjacent is a hive of activity at all hours. You can go up Rue de la Couronne or along Rue Espariat – a specific route is not necessary as every corner brings new delights. Place des Tanneurs had numerous small restaurants around a bubbling fountain and Forum des Cardeurs is similar, though the restaurants here specialise in oriental food.

Place Richelme has an outdoor market every day with fresh fruit and vegetables straight from the farms. Place d'Albertas must be seen for sheer placid beauty – ancient buildings around a cobbled deserted square with the façades unfortunately falling into decay. Nevertheless, it has been preserved in its original state and no sign of modernity or commercialism can be seen.

Hôtel de Ville, built in 1655, has an Italian style front and carved wooden doors which give it an unusually functional elegance.

You can combine sightseeing and shopping very effectively in the old town of Aix. On Cours Mirabeau, you will see many shops selling 'Calissons'. These are almond paste sweets and an Aix speciality, though you will see them all over France. The magnificent clock tower of the 13th-century Couvent des Augustins on Rue Espariat houses Caves Espariat with a fine selection of wines, and adjacent is Comtesse du Barry with an extensive range of gourmet specialities. Paul Fouques on Cours Gambetta sells the popular 'Santons', the native-costumed dolls. Rue Gaston de Saporta has many shops selling local produce and Rue des Cordeliers is lined with boutiques, local produce and gourmet foods and wines. South of the Cours is the Quartier Mazarin which contains most of Aix's museums.

The Musée Granet is on Place St. Jean-de-Malte and was once the Priory of the Knights of Malta. The work of Paul Cézanne, an Aix resident, is here of course – in fact, he attended the art school which was housed in the building at that time. Also on view are paintings by Ingres, Rembrandt, Rubens, Corot, Matisse and Cranach as well as sculpture, furniture, tapestries, ceramics, weapons, stamps and coins. None of these are as well displayed as they might be and for many the archaeology section is the most interesting. It contains the finds from the old Ligurian settlement which existed when the Romans came. *Open 10-12 and 2-6, closed Tuesdays.*

The former Bishop's Palace houses the Musée des Tapisseries et de l'Ameublement Ancien. Outstanding among the tapestries are the nine scenes showing the Life of Don Quixote, woven from 1735 to 1745, and a hanging of four pieces of 'Russian Games', dating from a few years later. An exhibition is held every year which offers free expression to contemporary artists. *Open 10-12 and 2-5, closed Mondays.*

Musée de Vieil-Aix on Rue Gaston-de-Saporta features exhibits showing regional arts and traditions including nativity cribs, puppets and dolls.

Anyone with an interest in art will not want to miss Cézanne's studio just north of Aix on Avenue Paul Cézanne. It is not easy to find and you will see the small wooden door in the wall and think there is another entrance. There isn't. Atelier Cézanne is just as the artist left it when he died in 1906. His coat, hat and pipe are there and many of the objects he painted – jars, bottles, glasses, skulls. You will see his easel and palette, paints and brushes, even canvases waiting to be used.

The garden is delightfully uncared for and a small bridge of tree branches crosses the stream. *Open 10-12 and 2-5 in the winter and 10-12 and 2.30-6 in the summer. Closed Tuesdays and holidays.*

In stark contrast to the older and mustier museums is the Vasarely Foundation, probably already familiar if you have driven along the A8 autoroute past Aix. No driver can miss seeing the massive black-and-white cube building and the interior is even more striking.

The Hungarian-born artist built this museum in 1975 to house his own works. 'Beauty is relative,' said Vasarely and his works are intended to show the necessity of combining taste and love with architecture now that 'modernity has abolished the human scale'. Le Corbusier and other architects have enthusiastically endorsed his views and welcomed his support.

You will certainly admire the exhibition even if you don't agree with it. The permanent part consists of vast hexagonal rooms with 40 foot high ceilings, each of the six walls covered by geometrical works, some in wood, some in tapestry, some in metal, some in double panels of glass. Many are optically illusionary and change as you walk past them. Many are black and white only, some black and silver only but others consist of cleverly selected colours.

Upstairs, sliding panels explain the designs and show how the dimensions were mathematically calculated. It is all far more pleasing to the eye than might be supposed and might well arouse your admiration for something unusual and different – a commodity rare in the art world.

Various exhibitions are held throughout the year in another part of the museum and these are more conventional but certainly not conformist.

Festivals

Aix Festival of Classical Music is one of the most famous in Europe. It is held every year from the middle to the end of July at various locations including the cloisters of Saint Sauveur Cathedral. An international dance festival is held in July also and in August there is a jazz festival.

Saint Christophe
(HR)S   *2 Avenue Victor Hugo   42 26 01 24   V, CB, EC.*

For convenience, price and quality combined – the Saint Christophe has to be the best value hotel in Aix. It is next to the tourist bureau and looks out at La Rotonde, the heart of the city and on Cours Mirabeau. A double with bath is 320f and with shower 260-295f. A single is 300f (or 250f). Breakfast is 35f and the garage 43f.

It is a modern building but colour and style are Provençale. The rooms are not large but are fully-equipped, tasteful and air-conditioned. The large and busy brasserie in front is handy for meals at any time. Meals 100-150f.

Le Manoir
(H)S   *8 Rue d'Entrecasteaux   42 26 27 20   All CC.*

You may feel that when staying in a town as historic as Aix, you should stay in a historic building. There are plenty of such hotels in France but most are expensive. Le Manoir is the answer as far as Aix is concerned.

It is a 14th-century cloister, right in the heart of the old town but sitting back inside its own courtyard so that it is calm and quiet. You walk through the lobby and into a long cloister, open to the sun, which has become a lovely outdoor dining area.

The public rooms have beamed ceilings and antique furniture. The bedrooms are modernised but not modern. Single rooms are 190-345f and doubles are 240-470f.

Le Pigonnet

(HR)M   *5 Avenue de Pigonnet   42 59 02 90   R cl. 1/11-21/11; 1/2-15/2. R cl. lunch only Sat and Sun o.o.s.   All CC.*

If you want to pamper yourself while staying in Aix, 5 minutes drive from the centre of Aix here is the perfect opportunity to do so. This charming Provençal farmhouse has every luxury yet retains an old-world atmosphere.

Cézanne painted in the grounds – especially his favourite subject,

Aix: Hotel Le Pigonnet

the Montagne Ste Victoire. Tables under the trees are among flowers and fountains for summer dining while indoors there is a small and a large dining room, several lounges and a bar.

Single rooms are 600-750f, doubles from 700-1050f but even the less expensive rooms are large and full-equipped. The extensive grounds include 2 acres of gardens and a pool.

The elegant restaurant offers meals at 220f and 300f.

Nègre Coste
(H)M   *33 Cours Mirabeau   42 27 74 22   All CC.*

The pretty four-storey façade of the Nègre Coste is right in the middle of the Cours Mirabeau. It is an elegant 18th-century residence which has received many famous guests, including Louis XIV. The great hall is in the style of Louis XV. Charge for the garage is 50f.

It has been completely restored to its original condition. All the rooms are tastefully decorated with appropriate period furniture. Prices are 400f to 700f; breakfast is 60f.

Le Moulin
(H)S   *1 Avenue Robert Schumann   42 59 41 68   All CC.*

A modern but pleasing building only a few minutes from the Cours Mirabeau yet quiet and calm.

Rooms are simple but pleasant and adequate. Prices are 150f to 340f for a single and 195f to 350f for a double. Eleven rooms have their own terrace. Breakfast is 36f.

Le Concorde
(H)M   *68 Blvd du Roi René   42 26 03 95   All CC.*

Only minutes from the centre of Aix but a pleasing and soothing atmosphere in the terrace and private gardens with a bubbling fountain.

The rooms are charming and furnished in different styles. They are priced at 195f to 345f for singles and 215f to 395f for doubles. All are fully equipped. Breakfast is available.

Hôtel de France
(H)S   *63 Rue Espariat   42 27 90 15   All CC.*

If you're looking for reasonably priced accommodation in the old town of Aix, the Hôtel de France is a good bet. On the edge of the Place des Augustins, just where the busy part of the old town begins, the hotel has recently been fully renovated. There is even a solarium.

The rooms are agreeably cosy and cost 180f to 280f for a single, 200f to 340f for a double. If you don't mind a little noise in the evenings, you can look out on to the fountain in the Place. Breakfast is 30f.

Hôtel des Quatre Dauphins
(H)S   *54 Rue Roux-Alpheran   42 38 16 39   V CB EC.*

In the old aristocratic Quartier Mazarin, this is an old private hotel near the Place des Quatre Dauphins and the Granet Museum. There are only twelve rooms, all decorated in traditional Provençal style. Prices are extremely reasonable for such charm, 250f to 300f for a single and 290f to 360f for a double. Breakfast is 35f.

There are no public rooms or gardens and no garage or parking facilities but otherwise this hotel is a very good choice.

La Caravelle
(H)S   *29 Blvd du Roi René   42 21 53 05   V CB EC.*

A five-storey hotel with an attractive façade. Most of the 30 rooms look out on to private gardens and it is preferable to choose one of these as there is a bus stop in front of the hotel on the busy Boulevard du Roi René. The rooms are 180f to 390f for a single and 240f to 390f for a double. Breakfast is 29f.

Abbaye des Cordeliers
(R)M   *21 Rue Lieutard   42 27 29 47   All CC.*

Value for money, this has to be the best restaurant in Aix. It is situated on the narrow Rue Lieutard in the charming, ancient old town . The menu at 95f could start with moules farcies then gigot d'agneau or poulet d'estragon then cheese or dessert. The 130f menu offers main courses that are a little more unusual. You might have soupe de poissons or jambon de Parme to start then the noix d'entrecôte au Roquefort and then cheese or dessert.

If you are in an expansive mood, you can go for the 185f menu – salade au saumon fumé followed by magret de canard in honey sauce then a choice of desserts. A good selection of wines are available around 100f.

La Cigalle
(R)S   *Place des Augustins*

For a really satisfying but inexpensive meal, you can't do better than La Cigalle. The 73f menu could start with terrine d'escargots flavoured with lobster bisque. For the main course, the carre d'agneau à la crème d'ail is deliciously unusual or you could have the truite aux amandes. Choice of dessert or cheese to finish.

The 98f menu is my favourite here. A salade des artichauts is a good way to start and then the filet of sole soufflé is a dish you see very rarely. Cheese or dessert to finish.

The location on the popular Place des Augustins means that La Cigalle is usually busy and its low prices make it popular with students from the university.

La Clémence
(R) *Place des Augustins All CC.*

> Equally popular with university students and others looking for a good but reasonably priced meal, La Clémence fills quickly though you mustn't be put off by the tiny interior – there is another room upstairs.
>
> Cassoulette de moules à la épinard is a most unusual starter and could be followed by gigot with onion confit but if you are really in the mood to have a local speciality, try pieds et paquets – tripe and calf's foot, a recipe from nearby Marseille. Cheese or dessert for the final course and this entire repast for only 86f.
>
> There is also a wide selection of à la carte dishes. Provence wines are 50 to 70f a bottle.

Les Deux Garçons
(R)M *53 Cours Mirabeau 42 26 00 51 V, CB.*

> A historic café which in the past has included poet Blaise Cendrars, comedian Raimu, aviator Antoine de St. Exupéry and actress/dancer Mistinguett among its patrons. After a disastrous fire, it has been reconstructed in the First Empire style reminiscent of the great cafés of Paris. It no longer enjoys the same reputation as in the past but its situation on the Cours Mirabeau means that it is still a place where people sit to be seen and to watch the world go by.
>
> It's best to eat à la carte and perhaps seafood such as oysters, mussels, clams and sea-urchins. Expect to pay 150f to 250f.

Map 3C **ANSOUIS** 84240 (Vaucluse) 8 km NW of Pertuis

 Thurs

> This is a charming village and very handily located. Just turn off the A51 autoroute and cross the bridge at Pertuis. The village sits on the flank of an isolated hill crowned by an unusually interesting castle.
>
> The castle is often referred to as a 'Château Double' for it does look like two different castles. Seen from the north, it appears to be an impregnable fortress, powerful and dominating. Its southern view shows the elegant façade of an 18th-century manor house built for sumptuous living. The flag which flutters bravely from the top depicts a white lion on a red background and is the heraldic symbol of the Sabran family.
>
> It was built sometime before 960 by the Counts of Forcalquier, then it was inherited by the Counts of Sabran in 1160 after a marriage between the two families. The extraordinary thing is that the château has remained in the hands of the Sabran family ever since and although they still live here (the Duchess writes best-selling historical novels), it is open to the public.
>
> Inevitably work throughout the centuries has introduced several different architectural styles. There are a number of feudal rooms including the old keep and the guardroom (now the village church) but

the interior still has its wooden panelling and many of the apartments have exquisite plasterwork. The kitchens (with all the old utensils) are fascinating. The gardens cover five terraces, the highest of which is like a hanging garden at the top of the rock into which the château is built.

During such a long and turbulent history, there have been many occasions when secret entry and exit were desirable – and sometimes essential. As a result, there are numerous tunnels running in all directions, the villagers say even as far as Pertuis.

The château is open 2.30-6.30, closed Tuesday.

Open about the same hours is the Musée Extraordinaire in the village, owned and run by a Marseillais named Georges Mazoyer. Well-lit and well-displayed panoramas show fish, shells, turtles and other denizens of the deep.

Ansouis has an extraordinarily well-kept look to it. You don't doubt that it is old, yet the village is so neat and tidy that if they ever run a contest for the best-kept village in Provence, I'll put my money on Ansouis.

Its typically mediaeval Provençal look has caused it to be used in films, like *Manon des Sources*, the recent version with Gérard Depardieu and Yves Montand. The film makers thought it looked like Aubagne ought to look but doesn't. It hasn't been invaded yet by many tourists, so don't expect much in the way of boutiques and artisans, apart from Roger Demuysère's wood sculptures, Antoine Calandra's pots and local wines, Daniel Galli's santons and Renée-Ann's ceramics.

The local wines are Vin de Pays A.O.C. Côtes du Lubéron and you can taste and buy at the Cave Co-opérative des Vignerons d'Ansouis from 8-12 and 2-6, Monday to Friday, mornings only on Saturday. Château Turcan is a privately owned vineyard run by M. Laugier and his sons. It is open all day, every day except Monday and has a small museum of wine and vines. Their reds are of very high quality.

Festivals

Ansouis has a Mardi Gras carnival and an artisan fair in July and August. There is a Fête of Notre Dame in September. The last Sunday in September is a very special one in Ansouis for that day fêtes Saint Eléazar and his wife, Sainte Delphine.

It is rare for a couple to be granted sainthood and even rarer is the fact that they were members of the Sabran family which still owns the château. Eléazar was the Baron of Ansouis and the Lord Justice of the Kingdom of Naples. In one of the rooms there you can see a triptych showing them being crowned with roses.

Proof of Ansouis' resistance to tourism to date is its lack of hotels and restaurants. The Bar des Sports in the village square will have to do for snacks and there are tables outside in a cheerful village atmosphere. They often have cheap specials such as a grilled meat and then a cheese course plus a quarter bottle of wine for 50f. There are several tea-rooms and some of these have rooms. These two chambres d'hôte offer extremely good value:

➤ Le Jardin d'Ansouis
(C)M   *90 09 89 27*   *Rue du Petit Portail*   *Open all year.*

> Arlette Rogers is a charming and vivacious hostess who works long hours to ensure that the guests in her two chambres d'hôte lack for nothing. She speaks excellent English, bakes superb patisseries and is locally renowned for her cheese and ice-creams.
>
> The two rooms are very large and each has its own bathroom and toilet. Both look out on to the flower-filled garden and patio where most of the meals are served in summer. They are priced at 275f for a couple and 25f extra for a third bed. A big breakfast is included. Lunch is served in summer and this runs into tea-time, for Le Jardin is known as a tea-room. Table d'hôte is available on reservation; 175f includes four courses, aperitif and wine. The personal touch is evident throughout and nothing is too much trouble.
>
> Arrowed for charm, hospitality, good value.

Lubéron Centre
(C)   *90 09 86 26*   *Rue du Grand Four*   *Open all year.*

> This has been active for some years as the Lubéron Language Centre, teaching English to French business executives. Now Clare McDonald and Michael Hankins have taken over several adjacent old houses and brilliantly converted them into 'The Lubéron Centre' in which to accommodate up to 14 people in eight rooms and offer courses in gourmet cooking, French and other subjects.
>
> The rooms are beautifully modernised, without losing the mediaeval flavour of ancient stone walls and views of the château, while adding skylights and all modern conveniences. A very large and well-equipped kitchen is available. The price is a remarkably modest 100f per person and the rooms are available to other guests if not occupied by course-members.

Map 3B   **APT 84400 (Vaucluse)** 40 km W of Manosque, 55 km N of Aix-en-Provence

---

> Apt would never claim to be one of the most picturesque towns in Provence but it has long been one of the busiest. A tribe known as the Vulgientes occupied the site when Julius Caesar stopped here on his way back to Rome after a victorious campaign in Spain. He created a Roman colony there which he named Apta Julia.
>
> From that time on, Apt remained the market centre of the entire region, of fruit orchards and chestnut groves, herbs and spices, fish and game and local produce too. The market is still held every Saturday and is a crowded, exciting affair which you won't want to miss. The best place to enter is through the Porte St Pierre in the ancient walls surrounding the town. To find the gate look for the Café Continental just outside the walls.
>
> The odours of garlic and lemons, baking bread, toasting cheese and wild lavender will tempt you to buy something. The crystallised fruits you will see on sale everywhere are a speciality of Apt and the market

has a wide selection to offer. While looking and buying, you may be entertained by itinerant musicians, mime artists, barrel organs and local characters in costume. You won't have any difficulty finding the market – it is centred around the Rue des Marchands which runs past the cathedral and the area is blocked off to traffic for the event.

Besides the market, Apt is of principal interest as a focal point from which to tour the countryside, but you might wish to see the Cathedral of Ste Anne, the grandmother of Jesus. A cathedral was first built here in the 5th century, on the ruins of an old Celtic temple. It was said to contain relics of Ste Anne, including her shroud, and these have been objects of pilgrimage for people from all over France.

The Emperor Charlemagne came here on Easter Sunday in 776 to consecrate the cathedral; in the 11th century extensive reconstruction and enlargement began and lasted about 150 years. Most of the cathedral you see today is this structure. The shroud which was believed to be that of Ste Anne was identified in the 19th century as having belonged to the Caliph Fatimide and brought back by the knight, Rambaud de Simiane, from the First Crusade.

Ste Anne's chapel (in the cathedral) is open 9-12 and 2.30-7. In addition to the shroud, there is some old porcelain from Limoges, some Arab ivories and *The Book of Hours* of Sainte Delphine.

The Archaeological Museum is on Rue Scudéry, two blocks south of the cathedral. Here there are Roman baths, traces of the arena, sarcophagi, oil lamps, coins, perfume vases, bowls and dishes. *Open 9-12 and 3-6 every day except Sunday.*

La Bonbonnière on Rue de la Sous-préfecture is one of the shops to seek out first when you go shopping in Apt. As well as the finest of crystallised fruits, it sells nougat, chocolate, Turkish delight and 'calissons', a local delicacy similar to marzipan. The Rue des Marchands – where the Saturday market is centred – has lots of good shops and wine can be tasted and purchased in Cave des Vins de Sylla on the Route d'Avignon, Château de Mille on Quai Général Leclerc, and at La Taste on Quai Léon Sagy.

The Pont Julien, a fine Roman relic, can be found just off the N100, about 8 km west of Apt. It was built to cross the river Calavon and was used by the legions marching between Spain and Rome. A visit to the bridge from Apt could be the first leg of a three-hour driving loop, going on to the villages of Roussillon, St Saturnin-les-Apt and Rustrel.

Festivals

Apt has several festivals throughout the year, most of them during the summer season:

The Fair of Ste Anne, patron saint of Apt, is naturally the biggest one. It is held on the last Sunday in July, with parades and wine tasting.

Corso de Pentecôte – floats, fireworks and costumes. This used to be for charity, a fund-raising occasion for the poor. Today this aim seems to have lost its importance.

Antiques Fair – last week in July.

Festival Tréteaux de Nuit – this is the summer festival, with concerts, plays and exhibitions every day from the end of July through August.

Fair of Ste Luce – December, festivals of local saints.
Fair of Ste Clair – January, dates vary according to the Christmas
calendar.

There is one other procession which you may encounter in Apt. In
time of drought, a statue of St Maur is paraded through the streets. If
the saint does not succeed in bringing rain quickly enough, he is
punished by being dunked in the fountain of St Martin and left there
until the next shower.

Auberge du Lubéron
(HR)M   *17 Quai Léon Sagy   90 74 12 50   Hotel open every day, all year   R cl.*
Sun eve. and Mon; first week in July and 15/11-15/12   All CC.

This has to be the best place to stay in Apt. There is an apartment at
700f but other rooms are fully equipped, nicely furnished and priced at
210 to 450f. Some of these are in an annexe so make it clear at the
time of booking if you particularly want to be in the Auberge itself.
There is parking and a garage.
   The Auberge is located in the centre of town on the river bank, very
convenient for sightseeing.
   The restaurant is elegant and the cuisine of a high quality though
perhaps a little over-priced for an auberge. Menus are 150, 215 and
290f and an à la carte meal could cost over 400f.

Relais de Roquefure
(HR)S-M   *90 04 88 88   On RN 100   Cl. 5/1-12/5   Visa, CB.*

The 15 rooms are clean and comfortable, at 170-300f. Demi-pension is
available at 200-260f. There is a pool, a pleasant garden and garage
parking.
   Locals use the restaurant, where the cooking is traditional and
reliable. In addition to the large dining room there is accommodation
for another hundred people in the garden and on the terrace, so you
can see it's popular. Menus start at 110f.

Brasserie Grégoire
(R)S   *90 74 10 26   Place Bouquerie   Open all year   Visa, CB, EC, MC.*

A vast busy place with straightforward food and a large clientele. The
enclosed garden area is delightful in summer. The plat du jour can be
relied on to be hearty country fare. Menus start at 75f.

Marie-Claire Frasson-Botton
(C)M   *90 74 04 88   'Les Mylanettes', Rue du Docteur Vallon   Cl. 1/11-1/2.*

A really fine example of a chambre d'hôte, complete with large living
room, library and television, lounge, plus a terrace and a loggia. All
the five rooms have private baths and toilets and you can swim in the
pool or in the lake.
   Room prices are 190-250f for two people and breakfast is included.
Meals are available if required at 70-110f.

Map 1C   **ARLES** 13200 (Bouches-du-Rhône) 40 km S of Avignon, 88 km NW of Marseille

Few towns in Provence can offer such a varied assortment of interests as Arles – it is associated with Van Gogh, bullfights and opera and has an extensive Roman and Provençal past coupled with a vivid and pulsating present.

Arles was a flourishing city when Rome was still a collection of mud huts. With the arrival of the Romans, Arles became the most important city in the region. The Consul Marius built a canal which turned Arles into a major port and it gained in stature when Julius Caesar destroyed Marseille, its only rival.

Valuable cargoes of olives, cloth and charcuteries brought in revenues which made it, by the time of the end of the Empire, the greatest city in Gaul and the granary of the western world. The crumbling of the Empire however saw Constantine the Great build a palace in Arles but this fame was short-lived and the city's power declined.

One fortunate result of this was that by being isolated in such a way and out of the mainstream of current events, Arles became a conservatory of the traditions of its past. This is why Arles was chosen by the Provençal poets and troubadors to be the symbol of 'Ancient Provence'. Any festival or spectacle presenting the past of Provence includes Arlésien costumes, songs and dances, equestrian displays and scenes involving the bull.

In the 19th century, Arles was a favourite residence of writers, artists and musicians. Alphonse Daudet was living here when he wrote his play *L'Arlésienne* from a story in his earlier work *Letters from My Mill*. Georges Bizet was asked to write music for it suitable for a 26-piece orchestra. The first performance was at the Vaudeville Theatre in Paris and it was an immediate success.

The music gives a wonderfully rich and evocative picture of Provence, the local atmosphere being created with several folk melodies and anyone who goes to Arles and hears Bizet's music will never be able to be hear of one without being reminded of the other.

Frédéric Mistral, the poet-laureate of Provence, created here his famous folk museum, using the money from his Nobel Prize award. It is known as the Musée Arlaten on Rue de la République and can be found just a few minutes south of the arena. It is housed in the 16th-century town house of a wealthy local family and is an unusually personal museum. The exhibits are a major source of information on Provençal arts, crafts, furniture, costumes, etc and are spread through thirty rooms. Many of the exhibits still have the labels with Mistral's own notations on them. *Open 9-12 and 2-7 in July and August; 9-12 and 2-5 the other months. Closed Mondays from October to June.*

The Roman Arena is one sight you will not want to miss. It is not the largest of Roman amphitheatres but it is certainly one of the most impressive. It is still in regular use (though no longer for its original purpose) and this helps to give it an air of reality that promptly brings to mind images of gladiators fighting one another to the death, wild beasts pawing the sand and seeking the human flesh they so often found.

The importance of the arena can be judged when you look at your map of Arles. The arena sits right in the centre of the city and all roads lead to it. 20,000 spectators could be accommodated then but today attendances are limited to about 12,000. Although the third and top tier which supported the purple canopy roof has gone, two tiers of sixty arches remain, making it a very impressive sight. Gone too are the vats of bubbling saffron – their purpose in Roman days was to camouflage the smell of blood.

The nearest that the arena can offer today to these gory spectacles is the bullfight. Arles is the leading place in France where these are held and you may see them two Sundays a month from the Easter weekend till November. Two kinds of bullfight are part of the entertainment – that in which the bull is killed and the other in which it is not. The latter may include other contests in which the bullfighters have to pluck a cockade from between the horns of the bull. If you wish to avoid the Spanish style bullfight, it is billed as 'Mise à Mort' (fight to the death). Posters will be everywhere with dates and times and prices.

The Antique Theatre was built in the first century BC as a theatre. It held about 8,000 people but has been severely pillaged through the centuries so that little remains. It is still used, though, to host the Festival of Arles in June and July and the International Photography Festival (one of the biggest in France) in July.

The chief mediaeval glory of Arles is the Cathedral of Saint Trophîme. It is situated on the main square, the Place de la République where its 12th-century porch shows the Last Judgement. Apostles and saints stand on either side of the door in richly carved niches between monolithic marble columns over lines of weird beasts. The Good march off to Heaven while below them the Damned trudge in chains towards the opposite destination. Around Christ are the symbols of the evangelists and a double row of angels watching. 'One of the Seven Marvels of Provence' is how the porch is described so it should not be missed. The cloisters of the cathedral should be approached from Rue du Cloître – Alexandre Dumas described them as 'the most curious in France'. They show saints and mythical animals in carved stone scenes from the Bible.

The Place du Forum is in the heart of the old town and just west of the arena. It used to be called La Place des Hommes because it was the place to hire farm workers, shepherds and help with the harvest but it has always been the principal meeting place for the people of Arles. In the square is a statue of Frédéric Mistral, poet-extraordinaire and a man to whom Arles owes much for propagating its history and traditions.

Underneath the Forum are vast underground galleries, larger than a football stadium, built by the Romans (perhaps the first Roman building in Arles) to store grain, oil and wine.

The Musée Réattu was once the Priory of the Knights of Malta and can be found on Rue du Grand-Prieure. Jacques Réattu was a local painter and the museum houses some of his works but they are mediocre in quality. Of much more interest are sketches by Picasso and paintings by Gauguin, Leger and Raspal but it is the recent installation of the Espace Van Gogh that is the principal attraction.

Van Gogh came to Arles in February 1888, seeking the light and colour that he so admired in the Japanese prints he collected. He found both and his fourteen months in Arles were the most productive of his life – he turned out about 300 paintings and almost as many drawings while he was here. They were equally the most traumatic months of his life for it was here that he cut off part of his ear, his friendship with Paul Gauguin foundered and he felt isolated due to a lack of appreciation for, or understanding of, his work.

He lived first in the Restaurant Carrel on Rue de la Cavalerie near the railway station. This has now been pulled down. He moved to the house in Rue Lamartine that he shared with Gauguin (*The Yellow House* painting) but this was destroyed during an alr raid in 1944. He lived then at the Café de la Gare where he welcomed M and Mme Ginoux. The Café du Soir is now a furniture store and the Café de Nuit on the Place du Forum is now a bar.

Clearly, little is left of the Arles that Van Gogh painted but a few of his subjects are still identifiable – the courtyard of the Hospital in Rue Wilson is unchanged and so are the Quais du Rhône at the end of the Pont Trinquetaille and 'the last mill in the Crau', in the Quartier des Mouleires.

It was an ideal place for Van Gogh who had to have subjects in nature to paint from, unlike Gauguin who preferred to use his imagination. *Starry Night, The Chair, The Sower* and *Sunflowers* were all painted in Arles as were *The View of Arles* and *Field at Arles*.

After his self-disfigurement, Van Gogh spent several weeks at the Hôtel-Dieu Hospital where he was treated by the sympathetic Dr Felix Rey whose portrait he painted. In March 1889, Van Gogh had himself placed in the 'Ancien Monastère de St Paul-de-Mausole' in St Rémy, an asylum which remarkably did nothing to hinder his creative flow.

In May 1890, Van Gogh returned north though not to his native Holland but to northern France. Two months later, he died.

The Musée Réattu is open 10-1 and 2-7, Monday to Friday; 10-7 Saturdays, Sundays and holidays. Small fee.

If you would like to take a guided tour called 'Traces of Van Gogh', the Tourist Office on Boulevard des Lices offers a two-hour visit to many of the places he lived and painted. *The tour leaves every Tuesday and Friday at 5 o'clock from the Tourist Office. Small fee.*

The Museum of Christian Art is on Rue Balze and has a collection of early Christian sarcophagi that is second only to that in Rome. It is from here that you can descend into the Cryptoportico (the underground granary storage). The Museum of Pagan Art is on the Place de la République. It was formerly the Church of St Anne and contains some fine specimens of classical Roman art. There are tombs, statues found in the Forum, mosaics and bas-reliefs.

A visit to a cemetery is not everyone's idea of an interesting way to spend a couple of hours but Les Alyscamps, a few minutes walk south of the arena, is unusual. The name is a corruption of 'Champs Elysées' and the cemetery was built by the Romans on the Appian Way. Les

Alyscamps is a long tree-shaded avenue lined with sarcophagi and leading to a ruined Romanesque church. It continued to be used as a burial ground long after the Roman era and wealthy Arlésiennes were buried here. Incursions of the railway passing through have greatly reduced its size which is why only this one avenue remains.

It has long been a favourite place to wander and meditate and – for many of the artistic residents of Arles – a place to encourage mental creativity. Mistral and Daudet often came here and so did Gauguin and Van Gogh – there is a marker showing the spot where Van Gogh used to place his easel.

The market on the Boulevard des Lices is colourful and bustling. It is held every Saturday and food is the main attraction including, of course, much local produce. Fruit, vegetables, olives, cheeses and the local saucissons are particularly inviting. Antiques, shoes and clothes are also on sale as well as Arlésien costumes.

Festivals

You might well expect that a town like Arles with such a tradition for romance and drama would have lots of festivals – and so it does. Some of these are:

Festival and start of the bullfights – Easter.
Fête des Gardians – May 1. Religious ceremony in the morning, entertainment in the evening in the arena. (Gardians are the cowboys of the Camargue.)
Potters' Fair – Ascension Thursday on the Boulevard des Lices.
May Commercial Fair – First Sunday in May.
Festival of Arles – end of June to beginning of July. 'Pegoulado' – a torch-light procession in local costume followed by a costume festival in the Roman theatre.
Annual Festival – July. International festival of music, drama, theatre, dance, opera. Held in several locations including Les Alyscamps, the Antique Theatre and the Courtyard of the Archbishop's Palace.
International Photography Exhibition – July.
Film Festival – August at the Antique Theatre.
Rice Harvest Festival – Mid-September. Traditional festival with a parade along the Boulevard des Lices including floats. Other entertainment such as bullfights.
Arlexpo – Mid-September at the Palais des Congrès.

Arles' two most prestigious hotels are the Jules César on Boulevard des Lices and the Nord Pinus on the Place du Forum. With room prices of 500-1,000f, I don't think they offer quite the value for money that the traveller can expect. Fortunately, the town is well off for accommodation and there is little problem in finding more reasonable prices and still maintaining quality.

Mireille
(HR)S-M   *90 93 70 74   2 Place Saint Pierre   Cl. H, Nov 15-Feb 16; R, Nov 15-March 1   All CC.*

Its only disadvantage is that it's just across the river but it's close to the bridge of Trinquetaille and barely five minutes walk from the arena and the heart of old Arles.

Since the rooms were re-modelled, they are bright and cheerful and fully equipped at 200-500f.

There is a pool which is overlooked by many of the rooms, a patio and a garden. Guy and Mireille Jacquemin are attentive and efficient hosts. Menus are reasonably priced at 105, 120, 170 and 180f and the emphasis is on Provençal food.

Le Cloître
(H)S-M   *90 96 29 50   18 Rue du Cloître   Open all year   All CC.*

Louis Thellier has no restaurant here but that helps keep the room prices down and as Le Cloître is right in the centre of the old town, there is a wide selection of restaurants within minutes walk.

The 33 rooms are 180-380f but you may wish to make sure that you get one of the 29 rooms that are fully equipped. There is a garden but parking is difficult.

Mas de la Chapelle
(HR)M   *90 93 23 15   Petite Route de Tarascon   Cl. R, Sun eve and Mon, all Feb   All CC.*

At least one old castle or priory or similar building that has been brought up to modern standards of accommodation is always included in this book whenever a town has one to offer.

The Mas de la Chapelle is a 16th-century chapel that was used by the Knights of Malta and it fits the above requirements perfectly. Situated in an 8 acre park, it has two swimming pools, three tennis courts and a delightfully mediaeval aura that is helped by the stained glass windows, the antique furniture and the Aubusson tapestries.

M and Mme Remillieux are the proprietors and are proud of the Mas as they should be. The 16 rooms are large and sumptuously appointed. They are priced at 460-660f.

The main part of the chapel is now a luxurious dining room and chef Phillipe Huot makes full use of the local ingredients to serve dishes which are essentially Provençal but with a distinctly classical touch. The fish with lasagne, garlic and basil is an excellent example.

Hôtel d'Arlatan
(H)M   *90 93 56 66   56 Rue du Sauvage   Open all year   Visa, CB.*

Long one of the best-liked hotels in Arles, this is a lovely 15th-century building just between the arena and the Rhône river.

It belonged to the Counts of Arlatan de Beaumont and still has its atmosphere of mediaeval days with antique furnishings. There is a patio, a bar, a walled garden and a private car park.

An unusual feature that you won't find in many hotels stems from the position of the Arlatan as adjacent to the old Roman baths. Part of the property belonging to the hotel has been dug to find further remains and these are visible through a glass floor.

The 10 apartments are 750-1250f but the 31 rooms are a more modest 380-680f. All are delightfully appointed and the level of comfort and concern for the guest is high throughout the hotel.

Auberge la Fenière
(HR)M   *90 98 47 44   Raphele-les-Arles   Cl. R only, Sat lunch, every lunch from May 15-Nov 1, Nov 1-Dec 20   All CC.*

An old Provençal farmhouse cleverly converted into a fine hotel. It's in the meadowlands of the Crau even though it's only 4 kilometres outside Arles and on the N453. There is a family atmosphere that everyone notices.

The 22 rooms are 280-470f. All are cosy and good-sized and have air-conditioning and TV. The menus are 160 and 230f and the kitchen uses local ingredients.

There is a garden also parking and a garage.

Longo Maï
(HR)S   *90 97 21 91   Le Sambuc   Cl. Feb   All CC.*

A fairly modern but Provençal-looking hotel with red-tiled roofs and managed with a firm hand by Jean-Etienne Raynaud.

The 16 rooms at 190-370f are very good value and so is the demi-pension at 230-305f. There is a garden, tennis and parking.

Menus are 95 and 115f and offer good, Provence cooking.

Le Vaccarès
(R)M   *90 96 06 17   Place du Forum   Cl. Sun eve, Mon, Jan 2-30   Visa, CB.*

One of the best places to eat in Arles. A bit higher in price than average but classical cooking, mostly in the Camarquaise style. There is a salon, a terrace and a balcony for the overflow from the dining room so it is clear that it is popular.

Bernard Dumas has a deserved reputation locally and you will particularly enjoy his filet d'agneau with aubergine, caviar and olives. This is a good place to try 'poutargue', made with roe of mullet. Menus are 180, 240 and 320f.

La Côte d'Adam
(R)S   *90 49 62 29   12 Rue de la Liberté   Cl. Mon and Nov 15-30   All CC.*

Chef Alain Collet is determined to offer meals at prices that make them available to everybody – and he is succeeding. The country-style restaurant is right in the heart of town and near the Forum. Ragout de canard in white wine is strongly recommended, and for a starter the mussel soup with saffron is delicious. Menus are 55, 70, 80 and 100f and a satisfying meal is assured.

Hostellerie des Arènes
(R)S   *90 96 13 05 62   Rue Refuge   Cl. Wed, Dec 1-Jan 31   Visa, CB.*

Well-situated opposite the arena, this is a family-run place and very popular because it offers very good food at very moderate prices.

As it is family-run, it cooks and serves family food so this is the next best thing to eating in a Provençal home. Menu prices vary but you can get a good meal at around 100f.

Map 3D   **AUBAGNE** 13400 (Bouches-du-Rhône) 18 km E of Marseille

 Tues.

Everybody knows Aubagne as Pagnol country. He was born here and wrote about it in several books but it was the recent films *Jean de Florette* and *Manon des Sources* which were most influential in promoting the area.

Well, if you come to Aubagne expecting to find a charming Provençal village with the pastoral air of the novels and films, you'll be sadly disappointed. For that you need to go to La Treille where Pagnol's family spent its summer holidays. It's about 15 kilometres to the north-west and on the other side of the autoroute. The 1986 films by Claude Berri were made near Cuge-les-Pins about 10 kilometres east of Aubagne on the N8.

Aubagne nevertheless makes the most of its native son. The Syndicat d'Initiative on the Esplanade de Gaulle in the centre of town has a huge tableau with santons representing Jean de Florette, Papet, Manon and all the Pagnol characters. Several ateliers in town sell such santons (models barely a foot high in full costume).

The two films stressed the importance of water but, with it, the local soil is rich and grows an abundance of fruit, vegetables and flowers. Aubagne is an important market town and very busy on market days. Otherwise, though, it's far from distinguished and perhaps the only other reason for visiting it might be the French Foreign Legion museum with an interesting array of exhibits. One of these is the wooden hand of Captain Danjou who, with his small unit of 64 men, held off a 2,000 strong Mexican army in 1863. The hand is paraded with honour every April 30 in memory. From Aubagne, take the D2 towards Marseille and then the D44A.

The museum is open 10-12 and 3-7 every day except Monday from June to September and the same hours on Wednesday and Sunday from October to May.

Hostellerie Manon des Sources

(HR)M   *42 03 10 31   Route d'Eoures   Open all year   Visa, CB.*

You'd best be warned that this is a popular hostelry for business meetings and seminars and is very well-equipped for such affairs. If you should be there at other times, however, it is a very lovely white mansion house and the rooms look out on to the pool. A 15-acre park surrounds it and there is tennis, horseback riding and a billiard room.

The 8 rooms and 8 apartments all have TV and mini-bar and at 190-240f are a bargain. Demi-pension is 410-460f and director André Farjon serves good quality meals using produce from the local farms.

I suppose the name is inevitable.

Hostellerie de la Source

(HR)M-L   *42 04 09 19   Hotel open all year, R cl. Sun p.m.; Mon; Nov and Feb All CC.*

It's not only the town that makes the most of its native son, Marcel Pagnol. The hotels do it too. This one is a charming 17th-century building in a park which lends an air of calmness and serenity, helped even further by views of the Massif de la Sainte Baume.

300-900f is a wide spread for the prices of the 25 rooms but all are very comfortable and cosily furnished. The rooms at the low end of the range are good value, those at the high end are a little over-priced. There is a large terrace and a pool. The swans on the adjacent pond augment the pastoral surroundings.

M et Mme Barral run the place and Patrick Varin is the chef responsible for the gastronomic renown of the restaurant. The langoustines et ris de veau au sesame is a good example of his imaginative cooking and le grand pot-au-feu de la mer à l'ail is a novel and tasty approach to fish. The breast of duck stuffed with pâté de foie gras is another dish you won't want to miss and no matter how full you may feel, the feuilleté aux poires with sauce caramel is a dessert to remember. Menus are 130, 170 and 260f.

Map 3B   **AUREL** 84390 (Vaucluse) 5 km N of Sault, 13 km W of Mont Ventoux

---

Located right in the heart of the Sault region, Aurel is 800 metres high and might be called 'Windy Village'. It even owes its name to 'Auro', the Provençal word for wind. It has been occupied as a site since prehistoric days and a vast Gallic-Roman cemetery underlies the whole area, but this exposure to winds has caused a steady decline in population so that today there are little over 100 people left.

Festivals

Aurel holds the Feast of St Pierre every August 20. The old chapel of St Pierre still sits on the hill, built on the site of a temple lost in time. There is a local fête around August 10 with a big aiöli feast, games and tournaments.

Le Relais du Ventoux
(HR)S   *90 64 00 62   R cl. Fri o.o.s., H cl. Jan, Feb   All CC.*

A village inn with a long history and popular locally. The 14 rooms are 135-190f and simple in the extreme.

Le Relais' reputation with the neighbourhood can be judged by the seating capacity of its restaurant, which is about 100. The garden and the terrace are ideal for outdoor dining and one unusual feature is the offering of vegetarian meals – not at all a common thing in the south of France.

Menus are 85f; you need have no fear about choice for there are always dishes like lapin à la tapenade, and jambon à la crème.

Map 3D   **AURIOL** 13390 (Bouches-du-Rhône) 20 km E of Marseille

---

The name comes from the bird, the oriole. In this part of the world, the oriole has bright yellow plumage and was called by the Romans 'aureolus', the golden bird.

The Greeks were here before the Romans though. This was a popular area for Greek traders to have second homes – so the Parisians and the foreigners of today are following a very early precedent.

Added proof of this was found in 1867; a farm boy, André Aubert, was digging up a stump of an olive tree when he found a cache of 2,000 silver coins. They had been struck on one side only and with the figures of animals, both real and mythical, from lions and dogs to griffons and sea-horses. Some had human faces with unmistakably negro features and the find was promptly dubbed 'The Devil's Hoard'. They were eventually identified as Greek and dating from about 500 BC.

You will want to make sure that when you eat around Auriol you consume plenty of onions. The local red onions are famous for their health-giving properties.

Festivals

Local fairs are held on March 19, September 14 and October 29. The Feast of Saint Pierre is at the beginning of August and there is an antique and bric-à-brac fair at the end of September.

Au Moulin de la Sambuc
(R)S-M   *42 72 90 46   On N560   Open all year   All CC.*

On the road into Saint Zacharie, the Moulin is popular with wedding parties and often has business meals and banquets but it is well patronised by individuals too. It is an old mill with a water-wheel and its own trout reserve. Game is always on the menu according to what is in season and what the hunters have brought in. Grilling over wood fire is used for meats, fish and fowl and so the choice of dishes is wide.

The Moulin is famous for its cellar and there are some great wines there but don't worry – there are less expensive ones too. Menus are available but you will probably choose the à la carte which will run to 100-200f.

Map 2C   **AURONS** 13121 (Bouches-du-Rhône) 5 km N of Salon

The seer and prophet Nostradamus who lived in nearby Salon didn't only predict the future. Occasionally, he related the past and it was in 1555 that he told how, in the previous year, a two-headed zebra came from Aurons.

The couple of hundred people in Aurons haven't accumulated a lot

Aurons: Hostellerie Domaine de la Reynaudé

of other local history so the town exists mostly on being confused with Auron in the Alpes-Maritimes and on having one very good hotel-restaurant:

Hostellerie Domaine de la Reynaude
(HR)M   *90 59 30 24   Open all year   All CC.*

Mixed blessings here. The hostellerie is an old post-house dating from the 18th century and on the ancient salt road. It is a charming two-storey stone building in a large park-like area. There is a heated swimming pool, two tennis courts and the 30 rooms look out to beautiful views of the countryside.

The bad news is that the place specialises in seminars but then this activity is what keeps the prices down for the normal guest so that you get high-priced accommodation and food at what are virtually subsidised prices.

There is parking, a bar and dining in the beamed-ceiling restaurant is a joy. The old well and the tables by the leafy pond are reminders of the post-house days. Demi-pension is 390f and full pension is 500f per person (based on double occupancy).

Map 4D   **BANDOL** 33150 (Var) 17 km W of Toulon

Ⓜ *Every day*

Aldous Huxley, Norman Douglas, Katherine Mansfield and D. H. Lawrence are among the writers who have lived in Bandol and found its lazy charm and ideal climate helpful in their creative endeavours. It's changed since then naturally and is rather more brash and commercial (and certainly bigger) but it is still a very pleasant resort. The principal change for the worse has been the rows of flat white apartments in serried ranks on the hills above the town. But you need not look that way. Look instead at the blue Mediterranean and the three sandy beaches.

The long promenade along the front contains shops, boutiques, cafés, crêperies, restaurants, bars and discotheques. There is a large marina full of yachts and just out of Bandol on the Route du Beausset is the Zoo-Jardin Exotique. It is well laid out and filled with exotic plants and birds. Despite its name, there are no animals larger than monkeys and pigs.

Bandol is a famous name in the wine world and if you don't want to go inland to the vineyards (which offer tastings), there are lots of opportunities in Bandol itself. Caves Bacchus on Boulevard Pierreplane, Caveau des Vins and the Maison des Vins, both on Allées Vivien and Caves de la Poste on Avenue 11 Novembre all offer good selections. Bandol is better known as a red wine but there is a rosé and also a white – look for the Blanc de Blanc.

Bandol has a casino that is quite lively and is open every day from 4 p.m. to 4 a.m. Roulette, blackjack, 30/40 and craps are all available and there is a restaurant, a café, a bar, a pâtisserie and snacks. To enter, you must prove that you are 18 or over and pay an entry fee of 56f.

The Ile de Bendor is only two kilometres off the coast and the boats which leave from the centre of the port take only ten minutes for the trip.

The island was an uninhabited rock forty years ago when it was bought by Paul Ricard, whose name you see on most bottles of Pastis. He planted it and developed it into a tourist centre of considerable charm containing numerous artisan shops, a fine modern art gallery, a Musée de la Mer with fish and boats, three hotels, three restaurants, a congress centre and – its main attraction – Ricard's museum of wines and spirits with 7,000 bottles from 45 different countries. *Open 10-12 and 2.15- 6.00 from Easter to September, every day except Wednesday.*

La Réserve
(HR)S-M   *94 29 42 71   Route de Sanary   Cl. 2/1-22/1. R cl. Sun p.m., Mon.   All CC.*

With its direct access to the beach and its shady terrace, this is a restaurant with rooms that has been popular for a long time and continues its success. The 16 rooms are 230-380f and there is private parking.

Proprietor Jacques Jacquet has recently improved the cooking considerably; you can have fine seafood on menus from 130f up.

Splendid
(HR)S-M   *94 29 41 61   Plage de Renécros   Cl. 30/10-1/4   All CC.*

On the small bay just across the tiny isthmus from the port of Bandol, the Splendid has a fine position and still has direct access to the beach which, being protected, is one of the best on this coastal strip. It is still only minutes from the port and the town.

The hotel looks calm and peaceful, all white with a red-tiled roof and its garden and terrace contribute to the serene atmosphere despite its proximity to a busy beach. Claude David has 28 rooms at 240-310f or 250-285f for demi-pension. There are menus at 100 and 120f and fresh seafood is featured on both.

Auberge du Port
(R)M   *94 29 42 63   9 Allée Jean-Moulin   Open all year   All CC.*

It has the reputation of being the best restaurant on the seafront and though it's a bit on the expensive side, the food and the cooking are well above average. A large terrace on the port side gives a fine view while providing welcome shade.

Jean-Pierre Ghiribelli makes full use of local produce and that means seafood primarily. Rascasse, langoustines, loup and rouget are usually featured and prepared in imaginative ways. Noisettes of roast lamb are often an alternative. Menus are 100-300f but you can select from the long à la carte list and keep the price down to a reasonable level. Bandol and Cassis wines are on the list, at 100-130f.

Le Bistrot du Port
(R)S   *94 29 41 39*   *Allée Jean-Moulin*   *Open all year*   *Visa, CB.*

Next door to the Auberge, cheaper, simpler. The Bistro has an outdoor terrace with shady umbrellas, and again the view of the port. The menu is adequate. Recommended are veal rolls in mushroom sauce at 95f, and the crevette and langoustine dishes. Salads are large and satisfying. Cassis wines at around 100f.

Hôtel Delos Palais
(HR)M   *94 32 22 23*   *1 Ile de Bendor*   *Open all year*   *All CC.*

Like so many of the islands off the Mediterranean coast of France, the Ile de Bendor has become an ideal place for seminars and the Hôtel Delos Palais is one of the best.

It accepts other guests however and with two tennis courts, golf, sailing, a pool, a diving centre, a bar and a disco, there is plenty to do besides explore the island.

The 55 rooms are priced on a full pension basis only – 530-620f.

Map 2C   **LA BARBEN** 13330 (Bouches-du-Rhône) 7 km E of Salon-de-Provence

---

The magnificent château that you see today has undergone a lot of changes. Originally known as the Castrum de Barbento, it was built in the 12th century on top of a large rock on the right bank of the Touloubre river where its waters cascaded down. In the religious wars of the 17th century it was destroyed, partly re-built and then burned.

Several restorations have been carried out and these are evident in the different styles – the simple straight lines of later parts of the castle are clearly designed for rooms and chambers, halls and passageways whereas the earlier towers with their battlemented turrets have defensive purposes.

It is eminently photographable from the outside and very visitable on the inside. All the rooms are furnished which means that you can get a very clear idea of what it was really like to live in a castle. You can see the bedrooms where Pauline Borghese enjoyed her numerous love-affairs and you can see the reception rooms of Roi René when he was ruler of Provence. There are dining rooms, kitchens, wine-cellars, a chapel, many other salons, rooms and bedrooms and underground chambers. The castle gardens were designed by Lenôtre who was responsible for the gardens at Versailles.

The castle is open every day in June, July and August. It is closed all January but open other months every day except Tuesday.

What used to be the park belonging to the castle is now a zoo of over a hundred acres with rhinos, hippos, elephants, cheetahs, panthers and kangaroos. The miniature train takes you through the park where there are waterfalls, picnic areas and a vivarium with crocodiles, snakes and turtles.

La Barben has only about 400 inhabitants but it holds an annual celebration at the beginning of August on the anniversary of its patron saint, Saint Sauveur.

Touloubre
(HR)H-S, R-M   *90 55 16 85   Cl. Sun p.m. and Mon and school holidays in winter*
Visa, CB.

From Salon, you have to drive 8 kilometres east on the N572 and then the D22 to find this typical example of a Provençal auberge. The accommodation is modest with 7 rooms at 240f but the restaurant is far more up-market. You can dine on the terrace or in the shady garden in the summer or by the big fireplace in the country-style dining room in the winter. M. Benayoun offers big portions in menus from 120-240f, making full use of regional produce and employing traditional cooking. The pieds et paquets is a favourite with the local clientele.

Map 2B   **BARBENTANE** 13570 (Bouches-du-Rhône) 30 km N of Arles, 6 km W of Châteaurenard

(M) *Every day except Sun.*

Barbentane claims to have invented the 'Farandole', the long line of swaying dancers which is so much a part of any Provençal festival. Mistral wrote about Barbentane and one of his legends *The Golden Islands* is set here.

Today, it does not have much to attract the visitor except perhaps the château, which used to be one of the most beautiful in Provence. Its construction was begun in 1674 and took over a hundred years.

It is open 10-12 and 2-6 in July, August and September, other times on Sunday only by appointment.

Castel Mouisson
(H)M   *90 95 51 17   Cl. 15/10-15/3   All CC.*

A typical Provençal mansion with 17 well-decorated rooms, at 240-270f. There is a pool, tennis court and a garden.

Map 5A   **BARCELONNETTE** 04400 (Alpes de Haute Provence) 70 km SE of Gap

(M) *Wed or Sat*

The name clearly comes from Barcelona and this little town was founded in the 13th century by Raymond Bérenger, Count of Barcelona and Provence.

It is perhaps the prettiest village in the French Alps. As the Italian border is only a few kilometres away, armies have marched and counter-marched through it but the Alpine terrain has been difficult for infantry, cavalry and artillery and Barcélonnette and the quiet highland valleys around it have remained much freer from war and devastation than most Provençal towns.

Winter is long here. Four or five months of snow are usual and there are several ski resorts in close proximity. Summer is still the main tourist season and the snow-capped Alps are visible in the clear air.

In the 19th century, many of the local inhabitants emigrated to Mexico and a large number prospered sufficiently that they were able to return to Barcélonnette and build comfortable villas. One reason for these emigrations is said to be the close similarity between the Catalan Spanish language as spoken in Mexico and the Provençal dialect. Many of the houses you will see on the main street, Avenue de la Libération (route d'Italie), are readily identifiable as having being built in Latin American style rather than French.

The town has little to offer the tourist. La Maison du Mexique on Avenue de la Libération shows displays of life in Mexico. *Open in July and August only, every day 10.30-12.00 and 3.30-7.00 except Sundays and holidays.*

The Museum Chabrand on the Avenue de la Libération has a fine collection of birds from all over the world and is an indication of Barcélonnette's prime activity – and that is as a centre from which to explore the botanists' paradise that surrounds it.

The Vallée de l'Ubaye is superbly scenic and there is an abundance of wild flowers in spring and early summer. Many of the local inhabitants spend the long winter days wood-carving and much of the beds and furniture you will see was hand-made.

The Parc National du Mercantour is only about 20 kilometres south of Barcélonnette so the town is equally convenient as a starting point for trips into it.

Rafts, boats, kayaks, canoes, inflatables and paragliders can all be rented. Swimming, fishing and camping, rock and mountain climbing are all available.

Information from the tourist office which is on the main square, Place Manuel. For more detailed information, the Office National des Fôrets at 9 Avenue de la Libération and the office of the Parc National du Mercantour on La Sapinière are very helpful.

The Wednesday and Saturday markets must be visited if you are in town on these days. On sale are all kinds of delicacies made from local fruit, herbs, nuts and plants. Along Rue Bellon are several shops selling similar products.

Barcélonnette is the starting point for a series of short trips in which you can see some of the most remarkable fortifications in Europe. The Marquis de Vauban, military engineer extraordinaire, began the series in 1693 when he built the Fort of St Vincent. The fort is located about 25 kilometres west of Barcélonnette along the D900. In 1880, more fortifications were added with the completion of artillery emplacements at Chaudon (south of St Vincent) and Chatelard (east of St Vincent). Both are accessible by car while at Col Bas (south of Chaudon) at an altitude of 2,500 metres is another battery accessible only by all-terrain vehicles or by foot.

You have to see these constructions to appreciate the enormous difficulties of building in such near-impossible territory – and there are more to come!

In 1843, the Fort de Tournoux was built – a long wall perched along the crest of a high ridge with towers and ammunition storage rooms spaced throughout its length. It is easily accessible in season – just take the D900 east from Barcélonnette. You will pass the village of Tournoux and you will also see another formidable fortress – the Redoute de Berwick.

Further east yet – and you are now close to the Italian border – are more fortifications, the Batterie de Mallemort and the Fortin de Viraysse. The latter is at 2,500 metres altitude.

Just off the D900 and west of the little village of Larche are more fortifications which make an interesting comparison. These were built to block the Route of the Col de Larche which leads directly into Italy – and they were built in 1931 as part of the Maginot Line. This is the line of defence begun after World War I with the intention of preventing the Germans from any further invasion of France. The line is best known for its existence along the Rhine river and, as is well-known, the Germans invaded France through Belgium, passing north of the Maginot Line and capturing it from the rear. It is not widely appreciated that the Maginot Line also served as a barrier between France and Italy. It is open to visits during the season.

Nowhere else in Europe is there such a staggering assembly of military fortifications in such a small area. The spectacular – and spectacularly difficult – region makes it all the more incredible. And on top of all this is the opportunity to trace the development of the mountain fortress from the earliest construction in 1693 to the Maginot Line which still played a part in modern history by its influence on the Franco-Italian conflict in June 1940 when the Italians invaded France after that country had surrendered to the Germans.

West of Barcélonnette on the N900, the tiny hamlet of Méolans is known as 'the village which loses the sun'. During the months of November, December, January and February, the mountains of the Séolans completely block out the sun. The villagers can watch the gigantic shadow move with the sun through the day and across the cliffs on the other side of the valley.

During these months, Méolans is continually in frozen darkness – except for the peak of one rock, on top of which rises the steeple of a church said to have been erected on the site of an ancient Druidic temple.

La Grande Epervière
(HR)M   *92 81 00 70   Route de Gap   Cl. Jan 11-18   All CC.*

Probably the best hotel in Barcélonnette, medium priced but good value for the money. The 10 rooms all have private bathrooms, and cost 350-380f.

There are views of the mountains from all the rooms and the setting is peaceful and in the middle of a large park.

The restaurant is not exceptional but quite satisfactory. Meals are 90-150f and demi-pension is available at 310-325f.

L'Aupillon
(HR)S   *92 81 01 09   Route de St Pons   Cl. Wed   Visa, CB.*

For low-priced accommodation, L'Aupillon is high on the list and well-known to tourists. The 7 rooms are only 150-200f though in summer, demi-pension is compulsory at 195-240f.

La Mangeoire
(R)S-M   *92 81 01 61   Place des Quatre Vents   Cl. Mon and all Nov   All CC.*

An old stone manor in appearance though it was once a barn. The cooking is quite sophisticated and there is a popular speciality known as 'la potence' which is a variety of grilled meats. Menus are 95 and 160f.

Le Passe Montagne
(R)S-M   *92 81 05 58   Rue du Colle de la Cayolle   Cl. Wed; mid Nov to mid Dec   All CC.*

A wooden chalet, mountain-style, 2 kilometres south of Barcélonnette on the D902, where chef Eric Danéri keeps the cooking simple but nevertheless tries to introduce a little something extra into it. The leg of lamb with tapénade sauce is a good example and there are some wonderful desserts such as the feuilleté chaud à la glace au miel. Menus are 110, 160 and 200f.

Map 2B   **LE BARROUX** 84330 (Vaucluse) 3 km S of Malaucene, 12 km N of Carpentras

---

There are two reasons for visiting Le Barroux. One is the château and the other is a hotel-restaurant.

First, the château and it is one of the most perfect you will ever see. It was built originally in the 12th century but fell into disrepair after heavy attacks by numerous enemies especially that most relentless of all enemies – time.

During the period from 1539 to 1548, a Frenchman of Italian origin named Henri de Rovilhasc devoted all his energies to reconstructing the château as a private home that was partly a fortress and partly a manor house in the current Renaissance style. In the succeeding centuries, the enormous walls, the angled towers and the numerous vantage points for archers and artillerymen presented a daunting façade of impregnability, while inside the lords of the manor lived a life of security and luxury.

You can wander around it at will. It is little visited today and its commanding position on top of a hill make it a lonely yet romantic structure. The restoration work which has kept it looking almost as exactly as it once did, was carried out in 1930 by M Vayson de

Pradenne and he deserves mention for such a fine job. It is rare to find such an old castle in such good condition and it is equally rare to find one quite so isolated with no surrounding village or any dwellings at all to mar the picture. There are magnificent panoramic views of Mont Ventoux from the château grounds.

The Chapel of Notre Dame la Brune, dedicated in 1593, once belonged to the owners of the château. It is not remarkable enough to be of special interest other than its attachment to the château although it does contain a Black Virgin – a statue of the virgin carved in dark cedar. It is quite old and is believed to have been brought here by the monks of Saint Victor when the parish was first established here in the 12th century, contemporary with the building of the original château.

The nearby village of Le Barroux is quite ordinary and has only 500 population. If you should be here to look at the château during the period from June 15 to July 15, however, you can see the Apricot Festival. There is a village fête on the 14th to the 16th of August.

Les Géraniums
(HR)H-S, R-S-M   *90 62 41 08   R cl. Wed o.o.s. and Jan 5-Feb 15   All CC.*

A friendly auberge, more of a family house where you will be greeted warmly and made to feel at home. There are 22 rooms of which 17 are fully equipped and the room rate of 190-215f is within the reach of almost all pockets. The charge for breakfast is 28f and you will be tempted to take as many meals as possible on the magnificent terrace with its sweeping view over the plain.

The food is rustic and there are several Provençal specialities such as tripes à la Provençal, pieds et paquets marseillais and andouillettes grillées. Menus range from 65 to 215f but there are à la carte choices which amount to around 200f for a meal.

Map 3C   **LA BASTIDE DES JOURDANS** 84240 (Vaucluse) 14 km NE of Pertuis, 21 km SW of Manosque

---

The Knights Templar are part of the history and legend of Provence and many locations claim to be Templar buildings.

Here the history is true. East of the village can be seen the ruins of an old convent known as the Cavalerie. It sits in a ravine marking the division between Vaucluse and the Alpes de Haute Provence and near a preserved Roman church. The Ferme des Templiers nearby supplied the victuals and stabled the knights' horses.

Festivals

On 16th February, there is a great Aïöli feast. The local day of fête is the first Sunday in September.

Le Mirvy: La Bastide des Jourdans

Le Mirvy
(HR)S-M   *90 77 83 23   Route de Manosque   H open all year   R cl. Wed noon
and Feb 15-28   Visa, CB.*

A very pretty Provençal farmhouse and located in the park of the
Lubéron. Everything is rustic and charming and the garden and the
pool are extremely inviting. There are ten rooms, all fully-equipped
and priced at a very modest 265-300f. All have a terrace with a fine
view. Mireille Abello is hostess and she will make your stay an
enjoyable one. The food is good Provençal cooking using mostly local
produce. Menus at 100, 138, 168 and 220f.

Auberge du Cheval Blanc
(HR)S-M   *90 77 81 08   Cl. Weds, Thurs o.o.s., Jan, Feb; June 18-25; Oct 15-22*
Visa, CB, EC and MC.

> You will fall in love with this place at once – a smart little stone
> building with white shutters and a large glass door with a white
> awning. It's on the edge of the village and the eight charming rooms
> are priced at 180-320f. There is a lovely garden for summer dining and
> menus start at 120f for a three course meal and go to 200f for four
> courses. The Daube made with lamb is an unusual variation on the
> traditional dish.

Map 2C   **LES BAUX** 13520 (Bouches-du-Rhône) 10 km S of Saint Rémy-
de-Provence

> In a land of mystery, few places are more mysterious than Les Baux. I
> had never experienced, anywhere in the world, a feeling of a location
> being haunted until I came to Les Baux for the first time.
> It is a half-ruined village today and the remains of the 11th century
> fortress seem to grow out of the rock into which it was built. Shattered
> building stones reach fifty feet into the air, giant ruined pillars climb a
> hundred feet and overlook sheer cliff faces which may or may not be a
> part of them. In places, the jagged rock faces have become natural
> stairways while paths both natural and man-made lead to nowhere.
> Blocks of masonry bigger than a house lay as if tossed by a monster
> hand yet all is so eerily desolate that it seems as if Les Baux could
> never have been inhabited.
> The desolate plateau that lies only a short walk north of the village
> has been aptly named the Val d'Enfer, the Valley of Hell. It was here
> that Dante conceived the idea of his Inferno. Some of the deep
> underground caverns are natural while some have been quarried for
> their rock in the building of the château.
> In the 11th century, the lords of Les Baux owned a considerable part
> of Provence and territories overseas. Their power was enormous and
> it grew until 1372 when Viscount Raymond of Turenne, nephew of
> Pope Gregory XI, became the most powerful and the most feared man
> in Provence. His wicked oppression and cruelty included forcing local
> villagers to jump to their death from the top of the château walls. His
> excesses eventually forced the king to gather together all the enemies
> of the Viscount and march against him. They were so numerous that
> he was forced to flee from France.
> The new counts of Provence were the de Manvilles but their strong
> support for the Protestant cause incurred the displeasure of Louis XIII
> and Cardinal Richelieu sent an army which spent a month blowing up
> the château and its fortifications.
> To see the village itself, you must park where indicated and walk
> through the Port Mage. The Hôtel de Ville is 17th century; the Hôtel
> des Porcelets is 16th century and now houses the Musée d'Art
> Contemporain with seven rooms of paintings, some of them showing
> landscapes of the region. The 12th-century Church of Saint Vincent is

Les Baux: Eglise St Vincent

in the Place Saint Vincent, which has a terrace with fine views to the north. The column on the right of the church entrance has graffiti carved into it but as it is the signature of an aspiring poet called Frédéric Mistral, its continued presence is tolerated.

The 14th-century Tour de Brau on tlle narrow Rue Turcat is now a lapidary museum with a good display of rocks and stones found in the ruins. You will also see the communal ovens where the villagers came to bake their bread.

This tour makes a convenient circuit which brings you to the ruined château. The 'Ville Morte', the dead city, as it is called and the plateau on which it stands are all open 8.30-8.00 every day in July and August and 9.30-5.30 the rest of the year.

The Hôtel de Manville has a 16th-century façade and inside a fine collection of documents and photographs relating to Les Baux, past and present. The Maison des Santons is a 17th-century chapel transformed into the Musée des Santons Provençaux and the Musée de l'Olivier is housed in the 12th-century Chapelle St Blaise.

As you drive out of the car park area and head downhill, you will see the Son et Lumière show, Cathédrale des Images which runs continuously as you walk past 50,000 square feet of giant images coming from 32 projectors, in a series of caverns inside an old quarry. Strangely effective. Every year, the show has a different theme.

Parking is free. Open from 10-7 every day.

Les Baux gave its name to bauxite, the ore of aluminium which was first found here. It is the reddish-brown clay you see as you drive anywhere in this region; the colour comes from the iron impurities. In 1855, the French chemist Henri Deville showed a shiny bar of aluminium metal to the Emperor Napoleon III, produced from Les Baux ore. The Emperor got so excited that he financed the building of a plant to produce enough metal to equip his entire army with aluminium armour. Deville found that he could not get the price of making the metal down below £10 per pound and the ambitious project was never realised.

This red clay soil and the bleached bone-white rock does not look like suitable terrain for growing grapes but there are vineyards around Les Baux. Two of them produce A.O.C. wines and one produces excellent vin du pays. All encourage you to come and taste and, of course, buy. These are: Le Mas Sainte Berthe, Le Mas de la Dame and Les Caves de Sarragan.

Over one and a half million people visit Les Baux every year so there are plenty of boutiques and shops. L'Herbier de Provence on the Rue Neuve sells all kinds of herbs and plants for health and beauty, La Fenêtre sells sculptures carved from olive wood and Le Cellier on Rue des Fours has santons, pottery and wines.

The Feast of Saint Vincent is the big feast day – on January 22.

L'Oustau de Baumanière
(HR)L   *90 54 33 07   H cl. 20/1-4/3   All CC.*

It costs around 1000f for a room and that is more than most people may want to spend for a night but L'Oustau has got to be on the list of the top half-dozen hotels in Europe and at least you should know about it.

Queen Elizabeth and Prince Philip stayed here, and after them the guest book looks like a copy of *Who's Who*. Whoever they are, they've stayed here.

The building itself is a cross between a Spanish hacienda and an Italian monastery. The gardens are exotically laid out with olive, peach and fig trees, spectacular at night when the ghostly gleam of the white rocks looms in the floodlights. The pool is immaculate, the terrace is gorgeous and the whole effect is that of an oasis of luxury.

Two tennis courts, horseback riding and a helicopter landing pad are here for the convenience of guests. Jean-André Charial is now the director, taking over from Raymond Thuilier who made L'Oustau into a world-renowned establishment. If some parts of the building and grounds look familiar, it is because they have been used in so many films.

The 11 apartments and 15 rooms have every luxury and comfort and are furnished throughout with antiques. All look out onto spectacular views, some of the gardens, some of the white rocky slopes and some of the ancient village.

Whether you eat in the vaulted dining room or out on the terrace, you will find that the food still has the Lyonnaise basis that has existed here for years although Alain Burnel is now chef de cuisine. An occasional guest complains that the cooking lacks originality, though when the standard and prices are thus high, anything short of perfection is open to criticism. Petit homard au Châteauneuf-du-Pape and gigot d'agneau en croûte are two of the well-known dishes, while the veau aux pruneaux and sauce à l'orange and for dessert the ices and sorbets are outstanding. A meal will cost about 600f and the wine list is extensive – and predictably expensive.

Les Baux: Le Mas d'Aigret

Le Mas d'Aigret
(HR)M-L   *90 54 33 54   H cl. 6/1-27/2, R cl. Wed lunch   All CC.*

Below the ruined fortress of Les Baux an Englishman, Pip Phillips, runs a delightful establishment that has all the accoutrements of a luxury hotel and still exudes a feeling of homey comfort. The views are magnificent, looking out towards the Camargue and the Mediterranean.

Fifteen rooms and one apartment all have a private entrance, bath and toilet, satellite TV and mini-bar; most have private terrace, balcony or garden and two are built into the natural rock. Demi-pension only in season at 1140-1440f for the rooms and 1540f for the apartment, occupancy by two people. There is a pool and seven acres of gardens.

The food is imaginative and prepared with a light touch that does not detract from the quality. It is helped further by the unique dining room which is built into the natural rock around a huge fireplace and furnished with antiques. Menus are 180, 260 and 300f. Sandre and rascasse are two of the fish dishes often featured and the noisettes farcies de gigot is excellent.

Bautézar et Musée
(HR)M   *90 54 32 09   Grande Rue Frédéric Mistral   H cl. 5/1-20/3; R cl. Mon. Visa, CB.*

Modestly-priced accommodation is hard to find in Les Baux – with a million and a half visitors a year, it is understandable that hoteliers can keep prices up and still fill all the rooms and tables.

This is an old hotel with 2 apartments and 10 rooms at 300-400f. The panoramic terraces give fine views over the Val d'Enfer and the dining room has ancient vaulted ceilings. There are menus at 130 and 200f and snacks are available.

Hostellerie de la Reine Jeanne
(HR)S-M   *90 54 32 06   Cl. Jan   Visa, CB.*

Further down the price range, the Hostellerie is at the entrance to the old village and has 11 old but serviceable rooms at 200-300f, including panoramic views. Seminars are held but only out of season.

The meals are as serviceable as the rooms, at 95 and 140f, and you can eat out on the shaded terrace. Demi-pension at 500f for two people is good value in such an expensive area.

La Reboto de Taven
(R)M-L   *90 54 34 23   Cl. Sun p.m. o.o.s.; Mon from 9/1-25/2   All CC.*

At the entrance to the Val d'Enfer, La Reboto has been here a very long time and has a deserved reputation. It is a charming old house and you feel the hospitality and know that the food will be good when you walk on to the terrace shaded by mulberry trees or into the garden.

Menus are 250 and 390f although you might prefer the à la carte. The carreé d'agneau is succulent and the éventail de canard au miel et aux cannelbages (cranberries) is a real treat. The wine list is a good balance between old vintages and recent local wines.

La Bérengère
(R)S-M   *90 54 35 63   Rue du Trencat   Cl. Tues p.m.; Wed; Nov   Visa, CB.*

A cosy little place in the village, full of flowers, paintings and pots – little is the right word for there are less than twenty covers. It is hard to say what you might eat because every day's menu depends on what looks best to proprietor Bernard Auzet at the market that day. Everything will be good though and full use will be made of local wines and produce. Menus at 145 and 215f.

Map 1C   **BEAUCAIRE** 30300 (Gard), 20 km N of Arles, 25 km SW of Avignon

---

Its imposing castle is one of the great sights. You get two sights for the price of one for, facing the castle of Beaucaire on the west bank of the Rhône, is the equally imposing castle of Tarascon on the east bank.

The building of the castle of Beaucaire was begun by Count Raymond IV of Toulouse in the 13th century and continued by King Louis IX. It was largely destroyed by Cardinal Richelieu as part of his plan to weaken the nobility by razing to the ground all fortifications not needed for defence. Only the walls which look out over the river, the great staircase, the chapel and the triangular tower remain. (The latter is known for some mysterious reason as the 'Tour Carrée'!)

Despite this destruction, the castle looks impregnable with its battlements and towers. From the top, you can readily understand why it survived for four hundred years. *Open every day from 10.00 till dusk.*

In the old part of the town of' Beaucaire and near the castle are some fine 17th-century buildings and the Town Hall, built in 1679, is very impressive. Its flat roof is covered with Roman tile and the building is elegant without being ostentatious.

Hôtel Les Doctrinaires
(HR)M   *66 59 41 32   Quai Général de Gaulle   R cl. Sat lunch; Sun p.m. o.o.s. Visa, CB.*

Run by the Sauvage-Dijol family and right in the heart of Beaucaire, this is a charming 17th-century building. The 34 rooms are 320-370f but full pension is obligatory in season at 700f for two. Breakfast and dinner are served on the lovely patio and the cuisine is gourmand, making full use of local produce.

Map 3C   **LES BEAUMETTES** 84220 (Vaucluse) 14 km E of Cavaillon

---

The name derives from 'baumo', grottoes. Earlier inhabitants lived in the numerous grottoes around while the N100 which goes through

Les Beaumettes was once the Domitian Way, one of the great Roman roads.

Festival

First Sunday in October – local fête.

Domaine le Moulin Blanc
(HR)M-L *90 72 34 50   Open all year   All CC.*

It's expensive but it is one of the great hotels of Provence and it would be a shame not to mention it.

It is a former post house and also a flour mill, two large stone buildings with a common entrance and shallow, sloping red-tiled roofs. The 7 acre park surrounding it is delightful for walks and there is a pool and tennis.

The 18 rooms are 480-1150f and are beautifully furnished with antiques. The huge fireplace is enjoyable to look at even in the summer.

Gourmet food is served in the great vaulted dining room amid splendour and elegance. Menus at 190, 300 and 350f.

Madame Marthe Deneits
(C)M   *90 72 39 22   Le Ralenti du Lierre   Cl. 1/11-1/4*

In the village, Madame Deneits' friendly chambre d'hôte is a definite alternative to hotel accommodation. There is a pool on the terrace, a large lounge, a living room with a fireplace and a separate dining room.

All five rooms are furnished differently. Three of them have private bathroom and toilet, one has a mezzanine, private bath and toilet and the fifth has toilet and washbasin but no bath or shower. Prices are 250-400f.

Map 2B   **BEAUMES-DE-VENISE** 84190 (Vaucluse) 20 km E of Orange, 30 km NE of Avignon

---

In the Vaucluse, you are continually aware that you are deep in the wine country. So many towns and villages are names familiar from wine lists and Beaumes-de-Venise is no exception – though it is a little different.

It takes its name from 'Baumo', the Provençal word for grotto, and these perforate the cliffs overhanging Beaumes-de-Venise while the district of Venaissin has been corrupted to Venise.

You will want to taste the wine from here because it is different – it is sweet. Sweet wines are popular in many Mediterranean countries, most being based on the muscat grape and fortified which brings the alcohol content up – as high as 15%. Frontignan, Lunel and Rivesaltes are three of the best-known of these but Beaumes-de-Venise is truly distinctive because it is not fortified and hence it is less sweet and less alcoholic. It is pale amber in colour and its taste is subtle so that it suggests a balance between sweet and dry. It is not expensive but it is not too common either and a visit here to its home village is a unique opportunity.

Legend insists that King René introduced the muscat grape into Provence and the statue of him on the Cours Mirabeau in Aix-en-Provence depicts him with a bunch of those very grapes in his hand. The Cave des Vignerons is on the D7 and a good place to try the wine. Open every week-day. Table wines are also on sale here.

Near the Cave is the church of Notre Dame d'Aubune, built in the 11th century and later enlarged. Local legend asserts that Charlemagne, Emperor of the Holy Roman Empire, built it to comemmorate one of his victories over the Saracens. Traces of these invaders can be found all over Provence and near Beaumes can be seen the Saracen Tower, the Devil's Rock and the Turk's Chamber. This is perfect hiking country if you want to see these and don't mind a little rock climbing.

Several 'wine routes' exist in this region – routes which you can follow, passing through villages and towns which offer excellent wines and centuries of history. One of these is La Route Lavande, the Lavender Route. About 70 km in length, it goes through more names that are familiar. Leaving Beaumes-de-Venise, it winds its way by Vacqueras, Gigondas, Sablet, Cairanne, Sainte Cécile des Vignes and Mondragon to Bollène on the A7 autoroute. This is a delightful means of spending a leisurely day driving through one charming village after another.

Particularly worth a visit is the Caveau de Saint Sauveur. It consists of ancient buildings converted into a modern winery without losing any of the charm. Just outside the village and you can taste Beaumes-de-Venise right on its home ground as well as Côtes-du-Rhône, Côtes-du-Ventoux and some good and extremely reasonably priced vins de pays and vins de table.

The ruins of the old château are strung along the hillside above the village, perched on a ledge in a manner so picturesque that it only just avoids being theatrical.

There is one very good place to stay in Beaumes-de-Venise which is only a very tiny village:

Le Relais des Dentelles
(HR)S   *90 62 95 27   Cl. Wed all year   All CC.*

Impossible to miss as it's right on the D7 road north out of Carpentras. As the name suggests, it is a relais, a pleasant, friendly place and a wayside inn rather than an hotel.

Michel Nicolai has only six rooms so booking is essential. The Relais is well-known and popular but if you can get in, it will be a stay you will enjoy.

The rooms are comfortable and cosy and only 150f each whether occupied by one or two persons. Breakfast is an additional 25f per person. Cooking is Provençal and correctly described as gastronomic. The menu is 80f which brings large numbers of diners from far and near so if you're dining among fifty or more, you will surmise that the Relais would be more accurately described as a restaurant with rooms.

Map 3C   **BEAURECUEIL** 13100 (Bouches-du-Rhône) 10 km E of Aix-en-Provence

---

I suppose it's a sad state of affairs when a village has nothing more to recommend it than dinosaur nests and two hotel/restaurants. Still, some villages don't have either ...

The Parc des Roques Hautes was classified as a geological site in 1964 after dinosaur eggs were found here. They will tell you in the village that the female dinosaur laid as many as a hundred eggs, moving in a more or less straight line and depositing four or five at a time.

Relais Sainte Victoire
(HR)S-M   *42 66 94 98   Cl. Sun p.m.; Mon; first week in Jan; Feb   All CC.*

At the foot of Sainte Victoire, the mountain that Paul Cézanne loved to paint, the Relais sits in a sheltered site on the plain of Aix.

It has been a popular place with the locals for many years and Messieurs Berges and Jugy have made it a favourite with many visitors too. It holds seminars but not during the months of June, July and August – a very wise procedure that many another hotel might follow. Keeping business guests and summer guests apart is a smart way to keep both factions as clientele.

There is a garden, swimming and tennis (on a half court), parking in the grounds. The 5 apartments at 400-500f and the 5 rooms at 250-300f have air-conditioning and TV and are cheerful and good-sized. Some have a terrace looking out on to the park and the garden.

The restaurant is, of course, what brings in the local residents. The fillet de loup aux truffes is a favourite and everybody asks, 'How do you prepare the boeuf Paul Cézanne?'

Menus are a bit pricier than the rooms on a comparative basis but the cooking is excellent and imaginative. Menus are 200, 250 and 300f.

Mas de la Bertrande
(HR)S-M   *42 66 90 09   Chemin de la Plaine   Cl. Sun p.m.; Mon; and 15/2-15/3   All CC.*

A fine old Provençal farmhouse in the woods, with a garden and a pool. The 10 rooms are priced at 300-500f, or demi-pension is offered at 385-535f.

The huge rural dining room opens up on to a large terrace which is in great demand for summer dining. Jean-Marie Merly is the chef and a former pupil of Jean-Pierre Robert. He had already established a reputation as chef at the Casino restaurant in Aix and the menus reflect his talent and elegant touch. He uses the finest ingredients from the local markets. You will enjoy his fillets de rouget avec sésame and tomato butter or you might prefer the pigeons au vin de noix. Menus are 130, 195 and 280f.

Map 3B   **BEDOIN** 84410 (Vaucluse) 15 km NE of Carpentras

 Mon

As you approach Bedoin from the west, you may wonder why it looks so familiar. This is because it is one of the most photographed views of Provence.

The vineyards in the foreground, the village of white houses with red-tiled roofs, the grey stone walls with the tall spire of the church surmounting the hill and – in the distance – the usually snow-covered peak of Mont Ventoux. Chocolate-box stuff and a photographic cliché it may be but it is nevertheless a scene of charm and serenity.

There are about 4,000 acres of vineyards around Bedoin and these are unusual in that they are shared about 50/50 between wine grapes and table grapes. The vines have been here a long time – since the 9th century for certain and possibly earlier. You will see numerous opportunities for tasting and buying vins des Côtes-du-Rhône and many are AOC grade, reds, whites and rosés. The Cave des Vignerons du Mont Ventoux offers a good selection of wines from local vineyards and there is the wine festival in August.

The Chapelle de la Madeleine is just outside the village on the way to Malaucene on the D19. It is a fine Romanesque edifice with carvings of steer heads on the outside. It contains a small museum with some rare exhibits including a 4th-century sarcophagus illustrated with biblical scenes.

In the opposite direction, that is on the D974 going east from Bedoin, is the minuscule community of Sainte Colombe. It is known locally as a 'relais gastronomique' where hunters of game, diggers of truffles and collectors of mushrooms bring their wares for sale.

Festivals

August 15 is the Feast of the Patron Saint Antonin but in July there is a shooting competition in which the competitors are allowed to use ancient firearms only.

L'Oustau d'Anais
(R)S-M   *90 65 67 43   Cl. Mon, Tues, Oct   All CC.*

'Only a simple Provençal village restaurant,' might be one description. A better one would describe it as a restaurant where chef Yannick Dauberte takes local produce and makes the most of it. Pieds et paquets isn't everyone's choice but few places cook it better than here. The daube is also extremely good. Menus are 90, 130 and 170f.

Map 3C   **BONNIEUX** 84480 (Vaucluse) 47 km SE of Avignon, 12 km SW of Apt

(**M**) *Fri*

At 425 metres high, Bonnieux has magnificent views of the neighbouring villages of Gordes, Lascoste and Roussillon. It is not just an isolated perched village though, but a busy little place with a 12th-century church and an unusual museum. This one is the Musée de la Boulangerie and tells the story of bread-making, with old ovens and other equipment, drawings, sketches and documents. *It is on the Rue de la République and is open 10-12 and 3-6.30, closed January and February but open weekends only in March, April and May, October, November and December.*

Also accessible from the Rue de la République is the Rue de la Mairie. Be sure to walk up it and then continue up the ancient rocky steps to the old church at the top with the massive fortified walls around it.

Most of Bonnieux's sights are just outside the village though. On the road to Apt is the elegant chapel of Saint Symphorien, built on to the remains of a 10th-century priory and today distinguished by its slender square tower. Le Pont Julien crosses the Calavon river near Bonnieux and is probably the best-preserved of the bridges built in Roman Gaul, about 300 BC.

The Château de Mille was erected on the successive remains of a mediaeval castle and a Roman villa while in still earlier times the primitive tribes living here showed that they were not so primitive, as they knew how to cultivate grapes and make wine. A cistern found under the present building held over 6,000 gallons of wine and a system of multiple level basins and channels cut into the rock demonstrate a high degree of wine-making sophistication. Visits and wine tasting are available.

Festivals

There is an asparagus market every day throughout April and May.

In August, usually at the beginning of the month, Bonnieux has a musical week. Throughout July and August there is a different planned event every Thursday. The local feast of Saint Symphorien is held on the first Sunday following August 15 and is accompanied by parades, games and wine-tasting.

➤**Hôtel l'Aiguebrun**
(HR)M-L   *90 74 04 14   Relais de la Combe   Cl. 1/1-mid Mar; mid Nov-31/12*
All CC.

This is a little higher-priced than I would normally recommend for this area but L'Aiguebrun is too well-known and too well-liked not to recommend fully. It is superbly elegant and the service and attention provided by Anne Ferraris are outstanding. There is no question that it is good value for money and the food is famous far and near.

There are only eight rooms, priced at 500-680f for a double. The location is about 15 minutes drive towards neighbouring Buoux and the ultimate in peaceful countryside.

The restaurant looks down on to the river and the waterfall and the magnificent wooded slopes, 150 acres of which belong to the hotel. A la carte is the best way to eat though be warned that the (almost) nouvelle cuisine does not offer large portions. Expect to pay about 200-250f per person.

Arrowed for elegance, good service, superb setting.

M. Mariette
(C)M   *90 75 89 78   19 Rue de la République   Cl. 1/10-31/3   No CC.*

At the very opposite end of the scale is this inexpensive chambre d'hôte right in the heart of the village. You have to park in one of the small village parking areas and carry your luggage up a short stone staircase but for a budget stay this place is difficult to beat. It's 175f for two people and all of the five rooms have a private bath and toilet. The rooms are a bit sombre with their dark flowered wallpaper but breakfast is included in the price.

Les Eydins
(C)L   *90 75 84 99   Route Pont Julien   Cl. 1/11-Easter.*

This beautifully restored old Provençal farmhouse 2 kms from Bonnieux on the road towards Pont Julien, the old Roman bridge, has opened just in time to be included here and it makes a welcome addition to the chambre d'hôte accommodation in the region.

Jan and Shirley Kozlowski have three double rooms, all with private toilet and bath. There is a common room near the pool with telephone, barbecue and kitchen and private parking. The property is extensive and there are magnificent views over the neighbouring olive groves and vineyards. A garden and a patio provide ample space for rest and relaxation while breakfast may be enjoyed on the terrace or in the vaulted dining room. Rooms are 420f with breakfast included and Polish Jan and English Shirley will make you feel really at home.

Map 2C   **BOULBON** 13150 (Bouches-du-Rhône) 19 km SW of Avignon, 8 km NW of Tarascon

---

Many people describe Boulbon as their favourite Provençal village yet it remains little-known. The locals would like to keep it that way – they have seen what happens to villages that become fashionable. Still, it seems strange that visitors have not spread the word and filled Boulbon with tourists.

It is pronounced 'Bourbon' and that was its name until 1792 when the town council decided to establish the individuality of their own village and avert continued confusion.

At first sight, it doesn't look extraordinary. The cobblestoned streets, the church with its ornate side-chapels and contrasting plain sanctuary, the wide Cours which becomes a beehive on market day – none of these appear too different from other Provençal villages you have seen. But Boulbon grows on you.

Its most striking feature is its massive fortress, looking like a Crusader's castle and perched above a great cliff. It was built in the 10th century, half embedded in the rock and might have been there for ever. Gardens and terraces added in the 17th century have mellowed its appearance a little but it remains a magnificent sight.

Boulbon's most popular event is the Blessing of the Bottles and thereby hangs a very unusual tale. Tradition says that Marcellin, a priest in the Rome of 304, refused to sacrifice to false gods and was thrown into a deep hole full of broken pottery. Before dying, he ran some of his blood into one of the jars around him and offered it to Christ whereupon it was changed into wine.

Festivals

Every year on June 1st, all the men of the village bring a bottle of wine each and they march through the streets, a drum and fife band playing and a bust of St Marcellin held high. The women and children tag along behind and this intolerably sexist behaviour probably originates in a pagan ceremony associated with fertility rites. The men have stoutly resisted all efforts at changing this however and when they reach the church, the bottles are blessed and each man makes the sign of the cross, pulls the cork and drinks the wine. Not all the wine though – a little must be left in the bottle for now that it has been blessed, it is kept to give to the sick and the dying throughout the year until the next ceremony.

As guests are not Boulbonnais, they are not allowed to carry bottles but don't despair – afterwards, the Mayor holds court and glasses will be offered to you. These will be ful! and there are plenty more bottles where the others came from. More festivities make it a long, noisy and exhausting day with carnivals, dancing, boules contests and fireworks.

The last week-end in August is another big event in Boulbon, the Feast of Saint Eloi, the patron saint of blacksmiths. The festivities begin on the Friday evening with a big boules contest for mixed teams (two men and one woman). On Saturday, there is the decoration of the horse-wagons and a judging of the best. This is followed by a grand ball which lasts past midnight.

Sunday is the biggest day of all, starting at 8 a.m. with a breakfast for the drivers of the wagons ('charrettes'). There is mass at 9.30 then a parade and blessing of the charrettes. At one o'clock, the whole village participates in a gigantic lunch under the shade of the trees in the square and then there is a parade of the 'gardians'. Another grand ball follows and there is also a discotheque.

It's surprising that Boulbon doesn't have recommendable hotels and restaurants but there are plenty in nearby Avignon, Tarascon and Graveson.

Map 3B   **BRANTES** 84390 (Vaucluse) 22 km NW of Sault, 32 km E of Vaison-la-Romaine

Hardly a village at all – just a cascade of houses tumbling down from the ruins of the old castle to the road below.

Brantes is still struggling hard to reach a hundred inhabitants but doesn't look like achieving that aim. It gets its strange name from the Latin 'Brantulae' (shaky rocks) which referred to its position, looking as if it is sliding down the escarpment.

The village is probably a lot more secure than it appears. Certainly it is ringed by a formidable wall of rounded stones, pierced only by a single gate and it has resisted human enemies and the elements for centuries.

From Brantes can be seen the grimmest face of Mont Ventoux.

Hôtel l'Auberge
(HR)S   *75 28 01 68   Cl. Oct 15-Nov 11   Visa, CB.*

Having described some auberges as 'modest', I am lost for words when it comes to this one. Perhaps sub-modest is the only expression. After all, accommodation in one of the five rooms costs a staggering 95f so you don't need me to tell you that it's simple even stark but you will sleep well in the clear mountain air of 550 metres altitude.

The restaurant is equally simple and very popular with the locals. More than a hundred of them pile in most nights and the garden and terrace are packed in the summer. Locally caught game features on the menus which are always a matter of what is available. Meal prices vary daily for this reason but you won't have to pay more than 60 or 75f for a good, enjoyable meal.

Map 3C   **BUOUX** 84480 (Vaucluse) 7 km S of Apt

There are only a hundred people living in Buoux so the village itself is not a Provençal metropolis. Much of its importance is attached to the countryside around it as the Valley of Buoux is one of the richest in Provence as far as prehistoric remains are concerned. There are scores of grottoes which were used as dwellings in Paleolithic times and the river Ayguebrun which runs through the area was at least a hundred times larger then, providing not only fish but irrigation for the fertile land which must have teemed with game.

La Brémonde, Salen, l'Escudette, Chaix and Baume les Peyrards are all sites near Buoux where thousands of flint objects, fossils and human bone fragments have been found. The use of fire by the local inhabitants has been confirmed. By the road leaving Buoux and all along it as far as Apt have been found what appear to be stone cannon balls. Speculation favours a different explanation and it is believed that during an earlier geological epoch, molten rock solidified while it still contained air bubbles. These bubbles slowly filled with rock at a later date.

The Château of Buoux is of mediaeval origin and was re-built during the 15th and 16th centuries. At the end of the 18th century, the Marquis of Galliffet undertook the enlargement of the château, starting with an imposing wing containing 36 windows. This gives the impression of a new ruin though it must be said that the effect generally is to complete the romantic appearance of the whole building.

The work that the Marquis began was never, in fact, finished. One reason given is that it was halted by the Revolution but the local story is that the Marquis de Sade, a later owner, returned from a hunt in a bad mood not having shot a single quarry. Furious at his lack of success, he fired shots at the masons and labourers who left and never returned.

South of the village is the fort of Buoux. It's not easy to reach – the trail leading to it is narrow and rocky. The ruins of the battlements and fortifications date back to the 14th century and they are made even more formidable by their position among the giant natural rocks.

Auberge des Séguins
(HR)S-M   *90 74 19 58*   *Quartier La Loube*   *Cl. Jan, Feb, Nov 15-Mar 1*   *No CC.*

Rather a strange place – it's part holiday camp and part youth hostel though the last time I was there, most of the guests were over 70.

It sits in a small valley near the entrance to the fort and is particularly popular as a base for hikers and climbers as the massive rocks behind the auberge are irresistible for their sheer and seemingly unclimbable faces. The 27 rooms are in a big old building along with a dormitory which sleeps 21 and is used by groups.

The whole setting is very rural and casual. It is quiet and serene and the world seems far away. The river teems with trout and there are as many fishing rods as hiking packs – which is a lot. During the day, the less energetic hang around the pool or the patio which adjoins the more modern building housing the restaurant and the kitchens.

Rooms are 200-250f and menus are 95f. The cooking is Provençal and daube and aïoli figure frequently.

Auberge de la Loube
R)M   *90 74 19 58*   *Quartier de la Loube*   *Cl. Tues. except fêtes; 2/1-2/2*   *No CC*

Even the Auberge's rival establishments in neighbouring Bonnieux recommend it so you can expect it to be good. The cooking is straightforward with only local fresh produce. Lamb from the Lubéron mountains is prominent and pintade is often available. The setting of the garden and terrace are very pleasant and the service is kept up to scratch by Maurice. A four-course menu is 150f and there is a good selection of inexpensive local wines.

The Auberge has no rooms but it is worth noting that there are several reasonable chambre d'hôtes in the immediate area.

P.S. If you're asking directions here, you may have trouble unless you remember that the locals call it 'Bee-ou'.

Map 2B   **CABRIERES-D'AVIGNON** 84220 (Vaucluse) 25 km E of Avignon

When the Great Plague swept through Provence in 1720, more than
half the population was wiped out in some villages. One of the
desperate measures taken by the local authorities here in Cabrières
was the construction of a wall to keep out all infected persons. As little
was known of the cause of the plague or how it was spread, this
effectively meant keeping out everybody.

The wall was over six feet high and consisted of loose rocks fitted
together. Towers were constructed at intervals and there were sentry
boxes and food storage silos. A thousand men were assigned the duty
of defending the wall and the guard was changed every two hours.

The Tower of Sabran in Robion was at one end of the wall and it
went through Cabrières to Monieux. Remains of the wall can be seen
today – take the D15 going towards Murs and at either the Col de la
Ligne or the Col de Regnagnade a forest road is marked to the west.

Festivals

The village has a local fête on the week-end nearest to July 14. The
bucolic atmosphere is well maintained by the country fair at the end of
July which features farm animals and the exhibition of local plants
with medicinal properties at the beginning of August.

Jacquy Truc
(C)M   *90 76 97 03   Open all year   No CC.*

It is very appropriate that this country village should have a highly
recommendable chambre d'hôte. It is in a large house about 100
metres from the village itself and has a private pool and a terrace.
There is a nice balcony and a large lounge.

There are five rooms on the first floor and all have a private shower
and toilet. At 180-220f (80f for another bed), this is extremely good
value for a budget stay.

Mas des Ortolans
(HR)M   *90 76 96 06   Chemin de la Bastidonne   H cl. 1/1-15/3; Nov; Dec.   R cl.
Wed.*

Should you prefer more conventional hotel accommodation, the Mas
is the place. Just outside the village, there are seven rooms at 345f. All
have TV and private bath. There is a pool.

Meals can be served on the terrace and the menu is 138f. The
speciality is cooking with fresh cream.

L'Escargotière
(R)S-M   *90 76 89 76   Cl. Tues, Wed lunch and mid-Nov to mid-Dec   Visa, CB.*

A fairly recent addition to the eating scene in this neighbourhood,
L'Escargotière is small and wisely stays with good Provençale
cooking.

The emphasis is on seafood, and there are some interesting variations like escargots, Biscay-style and epinard avec la crabe et les langoustines. There is an 89f menu for lunches only (except holidays) and menus at 135 and 190f. Daniel Lantuejoul deserves support in his efforts to offer fine meals at reasonable prices.

Map 3C   **CADENET** 84160 (Vaucluse) 12 km W of Pertuis, 35 km N of Aix

(**M**) *Mon*

Cadenet occupies an important position on the D973 which runs along the north bank of the Durance river. In earlier days it guarded the entrance to the Lourmarin valley.

It is not a particularly remarkable village today – even its famous statue portrays a character unknown outside the village. This is Etienne André, born here in 1777. As a boy, he loved to play his drums and he did this so loudly and often that the villagers were delighted when he joined the army to fight against the Austrians. His day of glory came when he made a solo attack on the enemy and allowed Napoleon's army to control the vital Bridge of Arcole. The statue in the Grand Place shows him making his great charge.

Festivals

Cadenet puts on a very creditable Mardi Gras carnival and there is the Fête of Saint Barthelemy on August 24.

Aux Ombrelles
(HR)S   *90 68 02 40   Avenue Philippe de Girard, Route de Marseille   Cl. Sun p.m., Mon, 10/12-1/2   Visa, CB.*

A small modern house, furnished throughout with Provençal furniture. There are 11 rooms, though only two have private bath and toilet. This accounts for the wide price range of 100-215f, all very reasonable.

The food is simple like the chicken in Côtes-du-Lubéron wine, but extremely good. Menus are 85, 105 and 150f.

Le Mas du Colombier
(HR)S-M   *90 68 29 00   Route de Pertuis   Cl. 25/1-29/2   Visa, CB, EC.*

Coming out of Cadenet on the road to Pertuis, you will find Le Mas, with its 15 rooms, a garden and parking. The rooms are good value at 250-310f, considering that a pool is among the facilities offered.

The restaurant is popular and I have seen over 150 people eating here – inside, on the terrace and in the garden. Menus start at 93f and the feuilleté d'escargots is a great start to a meal. Pavé de boeuf Colombier is the house speciality.

Restaurant Stefani
(R)S-M   *90 68 07 14   35 Rue Gambetta   Cl. Sun p.m.; Wed; 1/2-2/3   All CC.*

Don't be put off by the entrance. It doesn't look too prepossessing but inside, all is very different.

There is a lovely terrace with views and the large dining room is flanked by a bistro corner and a piano bar.

It is, of course, the food that people come for and Phillipe Stefani believes in traditional dishes which use the fresh produce available in the area which surrounds the market town. Phillipe says that the reason he specialises in seafood is that he lived so many years by the ocean. Try his bourride de poissons blancs on the 150f menu. You might start with the profiteroles d'escargots and conclude with the fromage du chèvre and the dessert maison. Other menus are 100 and 195f, while the Marseillaise style pieds et paquets at 85f is very popular with the local clientele.

Map 2B   **CAIRANNE** 84290 (Vaucluse)

 Thur

There can be very few villages which produce as good a red wine as Cairanne and still keep such a low profile. Surely such a wine deserves more publicity, more hype, wider sales...? Well, maybe the producers prefer it the way it is.

There are less than a thousand people in Cairanne and very little to attract visitors. The Musée du Donjon des Templiers is a wine museum but even the Chapel of Notre Dame-de-la-Vigne has been built as recently as 1962 as the result of a vow made during World War II. That all leaves nothing but the wine – and what a wine!

The Côtes du Rhône Villages wines are among the best of the full, rich reds that can also age. They combine a fruity flavour with the earthy taste of a wine from the southern dusty soil. The wines of Cairanne are richer than Beaujolais but lighter than claret. Don't take my word for it. Try them for yourself.

The Caveau de Belvédère is a syndicate of 14 private wine cellars. The Co-operative offers tasting and sales of wines which are largely different. La Grand Contadine is a label to watch out for at either of these. One of the outstanding vineyards is the Domaine Brusset where three generations of the family work together. Cairanne is called 'le haut village des maîtres-vignerons' and even among such talented competition, the Brusset family has gathered a gallery of medals. A warm welcome awaits you at Domaine Brusset from André, his son Daniel and grandson Laurent. On the last Sunday in July, Cairanne holds a wine fair which makes the village a very popular place that day.

Cairanne is not a hotel town but there is one very good chambre d'hôte:

Mme Pierrefeu
(C)S *90 30 82 04* *Domaine le Plaisir*

A pleasant, quiet garden and five delightful, simple rooms in which Charlotte Pierrefeu takes great pride. Two rooms have toilet and a shower, two have bidet and bath, one has a toilet and bidet. Anyone should be able to make a choice from all these, especially as the prices are 120f for one person and 140f for two, including breakfast. A meal is 60f, also simple, but satisfying local fare. Demi-pension at 150f per person is another option worth considering.

Map 3C   **CALAS-CABRIES** 13480 (Bouches-du-Rhône) 5 km SW of Aix

Located on the D9 going south out of Aix towards Marseille, Calas-Cabriès is on the edge of a reservoir and only minutes from the autoroute. All of this makes it remarkable that it is such a beautifully preserved little village.

No pretensions and nothing of outstanding value for the visitor, nevertheless it has a charm of yesterday and an unspoiled, untouched air about it.

It is a good alternate for an overnight stop if you prefer not to be in Aix for it has an excellent hotel.

Auberge Bourrelly
(HR)M   *42 69 13 13*   *Hotel open all year*   *R cl. Mon*   *All CC.*

A delightful old Provençal auberge, shaded by plane trees. There is a park all around, a large terrace and a very inviting swimming pool.

The 11 rooms and one suite all have TV and mini-bar and range from 300-490f. Breakfast is 45f. The restaurant prides itself on gourmet specialities and the menu changes frequently. Meals are 159, 180, 230 and 350f. Demi-pension at 580f is a good option.

Le Château
(R)M   *42 69 05 75*   *Route du Chemin du Réaltor*   *Cl. Wed; 2 weeks in winter; 2 weeks in August*   *Visa, CB.*

If it's remarkable to have a good hotel in such a tiny village as Calas, it's just as remarkable to have another good place to eat. M et Mme Delafosse have improved Le Château and that is in itself an achievement for it was already one of the the places to eat in this area near Aix.

The restaurant is in an old building hidden away in the woods. The generally rustic atmosphere houses classical Provençal cooking. Leg of duck in old port with foie gras is one example and other dishes include new approaches to escargots and even to sole which is usually the most routine of fish.

Menus are 110, 160 and 235f.

Map 2B   **CARPENTRAS** 84200 (Vaucluse) 24 km NE of Avignon

 Fri

From the capital of a Celtic tribe in pre-Roman days and then a trading post for the Greeks, Carpentras reached its peak of importance at the beginning of the 14th century when Clement V was crowned in Lyon as Pope at the instigation of King Philip of France and in direct rivalry to the papacy in Rome.

Although Avignon was chosen by Clement V as his capital, he intended it to be only temporary until his establishment in Rome. He lived in a few rooms in the Dominican monastery in Avignon until it was clear that a return to Rome was unlikely in the short term. Carpentras, being already a bishopric, was preferred by Clement V who spent much of his time here from 1309 to 1314 and his presence brought the town to a position of considerable power.

Jews were given protection here but it must be noted that this was not altogether a gesture of tolerance or good-will. The papal court in France was expensive as the fugitive pope became the first absolute ruler in history and dependents and petitioners, artists and troubadors, cardinals and professors, relatives and friends and thousands of others flooded here. To extract tax from all of these, Clement needed a strong and clever financial system and he selected Jewish financiers to run it.

This also had the advantage of making sure that the money stayed out of the hands of the Italian banks.

The synagogue stands today, almost in the centre of town and steps away from the cathedral. It is the oldest in France. It has a richly decorated interior and you can see the marble tables on which the bread was made and the ovens in which was baked both the unleavened bread and the cakes flavoured with sugar and rose-water. The ritual baths for purification can also be seen.

The synagogue is open Monday to Friday 10-12 and 3-5.

The Cathedral of Saint Siffrein has many fine works of art by French painters including Mignard and Parrocel and sculptures by Bernus and de Mazan. The treasury contains several objects of both religious and commercial value. The south door is gaily decorated and is known as the 'Porte Juive' for it was through it that Jewish converts to Christianity would walk to the baptismal font.

Behind the cathedral is the Arc de Triomphe built, like many others in France, to celebrate victory over the Celtic tribes. Many commentators have pointed out that the Celts are shown in the bas-reliefs as massively-built men with bulging muscles and power-packed shoulders – a tribute of course to the Roman soldiers who defeated them even if most archeological evidence does not support the stone images.

The enormous Hôtel Dieu is a few minutes south of the cathedral and dates from the 18th century. It is still used as a hospital but its main interest is in the pharmacy with its extensive collection of the pots and jars used by the apothecaries.

The pharmacy is open to the public from 9-11 on Monday, Wednesday and Thursday.

The museums of Carpentras are all a little disappointing but if you want to spend more time here, there are several. The Musée Comtadin deals with local history and has a collection of sheep bells, weapons, seals, coins, papal documents and santons. There are portraits of famous inhabitants of Carpentras and some paintings of the town in mediaeval times. On the next floor is the Musée Duplessis, named after a local painter and containing some primitive art, works by local painters Rigaud Parrocel and Laurens.

Both museums may be visited 10-12 and 3-6 in the summer, 10-12 and 3-4 in the winter, closed on Tuesdays. One ticket provides admission to both. They are located just west of the cathedral, on the Blvd Albert Durand.

In the same building is the Bibliothèque Inguimbertine. This belonged to Monsignor d'Inguimbert, bishop of Carpentras from 1735 to 1757 and a notable scholar who brought with him about 5,000 books. He bought a library of a further 15,000 volumes from Aix and added to it on every possible occasion. Today, the library contains about 225,000 books and at least half of them are old and valuable. There are also music scores and manuscripts, coins and stamps.

The library is open for consultation of the books from 2-6.30 on Monday, 9.30- 6.30 on Tuesday, Wednesday, Thursday and Friday, 9.30-12 on Saturday. It is closed for the month of July.

Between these museums and the cathedral is the Musée Sobirats which is a convincing reconstruction of an 18th-century private home and north of it is the Musée Lapidaire, installed in an old convent of 1717. It has displays of archaeological and mineralogical interest.

Both are open 10-12 and 2-6 in the summer, 10-12 and 2-4 in the winter, closed on Tuesdays.

The weekly market in Carpentras every Friday morning is a major affair and participants come from long distances. It spreads over most of the town. From the end of November to the beginning of March, there is a truffle market from 9-12 in Place Aristide Briand and at the end of November there is the Annual Fair of St Siffrein which comprises agriculture, commerce and industry.

Festivals

In April, May, June and July, Carpentras holds a cultural festival which is strongly attended. Song, dance, music, drama and ballet are all presented and many international artists participate.

Carpentras is a hub of roads leading in various directions and various circuits of discovery and exploration of Vaucluse are possible from here. Consequently, there are numerous hotels and restaurants available.

Le Fiacre
(H)S-M   *90 63 03 15*

An 18th-century family hotel located right in the heart of town, its ancient stone-arched entrance invites you immediately. A tree-shaded patio provides an oasis of cool tranquillity.

153 Rue Vigne
Open all year   All CC.

Twenty rooms are all furnished differently and very tastefully with pastel panels blending beautifully with the occasional piece of antique furniture. All the rooms are large and look out on to the patio. All have bath or shower, private toilet and television. Pricing at 180-350f is good value.

There is no restaurant but a delightful breakfast room. Breakfast is 32f.

Le Coq Hardi
(HR)S-M   90 63 00 35   36 Place de la Marotte   Hotel open all year   R cl. Sat noon and Sun, Dec 24-Jan 2, Aug 18-Sep 5   All CC.

Well-situated in the centre of town, Le Coq Hardi is new so it is trying hard to establish itself among the hotels of Carpentras.

It is also modern and you may prefer an old-world atmosphere but if you like comfort, you can't go wrong here. There are 19 rooms and 15 of them have private toilet, bath or shower and TV. Prices range from 170-360f plus 30f for breakfast. There is parking out front and a nice shady terrace.

The 'Romeo and Juliette' restaurant is becoming quite popular and offers menus at 89, 129 and 169f. There is also a good choice of à la carte dishes from 50 to 100f. The wine list is well-chosen and bottles of good regional wine start at 70f.

L'Orangerie
(R)S-M   90 67 27 23   26 Rue Duplessis   Cl. Sat noon   All CC.

Improvements here recently have introduced a pleasant atmosphere and the soothing soft colours make this perhaps the best place to eat in Carpentras.

Not that there were ever any complaints about the food and patrons will be glad to know that it is as good as ever. The terrace-garden is popular in the summer but whether you eat in or out, you will enjoy a fine meal and most likely a dish that you don't see on every menu.

Chiffonade de cailles aux airelles and filet de canard aux poires et sirop d'orange are two of the delights served by Madame Trillat and the menu prices at 85f to 200f are reasonable for such excellent quality and imaginative cooking. The goat cheeses from local farms are among the best in Provence.

Other recommendable places to stay or to eat are only 4 km out of Carpentras and can be found under the heading of 'Monteux'.

Map 2D   **CARRY-LE-ROUET** 13620 (Bouches-du-Rhône) 16 km W of
Marseille

A pretty little resort town on the Mediterranean, about midway
between Marseille and Martigues. The fishing port is very picturesque,
there are four good bathing beaches, lots of holiday homes, a casino
and an open-air cinema .

Once a Greek port, then Roman, Carry gets its name from a 'rouet',
a water-wheel used to bring seawater into basins for evaporation and
recovery of the salt. Its more recent fame has stemmed from one of its
residents – the great film comedian, Fernandel . Here he was known as
Fernand and was just another local inhabitant, drinking anis at the
café, playing boules and fishing. He is buried in the local cemetery.

February 3 is a little too early for most visitors to enjoy it but then
there is a great dégustation of oursins (sea-urchins) which are caught
in large numbers off the coast. Among the dishes enjoyed is
oursinade, a fish soup served with a purée of oursins, and also
omelettes made with fresh oursins. The oursin craze lasts about a
month.

La Tuilière
(HR)S   *42 44 79 79   34 Avenue Draio de la Mar   Open all year   All CC.*

Lillane Larribère has a winning formula here, with 22 rooms almost on
the beach. All have private toilet, bath, shower and TV. There is
private parking, terrace and flower-filled garden and all at 225-315f.
The restaurant serves a simple menu at 59f; there is a fish menu at
128f which starts with soup aux poissons then offers a choice of filet
de loup à l'oseille or cassoulette de supions plus cheese and dessert, a
Tourist Menu at 159f with four courses and four entrees *and* a Gascon
Menu, five courses at 188F, and if you order in advance the main
course could be bouillabaisse.

L'Escale
(R)M-L   *42 45 00 47   Promenade du Port   Cl. Sun; Mon   All CC.*

It's a gourmet restaurant and it has a privileged position with its
flowered terraces overlooking the port. You will want to eat out there
in the summer months but the Art Deco style of the indoor restaurant
is charming too.

It's expensive – but it is good. Chef Gérard Clor is renowned for his
masterly touch with seafood in the kitchen and moules à la crème d'ail
from Bouzigues are an irresistible starter. No-one knows what spices
he adds to the loup but it is a superb presentation of 'the king of fish'.
I've had to keep the price till last – an à la carte meal here will cost
about 500f.

Map 3C   CASSIS 13260 (Bouches-du-Rhône) 22 km E of Marseille

Ⓜ *Wed and Fri*

One of the prettiest ports on the Mediterranean and a particular favourite of mine for decades. One of the virtues of Cassis is that it has changed hardly at all in that time. It's still leisurely and seemingly uncrowded despite its popularity with tourists.

Cassis has been a fishing port since the Greeks were here. Mistral chose Cassis as the birthplace of his hero, Calendal, a simple anchovy fisherman who performed great deeds for the love of his beautiful Esterelle. Dufy, Matisse, Dali, Dérain and Vlaminck have all painted it.

The old château straggles about a quarter of a mile along the clifftop and dominating the port and the beach. It is magnificently mediaeval though clearly built at different periods and in different styles. It was bought some years ago by the Michelin family and they still live there so visiting is not permitted.

The Calanques are one of the unforgettable sights and experiences of the whole South of France coastline. A 'calanque' is a long, narrow inlet, created by the erosion of land by the Mediterranean and leaving huge white limestone cliffs sticking out like great fingers. The longest of the inlets is over a kilometre and the cliffs are almost 400 feet high. The water is an intense blue-green and you can see the bottom in most places.

There are two ways to see them and the first is by boat. There are lots of these operating from the port which is where everything is in Cassis. There are choices of trips visiting three, six or eight calanques but the first is best for a first visit. The trip takes 45 minutes and costs 40f. The boats carry 12 to 85 people and you might want to choose one of the bigger craft if the sea looks choppy – as it sometimes is.

After an exciting dash out into the open Mediterranean and with the port of Cassis looking far, far behind, your boat will take you into each calanque in turn. Among the sights on the way are scores of nude bathers on the rocks and on the small boats which find the calanques perfect mooring. The sheer cliffs will make you dizzy when you look up at them particularly when you see the climbers clinging like flies to invisible hand-holds or dangling from ropes.

You may also want to drive along the top afterwards and look down in order to fully appreciate these unique formations. The sandy beaches at the innermost end of the Calanques are enticing but not easily accessible except by boat. Whenever a pirate film is made, it is hard to imagine that the film-makers would look any further for more photogenically perfect pirate coves.

There are two wide sandy beaches – the Plage de la Grande Mer is below the old château and the Plage du Bestouan is north (or west) of Cassis. From the latter, it is possible to take the footpath to the Calanques. It takes at least 90 minutes but it is then possible to scramble down the rocks to the water. You need to be fit and foot-sure to do this.

There is a sparkling new casino just in from the port and locals keep it busy even out of the tourist season. Hours are from 3 p.m. to a rather sedate 2 a.m. It offers black-jack, 30/40, baccarat and roulette.

The Musée Municipal d'Art et de Traditions Populaires is near the Casino and has displays and material from the Greek and Roman periods together with others coming through the history of Cassis through mediaeval times to the present. There are sculptures, paintings, pottery, manuscripts, coins and Provençal costumes. *It is open from 9.30-12.00 and 3-6 every day except Sunday and holidays. Free.*

Boutiques and shops are clustered around this area which also contains the mairie and the post office.

In the world of wine, much confusion is caused by the name Cassis. The blackcurrant liqueur made in Burgundy can be added to any dry white wine to make the well-known aperitif but the wine produced in the district around the town of Cassis deserves better than to be mistaken for an aperitif.

The white is far the best-known and goes perfectly with the local seafood. It is light, fresh and fruity, the grapes being a blend of Ugni Blanc, Clairette and Marsanne sometimes with a little Sauvignon Blanc. Being low in acidity, it needs to be drunk young – 85% of production is drunk locally. As the vineyards cover only 500 acres, the total output (which includes small amounts of the less renowned rosés and reds) needs to command a higher price than Provence competitors. It is still quite affordable though especially in the neighbouring restaurants and shops. The Clos Sainte-Magdeleine is the main name to watch for and others are Domaine du Paternel, Clos Val Bruyère, Domaine Caillol, La Ferme Blanche and Clos des Quatre Vents. All can be visited and many have deep and extensive underground caves and storage rooms, some of which may date back to the 12th century when wine was first made here.

Festivals

In July, there are art exhibitions, concerts, music and dance festivals. The nautical feast of Saint Peter, the patron saint of fishermen, is celebrated with parades either at the end of June or the beginning of July. There is also a local fête around the middle of July and a wine festival at the beginning of September.

Cassis is just barely adequate for accommodation but with plenty of restaurants. Visitors arriving during the morning spend their time strolling up and down the quayside inspecting all the menus and trying to choose. Almost all are good. Prices differ moderately. Most have views over the port and with some a fresh fish stall is out front. At others, you will be entertained at the outside tables by itinerant performers on the quay, many of them animal acts. None are pretentious or pushy and in fact all of them are like Cassis itself, friendly and natural.

Liautaud
(HR)S   *42 01 75 37*   *Rue Victor Hugo*   *Cl. Nov 1-Dec 15*   *Visa, CB.*

I have to confess to a large degree of sentiment here because this was the first hotel I stayed at in Cassis and that was more years ago than I can remember. I have been back numerous times since and it has never failed me. Yesterday, I found it as good as ever.

The 32 rooms look out over the port and all have been modernised since my last visit but the friendly family atmosphere remains the same. Priced at 220-300f, the rooms are real value.

I have sometimes eaten here even when only visiting for the day and that is a good recommendation for any restaurant belonging to a hotel. Menus are 100-190f and there is a wide choice of fresh seafood.

Hôtel Provençal
(H)S   *42 01 72 13*   *Rue Victor Hugo*   *Open all year*   *Visa, CB.*

Almost on the port and some of the 10 rooms look out over it. The hotel has no restaurant and is minimally equipped but for a reasonable 220-250f, it is a good alternative to Le Liautaud.

Les Jardins du Campanile
(HR)M   *42 01 84 85*   *Rue Favier*   *Cl. Oct 15-Apr 1*   *All CC.*

You may be so enchanted by Cassis that you will want to find an up-market hotel and really enjoy yourself. If that is the case, then Les Jardins du Campanile is made to measure.

Amid lemon trees and palm trees sits an old Provençal farmhouse which combines comfort and style. There is a pool and tennis and a pleasant garden. The 4 apartments at 650-1250f may be a bit over the top but the 32 rooms are all furnished differently and well equipped. They are priced at 300-500f. There is closed and guarded parking.

Meals are available to residents only and offer reasonable choice, well-cooked meals at 90f up. Seminars are held all the year round so you might wish to avoid them.

Les Roches Blanches
(HR)M   *42 01 09 30*   *Route des Calanques*   *Cl. Dec and Jan*   *All CC.*

If you don't mind being away from the port or indeed if you want to be away from it and in a quiet scenic spot, Les Roches Blanches is in a commanding position about a kilometre west of Cassis. It is an old villa with a private beach (not sandy though). There is a nice garden and parking. The 35 rooms are not large and could be a bit more cheerful but all in all, they are good value at 350-650f. The restaurant is for residents only and though it is marginally above competitive prices, should you not want to go out to eat, the meals at 165-200f are well-prepared and offer some alternatives to the excellent seafood.

L'Oustau de la Mar
(R)S   *42 01 78 22   21 Quai des Baux   Open all year   Visa, CB.*

One of the best of the many restaurants on the port and one which
has maintained a reliable standard for many, many years.

Part of the restaurant is inside and part is outside but if it's summer,
make sure you have umbrella shade. The gambas grilled and
flambéed in cognac at 85f are exceptionally worth the money, six or
seven very large and very succulent ones served with steamed
potatoes. The brochette of lotte and gambas at 87f is another popular
dish. All of the seafood is in fact very good although meat-eaters are
catered for too. Menus range from 85 to 103f.

There is a choice of Cassis white wine from three local vineyards. All
are enjoyable but I would recommend the Château de Fontcreuse at
110f for the Blanc de Blanc.

Nino
(R)S-M   *42 01 74 32   Quai Barthélémy   Cl. Sun p.m.; Mon; Dec 20-Jan 15   All CC.*

Right on the port and always busy. Seafood naturally but with an
Italian flavour which makes it a little different. Bar braised on the grill
is excellent and there are occasional touches such as the grilled
peppers and anchovies. There are menus at 100 and 140f. The staff are
smiling and helpful.

La Vieille Auberge
(R)S-M   *42 01 73 54   Quai Barthélémy   Open all year   All CC.*

Its address suggests that it is on the port and it is – almost. Actually, it
is on a balcony up above the port. It's another old favourite in Cassis
and you can choose either the 99f menu or the 160f menu. The former
is three courses and might consist of escabeche of sardines then
gratin de fruits de mer then dessert. The 160f menu is also three
courses but with some more expensive dishes such as the filet de
turbot in ginger as the main (and very unusual) course. You will need
to be very stern willed to decline the îles flottantes for dessert.

There is a choice of Cassis white wines at 105-120f.

Chez Vincent
(R)S   *42 01 35 19   Quai les Baux   Open all year   Visa, CB.*

The special here is the bouillabaisse. It's perhaps a bit richer than
some you may have tasted but if you are not familiar with this
uniquely Mediterranean dish, here is a good place to try it. At 340f for
two people, it is a golden opportunity.

There are menus at 85 and 108f and rascasse is often featured from
the day's catch. Don't miss the chance to drink the Clos Sainte
Magdeleine at 115f, either the rosé or the white.

Map 4D **LE CASTELLET** 83330 (Var) 9 km N of Bandol, 20 km NW of Toulon

Most visitors to this region are either speeding along the autoroute between Marseille and Toulon or sunning and swimming at one of the beach resorts such as Bandol, Sanary, La Syne or Six-Fours. Few bother to come these few kilometres inland to see one of the most delightful perched villages in the Var.

It isn't that high – only 283 metres – but it sits on top of a hill and offers charming views of rolling landscapes and acre after acre of vineyards.

Le Castellet is associated with Marcel Pagnol and the Lumière Brothers. It was on the place in the mediaeval village of Le Castellet that Pagnol set much of *La Femme du Boulanger*. The baker's shop itself is now an antique shop but the café which features prominently in the book is still there. The 1986 version of *Manon des Sources* was partially shot here and you will appreciate why when you see the old castle with its powerful ramparts, the narrow streets and the old church of Saint Sauveur built by the Knights Templar in the 12th century.

This immediate region is said to have exceptionally intense light and it was this that attracted the Lumière Brothers who came here to work out their ideas for making motion pictures. The house which they bought and used to conduct their experiments in is now the hotel (see below).

The vineyards you can see from the village produce some good Vins des Côtes-de-Provence. Château Romassan is one that is particularly recommendable.

Festivals

July 26 is the Feast of Sainte Anne and July 15 sees an antique and bric-à-brac fair.

Castel Lumière
(HR)M   *94 32 62 20   Rue Portail   H cl. 10/1-20/2; R cl. Sun p.m., Mon.   All CC*

This was once the house where the Lumière Brothers put together their ideas for making the first motion picture *L'Arrivée d'un train en gare de La Ciotat* in 1895. Now it is an elegant and refined restaurant with six rooms. As the name of the street implies, it stands beside the gateway to the old village.

The six rooms are priced more reasonably than you would expect for such charm – 350-410f. All are fully-equipped. There is parking but no garage.

As you might suppose, the restaurant is dominant and Bernard Laffargue offers what he describes as 'Var gastronomy'. The foie gras with Banyuls is a starter not to be missed. L'agneau au basilic and suprême de loup aux truffes make the main course a difficult choice. Few diners can resist the soufflé aux liqueurs. Menus are 200, 290 and 400f but the quality of the food and the cooking fully justify the prices. A fine selection of Bandol wines is on the list.

Map 2B   CAUMONT-SUR-DURANCE 84510 (Vaucluse) 8 km NW of Cavaillon, 6 km E of Avignon

(M) *Thurs*

In the heart of the village is a most unusual structure known as La Lanterne des Morts, the Lantern of the Dead. It is a tall chimney of nearly fifty feet and has a circular top with eight small windows in it. In earlier days, the lamp inside would be lit whenever a person of note in the village died or when there was the threat of the plague.

Two kilometres south and towards the Durance river valley and Aix, the Chartreuse de Bonpas is in a naturally commanding position over the only practicable crossing of the river. It is a monastery, of course, but was built in the 12th century when it was common for such buildings to be heavily fortified. It has been restored and re-built numerous times but it still presents an impressive aspect with its towers and crenellated battlements.

Festivals

Caumont has the Feast of Saint Symphorien on August 20 and a grape festival and market in August and September.

Cavaillon and Avignon being so close, there are plenty of hotels and restaurants within a short distance. Still, it is worth mentioning two very good chambre d'hôtes in Caumont:

Janet Shackleford
(C)M   *90 23 03 48   Cl. mid Nov to mid March   No CC.*

Mrs Shackleford is English and is delighted to welcome you to her village house. There is a large lounge, a terrace and a television room. The three rooms are all on the first floor and all equipped with a wash-basin. Bathroom and toilet are common to all three rooms. The cost is 150f. Meals are up to 65f or demi-pension is available at 185f per person.

Bernard Lefèbvre
(C)M   *90 23 07 49   Chemin des Terres de Magues   Open all year   No CC.*

Just outside the village and in a villa on a hillside in a heavily wooded area, M. Lefèbvre has only one room and it is priced at 150f. It has a private bath and toilet. A meal can be had at 60f.

Map 3C   CERESTE 04110 (Alpes de Haute Provence) 18 km E of Apt

(M) *Thurs*

Located on the N100 road which runs east to west on the north side of the Lubéron mountains, Céreste was also an important stopping place for the Roman army and the Tour d'Embarbe was built to protect the encamped legions by the Consul Ahenobarbus.

North-east of the village can be seen the ruins of the Prieuré de Carluc. The site is immeasurably old. The oak forest and the spring were considered sacred and there are cave-drawings. The Priory was built in the 12th century on the remains of a Gallic-Roman sanctuary and the monks came from Montmajour to settle here.

There is a small museum which concentrates on prehistoric fossils. Céreste has a big fair in July.

→ **Hôtel Aiguebelle**
(HR)S-M   *92 79 00 91   Cl. Sun p.m.; Mon (except in July and Aug); Dec; Jan Visa, CB, EC.*

One of the fascinating discoveries which can constantly be made in Provence is the gem of a hotel and restaurant in the smallest village.

Céreste looks nothing as you drive through it and it has less than a thousand people. The 13 rooms at 150-250f are more than adequate though it is the restaurant here which is the principal attraction. The cooking tries to be different (and succeeds). Menus are 80, 120 and 180f and the 120f version is a very satisfying four-course affair. Cassolette d'escargots à l'anis was an imaginative starter, the carrée d'agneau à la crème d'ail were substantial, while cheese and then patisserie completed.

An unusual variant offered is the all-cheese meal. So many good ones are produced in the area that the Aiguebelle had the idea to serve a meal which is a different cheese for each of three courses, all prepared in different ways and each served with a different wine. There was a choice of dessert and the total cost is 140f.

Arrowed for comfort and excellent food.

| Map 4B | **CHATEAU ARNOUX** 04160 (Alpes de Haute Provence) |
| | 15 km S of Sisteron, 25 km W of Digne |

When you see its imposing château dominating the Durance river crossing, you will appreciate Château Arnoux's strategic position at the junction of the main roads from Grenoble to Nice and Marseille.

The château is now the Mairie and you can visit it in summer between the hours of 9 and 7. The park around it has nearly 200 varieties of trees and bushes including some that are rare in Europe such as bananas, ebony and Chinese mulberries. The best time of the year to enjoy them is in the autumn.

Festivals

A jazz festival is held every year at the beginning of July and an international exhibition of paintings in September and October.

La Bonne Etape
(HR)L   *92 64 00 09   Chemin du Lac   Cl. Sun p.m.; Mon o.o.s.; 1/12-9/12; 5/1-12/2
All CC.*

Once known as the Hôtel de la Gare and before that a 17th-century
coaching inn, La Bonne Etape opposite the château is one of the great
hotels of France. It rates four of everything for its hotel and its
restaurant. Pierre and Jany Gleize deserve great credit for bringing it
up to this standard and though it is expensive, no effort is spared to
bring you every conceivable luxury.

There is a pretty garden and a lovely heated pool. The seven
apartments and the eleven bedrooms are beautifully furnished in
Provençal style with rustic furniture, hand-printed wallpaper and
flagstoned floors. Some of them have private terraces and all have air-
conditioning. The apartments are priced at 900-950f and the rooms at
450-850f. Breakfast is 85f.

The cooking is up to the same high quality as the hotel. Elegance,
imagination and local fresh ingredients are paramount. Typical dishes
use the very finest lamb from Sisteron (the best in France) and there is
the frequent flash of ingenuity such as the loup de mer à la tapenade.
Even a dish as mundane as lapin farci becomes a culinary delight.

Menus are 200, 330, 390 and 440f. The wine list is extensive and
there are many excellent Côtes du Rhône wines, not too expensively
priced.

Map 2B   **CHATEAUNEUF-DU-PAPE** 84230 (Vaucluse) **13 km S of**
Orange, 18 km N of Avignon

No self-respecting drinker of wine could possibly be in this part of
Provence and miss the opportunity to come here – the home of one of
the most prestigious names in wine.

The old castle which gives the wine its name was erected by the
popes in the 14th century and is a little way north of Avignon. The
castle is now in ruins but the vineyards surround it, following the
Rhône river for ten kilometres or so and reaching almost to Orange.

Jacques Duèze is better known as Pope John XXII and is notorious
for his activities as an alchemist but his interests were diverse and he
is credited with the planting of the vineyards. The growth in status of
Châteauneuf-du-Pape is all the more remarkable as the soil is partly
sandy and partly pebbly – although one explanation is that the heat of
the sun during the day is concentrated in the pebbles which retain it,
releasing it slowly during the night. Thus the vine roots remain warm
continuously.

Vine growers claiming the right to the appellation of Châteauneuf-
du-Pape may cultivate as many as thirteen different grape varieties
and many producers use all of them. Grenache, Syrah, Mourvèdre,
Cinsault and Clairette are the principal grapes and Château Rayas and
Château de Beaucastel are among the leading estates. Châteauneuf-
du-Pape is a powerful, warm wine with a strong bouquet and is
particularly recommended to accompany a game dish, though it is

equally enjoyable with beef. There is even a white Châteauneuf but production is very limited; if you see a bottle, grab it.

Festivals

At the end of April and on the occasion of the Feast of Saint Mark, there are wine tastings of the previous year's vintage at the Echansonnerie des Papes in the village. This is the name of the chief wine brotherhood of this region; don't miss the chance to be there.

The Echansonnier is like a sommelier but much more important. He was a trusted nobleman in the days of the great castles and the great feasts. He did not merely pour the wine but had the responsibility of tasting it. This was not only to ensure that it was of suitably good quality for his master but also to make sure that it was not poisoned.

The Echansonniers still appear richly attired in purple and white robes and bear a symbolic golden key. The banquet for the Feast of Saint Mark usually serves chicken in a rich sauce of chicken and veal stock with onions, carrots and herbs and – of course – Châteauneuf-du-Pape wine.

Another eagerly awaited day is when the grapes change colour and achieve maturity. This is usually at the beginning of August and signals a wine festival which is held over the week-end following. There are parades, a Provençal mass in the church of Saint Théodore, folk-dancing, equestrian displays, pageants, processions, feasts and – yes, you guessed it … plenty of wine drinking opportunities.

In the Caves de Père Anselme is an interesting museum which shows the history of a wine in sequential detail. The preparation of the ground, the treatment, the tools, the equipment such as vats and presses. Little is omitted, even to weights and measures, insects which destroy the grape vines, the corks and the bottles. Wine is naturally on sale.

Hostellerie Château Fines Roches
(HR)M   *90 83 70 23   Cl. 23/12-14/2   R also cl. Mon   Visa, CB.*

Mistral, Daudet and other poets and writers of the early 19th century used to gather here when it was the home of the Marquis de Baroncelli. He had it built in mock-mediaeval style on top of a hill looking out over the vineyards south of the village. Now it is a small and beautifully appointed hotel.

There are only seven rooms, which makes the château a very cosy hotel. They are priced at 390-690f and all have antique furniture as well as all mod cons. Breakfast is 60f. Maybe at the higher priced end of the range for an overnight stop but the charm of the place is undeniable – even if the mediaevalism is not fully authentic.

Proprietor Henri Estevenin's sons handle the cooking and the restaurant has a well deserved reputation. The home-made terrines are exceptional and there is usually some speciality of the house which uses the local Châteauneuf-du-Pape wine. Menus are 195 to 240f; à la carte will run over 300f.

Logis d'Arnavel
(HR)S   *90 83 73 22   Route de Roquemaure   Open all year   All CC.*

If you're looking for a lower-priced alternative, this is it. There are 15 rooms in an old country house converted into a small hotel. The furnishing is comfortable, there is a garden and a pool and the setting in the quiet countryside is very relaxing.

Rooms are 270-300f and breakfast is 33f. In summer, you can eat out on the terrace. Meals are simple but satisfying and well-prepared from local ingredients. Menus are 180-220f.

Map 2B   **CHATEAURENARD** 13160 (Bouches-du-Rhône) 6 km S of Avignon

---

Two towers remain of the ancient fortress, the Tower of the Griffon and the Tower of the Three Daggers. The Reinardus family built the castle and gave their name to the town. They also have their name securely in local tradition and history for the original Reinardus was a friend of Charles Martel and assisted him in repelling the Moslem invasion of the 8th century. The ghost of Reinardus' wife, Emma, still haunts the Tower of the Griffon (well, so they say).

From the château (so they also say) runs an underground passage which passes under the Durance river and was used by Pope Benoît III at the time of the Great Schism. The château was besieged many times and passed into many different hands through the centuries. One of its owners was the Bishop of Gap, Louis Saporta, who had the reputation of being more of a warrior than a monk and preferring the sword to the sceptre. He travelled well-armed and it was he who gave the name to the Tower of the Three Daggers.

It is unfortunate that a building with so much history should be only a ruin today but you can climb the Tower of the Griffon (*open 10-12 and 2-6 every day, closed December and January*). There is a small museum in the tower. There is a magnificent panorama over the valley of the Lubéron and the Durance. Concerts are often given in the château ruins.

Festivals

One of Provence's most popular saints is Saint Eloi, he who miraculously put back the leg of a mule and has ever since been accepted as the patron saint of blacksmiths. He is celebrated every year in Châteaurénard by a parade of the 'Carreto Ramado'.

These are chariots drawn by teams of horses in elaborate harness. Their passage through the town is accompanied by a great deal of wine drinking (by the townfolk).

Hôtel Le Central
(HR)S   *90 94 10 90   Cl. Sun p.m.; Mon lunch o.o.s.   Visa, CB, EC.*

18 rooms in a small hotel in the centre of town and near the railway station. Priced within everybody's range at 115-215f they are decidedly

unfancy but more than adequate. There is parking and the restaurant is large (seating nearly 200 including the outdoor areas). Provençal cooking is featured and the hot fruit tarts are renowned. Menus are 65 and 100f and there is a piano bar and a show on Saturday nights.

Hôtel La Pastourelle
(HR)S   *90 94 10 68   Cl. Jan   Visa, CB.*

Rock-bottom prices of 80-140f per room make the nine rooms here eagerly sought after. There is parking and the restaurant is large and has a terrace for summer dining. The menu at 45f is the popular one and features entrecôte au Roquefort.

Map 2C   CHEVAL-BLANC 84460 (Vaucluse) 5 km SE of Cavaillon

 Sat

On old maps you will find Cheval-Blanc called Blanc-Montagne, the name it adopted when separating from Cavaillon in 1790.

It sits on the north bank of the Durance river but it is the smaller Regalon river which irrigates it. There are some very attractive – if occasionally fairly difficult – walks along the gorges of the Regalon, though it seems to get drier every year. You will see entrances to grottoes – Les Dentales, Le Puceau and La Baume des Enfers – which were the homes of prehistoric man, especially if you follow the direction north towards Vidauque.

Festivals

In February, Cheval-Blanc has a strange festival. The young men of the village disguise themselves, some as girls in white robes gaily decorated with spangles and some as hermits in tatters and rags. They visit the houses of the village girls where they are welcomed with a glass of wine. An invitation follows to a ball that evening. The origins of this unusual ceremony are not at all clear, even to the villagers, but it seems that no objections have been put forward by either the boys or the girls.

Restaurant Nicolet
(R)M   *90 78 01 56   Route de Pertuis   Cl. Sun p.m.; Mon   All CC.*

Alain Nicolet was voted one of the Maîtres Cuisiniers de France last year and it is no wonder that enthusiastic gourmets come from afar to enjoy a meal at the restaurant that Alain and his wife Mireille run so well. Don't take a chance – you'll need to book.

The restaurant is on the road to Pertuis, in the middle of nowhere, and you wonder such an outstanding chef should choose to be here.

But film stars, writers, producers and artists all come to have the fistou Provençal aux escalopines de lotte au basilic and the gigotin d'agneau rôti, with sauce romarin. The bread is baked on the premises and every single item used in the cooking is fresh. Full use is made of the many and varied Provence spices and flavours. There are two menus, one at 205f and one at 340f. Either one will be a meal to remember and both are value for money that you won't be able to equal in many other restaurants. There are even five kinds of coffee to choose from!

Map 3D **LA CIOTAT** 13600 (Bouches-du-Rhône) 32 km E of Marseille, 37 km W of Toulon

---

The Greeks established an anchorage here in the 4th century BC and called it 'Cithatista' although the Provençals, always romanticising, insisted that the wind blew through the maritime pines and produced the sounds of the 'cithare' (the zither).

Half-way between Marseille and Toulon, the harbour of La Ciotat continued to be a valuable location and shipbuilding was the major industry here for many years. With that business now in severe decline, the active administration has focused on tourism and made great efforts to attract visitors. The six kilometres of beaches, some sandy, some shingle, and the picturesque old port have become the featured attractions and La Ciotat is an uncrowded and inexpensive option for those seeking sun and water.

Away from the cranes and skeleton structures of the shipyard at the western end of the town, La Ciotat is quite pretty and blends Provençal buildings with modern hotels, restaurants and shops along an extensive seafront. Water sports and beach activities dominate, of course, on the 'Golfe d'Amour', as La Ciotat now calls it.

Georges Braque painted here and Stendhal said that if he had to live in Provence, he would choose La Ciotat. You will see signs referring to La Ciotat as 'La Ville des Lumières'. This has nothing to do with lights. Auguste and Louis Lumière were the two brothers who are credited with the invention of cinematography. They made about a dozen films, one called *L'arrivée d'un train en gare de La Ciotat* which doesn't sound too exciting today but must have been to the audiences who saw it at the Château Lumière on September 21, 1895. There is a monument on the beach at the Boulevard Beaurivage near the spot where the château stood.

Boats depart at frequent intervals from Le Vieux Port for the half hour ride out to L'Ile Verte, a small island a kilometre long and less than a kilometre wide. It is densely covered with magnificent pines and its perimeter is all sandy and pebble beaches. There is a restaurant 'Chez Louisette' which serves pizzas and grills. It makes a pleasant day's excursion and you can wander around the island at will and see the small fort which once defended it.

Festivals

The Feast of Saint Peter is more so – the fête of the patron saint of fishermen is held on the second Sunday in July. There is a bric-à-brac fair the third Sunday in every month. In June, July and August, La Ciotat holds various international events, both sporting and cultural including music, dance, tennis and sailboarding. Late in July, the traditions and folklore of Provence are presented in 'Les Provenciades', a week of parades, plays, markets, music and dance festivals and other spectacles involving bulls, horses and gardiens from the Camargue.

Ciotel Le Cap
(HR)M   *42 83 90 30   Corniche du Liouquet   Cl. Sun p.m. o.o.s.; 30/11-1/3   All CC.*

An elegant and modern hotel in a calm and beautiful park 6 km E of La Ciotat on the edge of the Mediterranean. There are two pools and two tennis courts and various watersports on a private beach.

The 43 rooms are in separate stone bungalows and all have a private terrace, bathroom, toilet and TV. At 465-600f, these are good value if you take advantage of all the facilities that are offered for you can make a full holiday without leaving the grounds.

Guy Boissi also offers a gourmet restaurant, Le Séréno. You can dine in the elegant dining room with its vaulted wooden ceilings, planked like a yacht, or on the terrace, both overlooking the sea and the swimming pool. The cooking is classical but with regional overtones. The bourride de chapon is one speciality that I can recommend and as a starter try the sardines marinated in balsamic vinegar, olive oil and with tapenade.

Menus are 140 and 220f and these prices are reasonable for the high quality of the food.

Hôtel Rose-Thé
(H)M   *42 83 09 23   4 Boulevard Beau Rivage   Cl. 15/10-31/3   All CC.*

A flat-topped, white stone building on a corner looking out over the beach, given an unusual appearance by the columns around the second floor. The beach opposite is sandy and quite shallow – it is startling to see bathers far out standing with water only to their waists.

Since recent interior renovation, the 21 rooms are pretty and cheerful and many look out to sea. They are 270-430f.

Jean-Pierre Masson plans on opening a restaurant soon.

La Coquille
(HR)S-M   *42 83 12 18   18 Avenue Franklin Roosevelt   Cl. 15/1-1/2   Visa, CB.*

12 rooms at 250-450f or 300-400f for demi-pension. It's on the beach and near the monument to the Lumière brothers.

The restaurant is patronised by locals and tourists alike so it stands on its own reputation aside from the hotel. It offers every conceivable kind of seafood – there's no point in listing them, you will have a hard time thinking of a fish or shellfish that is available and not on one of the menus which range from 90-250f.

Map 2B **COURTHEZON** 84350 (Vaucluse) 8 km S of Orange.

 Fri

The name of the village is, for some reason, used throughout France for when a boules player drops his shot short, a cry will arise 'C'est un peu courthézon!'

The magnificent Château de Val-Seille is today the property of Courthézon but it used to belong to Elie Dussaud, the engineer who built the Suez Canal under the instructions of the diplomat, de Lesseps.

The old ramparts of Courthézon remain and Mistral referred to them as being 'gilded by the sun'. The old church is worth a visit too, mainly to see its famous organ which is classified as an historical monument.

Festivals

The autumn fair at the beginning of September is an occasion of much joy – and wine drinking. It seems a long time through the winter to the Spring Fair which is held early in May.

La Porte des Princes
(HR)S   *90 70 70 26*   *Open all year*   *All CC.*

Really a restaurant with a few rooms, which usually means a good and inexpensive place to stay (and often eat). The eight rooms are only 120-180f but they *are* simple. Breakfast is 25f.

Despite its emphasis on being a restaurant, La Porte des Princes is not expensive in that area either. Menus are 65, 85 and 150f and Jean-Marie Tramier keeps the food and the cooking simple too. Filet aux morilles and rognons de veau à la crème are two examples while the escargots à la bourguignonne are always very popular.

Map 2B **LE CRESTET** 84110 (Vaucluse) 4 km S of Vaison-la-Romaine

The village is dominated by the imposing ruins of its ancient castle built in 850. The building was a remarkable survivor and must have remained largely unchanged until the French Revolution. It was certainly equipped to do so – inside it were grain storage chambers, a mill for grinding wheat, ovens for baking bread and all the means of withstanding sieges.

The most important requirement – water – was provided by a huge well six feet in diameter and two hundred feet deep, dug through the solid rock on which the castle stands. Restoration work has been under way for some time and by the time this appears in print several parts of the castle should be open to visitors.

Going out of Le Crestet on the Chemin de La Verrière, you will see the Chapel of Notre Dame de Prèbayon. This was a monastery, built in the 7th century. A spring was found here which was considered to be miraculous. It was called Malezieux because it was believed to cure various illnesses of the eyes.

Every Easter Monday (and the villagers insist that this means every Easter Monday since the 7th century), there is a pilgrimage to the site.

Festivals

There is a village fête in Le Crestet on June 30 and a fête to celebrate the patron saint, Saint Sixte, early in August.

La Garenne
(R)S   *90 36 05 01   Route de Malaucene   Cl. 2/1-31/1   All CC.*

Something of a meeting place for the residents of the neighbourhood – especially when there are almost 400 people here, between the indoor restaurant, the outdoor one and the shady terrace. Dinner dances are held here too.

The taste of the locals is very clearly for game. There are few game dishes that you won't find here from pheasant and partridge to quail, duck and guinea fowl. Other preferences are catered for too though with specialised regional dishes like pieds et paquets. Menus are 70 and 130f.

Map 2B   **CRILLON-LE-BRAVE** 84410 (Vaucluse) 17 km NE of Carpentras

In the square of this tiny village stands the statue of its most famous lord – Louis de Balbes de Berton, known as 'Crillon'. His exploits as a warrior fighting with King Henry III and then IV led to his nom de guerre of 'Crillon le Brave' and the village took his name in the 16th century.

Near the D138 going towards Bédoin are the ruins of the Chapel of Saint Michael. It is Romanesque and the apse with its 14th-century frescoes can still be seen. The one depicting the Last Supper is unusual as it shows only the twelve apostles, the painter refusing to acknowledge Judas' existence.

Festivals

The Feast of St Romain is celebrated from July 4 to 6 and there are local fêtes on September 8 and November 18.

➤**Hostellerie de Crillon le Brave**
(HR)M-L   *90 65 61 61   Open all year   All CC.*

As occurs so often in Provence, here is a luxurious and elegant hotel, combined with an excellent restaurant, located surprisingly in a nearly unknown village.

This was a large and ancient house which has been fully restored. It is in the village itself, near the church and has panoramic views across the plains of Carpentras.

The four apartments and the 16 rooms all have white walls with the Provençal wall hangings known as 'soleiado'. All are furnished differently. If you want to be in the main building, you should specify when booking as some of the rooms are in an annexe accessible from the garden. Prices range from 650-1450f which is high but for a special treat the Hostellerie is really something rare. Tennis and a pool complete the picture.

Under the vaulted ceilings of the restaurant with its enormous fireplace, you will feel pampered – and that applies to both the food and the service. The bourride méditerranée is superb – better than a bouillabaisse. The local lamb in one delicious form or another is usually on the list and menus are not too high-priced at 190 and 240f.

Arrowed for luxury, lovely building, fine food.

Map 3C   **CUCURON** 84160 (Vaucluse) 8 km NE of Cadenet

The thousand or so inhabitants of this small village delight in its unusual name. They dispute the claim though that it comes from the question asked by Julius Caesar when he wanted to know 'Cur currunt?' ('Why are they running?') in reference to the local inhabitants fleeing before the Roman army.

This is one of the richest regions in Provence for prehistoric remains. Bones of hippos, an early horse, gazelles and sabre-toothed tigers have been unearthed and dated at 20 million years old. An unusual find was a fossilised turtle, seven feet long. This local menagerie of the past also contains a gigantic snail, called a 'Barbaroto' in the Provençal language, which can be seen painted on the Tour de Beffroi (the belltower).

Festivals

The big day of the year in Cucuron is May 21, the Feast of Saint Tulle, the local patron saint. The youths of the village pass through the streets in procession to plant a poplar in front of the church. This ceremony commemorates the saint's success in stopping the spread of the plague in 1721. The poplar figures strongly in village mythology in other ways too – when village girls want to find a husband, they tie a ribbon to it.

There is a small museum in the old Hôtel des Bouliers opposite the church. It has a surprising amount of exhibits on local traditions and history. *Open 3-6 every afternoon through the year and 10-12 mornings from June to September.*

Otherwise, Cucuron is a quiet village and frustrating for a driver of anything bigger than a VW Beetle – the streets are very narrow with sharp right-angled turns and most are one-way with obscured signs.

L'Arbre de Mai
(HR)S-M   *90 77 25 10   Cl. Mon; Tues o.o.s.; 1/11-15/12   Visa, CB, EC.*

There are only six rooms here, small and simply furnished. They are priced at 155-280f.

L'Arbre de Mai is right in the heart of the village and near the church. It is best-known for its restaurant which is very popular. There is a terrace and a garden which are essential in the summer when the interior of the tiny restaurant with its low, beamed ceilings may become hot and airless.

Menus are 70, 95 and 110f and all the traditional Provençal dishes are here. They are cooked in the traditional ways and you can enjoy daube provençale, pieds et paquets and ris de veau à l'orange just like a Provençal grandmother used to cook them.

Map 4B   DIGNE-LES-BAINS 04000 (Alpes de Haute-Provence) 31 km SE of Sistéron

---

(M) *Wed or Sat*

The capital of the Alpes de Haute-Provence departement, Digne is also the largest town in the north-eastern quarter of Provence and situated at a strategic location on the Bléone river.

To tell the truth, this is a rather bleak, arid part of Provence and not at all like the charming areas that make up the rest of it. Driving through it, there are extensive horizons with distant views of blue hills, crisp in the sunshine – but most of is not really vacation territory which is why most guide books pay little attention to it.

Whether you read the book or saw the musical, you will remember that when Jean Valjean stole the candlesticks in *Les Miserables*, he took them from the Bishop of Digne.

One reason for Digne's sombre demeanour is probably its reputation as a spa which accounts for the last part of its name. In the 17th and 18th centuries, Digne was one of the great spa towns of France and people came to have their gout or rheumatism cured. Such places – and there are many throughout Europe – tend to be sober-sided as their purpose was not pleasure but the restoration of health. A few (like Wiesbaden) have succeeded in becoming more cheerful and spirited but some retain the aura and Digne is unfortunately one of them.

The Boulevard Gassendi is the main thoroughfare and lined with cafés and hotels. The narrow streets of the old city climb up to the Town Hall and to the cathedral which is right on top of the hill. This is the Cathédrale Saint Jérome, which was built as a small church in the 15th century and enlarged several times. Restoration has also been carried out and more is now essential if the building is to be considered as a site to attract visitors.

On the Boulevard Gassendi is the Municipal Museum which has paintings representing work from the 16th to the 20th century. There is some sculpture and items of archaeological and natural history interest. *Open 10-12 and 2-6 weekdays and 10-12, 2-5 on Sunday.*

There is another museum in Digne which is unusual – the Museum of the Second World War. It is a few minutes walk east of the Municipal Museum on Rue Colonel Payan. Bitter disputes have taken place ever since the museum opened, owing to different viewpoints on who collaborated and who did not and on the occupation of Digne by the Italians (many of whom settled here) as well the role played by the Communists. For the visitor, though, it is a fascinating slice of local history. *Open from 3-6 Monday to Friday from May to September, 2-5.30 Wednesday only the rest of the year.*

One of the most illustrious residents of Digne was Alexandra David-Neel who died here at the age of 101. She was a renowned traveller and is most famous for her journey to Lhasa, the capital of Tibet when it was still known as 'the Forbidden City'. She spent two months there in disguise as a Tibetan beggar and her book describing her experiences is one of the great travel adventures.

Her house, Samten Dzong (which means 'the fortress of meditation') is on the Avenue Maréchal-Juin and may be visited from 10.30-5 from July to September and 10.30-4 the rest of the year. There are guided tours. Tibetan products are also on sale.

At the confluence of the Bléone river and the torrent of Eaux Chaudes about 2 kilometres east of Digne and on the Avenue des Thermes, is the Etablissement Thermal. Nine sources of water spout up, all 38 to 42 degrees Centigrade. At nearby Saint Pancrace, the Romans had already installed a small thermal station.

Le Grand Paris
(HR)M   92 31 11 15   19 Boulevard Thiers   R cl. Sun p.m.; Mon o.o.s.; 20/12-1/3 All CC.

The building was once a 17th-century convent and has been converted into a very high quality hotel and restaurant.

The five apartments at 550-675f and the 31 rooms at 265-435f are all fully-equipped and beautifully furnished. Breakfast is 50f.

The restaurant is equally high quality with imaginative cooking on a classical basic. The selle d'agneau en croûte is recommended. The truite à la crème de poivrées is an unexpected variation on what is too often treated as a routine fish. Menus are 160, 200, 225 and 340f.

Mistre
(HR)S-M   93 21 00 16   Boulevard Gassendi   Cl. Sat; 10/12-10/1   All CC.

A landmark in Digne, Mistre has been run by the same family for three generations. The 19 rooms are fully equipped and priced at 300-425f. Breakfast is 40f. There is a pleasant terrace on the first floor. The current owner, Rolland Comte, serves local produce, cooked with care and attention, on menus at 150, 210 and 310f.

L'Origan
(HR)H-S, R-S-M   *93 21 62 13   6 rue Pied de Ville   Cl. Sun; 15/11-30/11; 23/3-30/3*
All CC.

In one of the pedestrians-only streets, L'Origan is really a restaurant with rooms. There are only 9 of them and though they are simple and ordinary, the price of 100-150f makes them attractive.

One of the specialities of the Digne area is truffles and you will have an excellent chance to enjoy their peculiar appeal here. Several opportunities are taken by Phillipe Cochet to use them in his classic cooking with an individual touch. It was selle d'agneau aux truffes when I was there but it will perhaps be some imaginative variation on another dish when you dine. Be sure to have the game when in season.

Menus are 100, 145 and 240f.

Map 2C   **EYGALIERES** 13810 (Bouches-du-Rhône) 12 km E of St Rémy

You have a choice – you can believe that the village takes its name from 'aigo', the Provençal word for water, or you can agree with those who point out that it must come from 'aigle' as there is an eagle on the village coat-of-arms.

The most noticeable building is the Chapel of Saint Sixte which is perched on a hill just outside Eygalières on the D24B heading for Orgon. It is 12th century and with an unusual angel weathervane.

If you wish to do some archaeological research – strictly unofficially, mind you – keep your eyes on the ground in the vicinity of the village. This area has been quarried for stone for tens of thousands of years and people still find the occasional weapon or tool, such as the head of an axe, a hammer, the point of a spear or the head of an arrow.

The old village, with its typical maze of narrow, winding streets, is worth exploring. The Château de Romanin lies in ruins but among those ruins is the shaft of a well, chopped right through the solid rock by the Romans. A look around the arid countryside will explain why this was necessary and it will also give credence to the old Provençal saying 'L'Aigo es d'or' – water is gold. The well is believed to have been the work of the Roman Sixth Legion on their way back to Rome from the garrison at Arles.

→**Le Mas de la Brune**
(HR)M-L   *90 95 90 77   H cl. 2/11-3/4   R cl. Tues; Wed lunch   All CC.*

It's expensive but is one of the finest hotels around.

The building is a 16th-century residence of great charm and style, classified now as a historical monument. There is attention to detail throughout, in the carpets, the moulding, the door handles and hinges and the entire effect is authentic and delightful.

It sits in a park full of chestnut and plane trees, and there is a pool.

The 10 rooms, priced at 445-760f, are magnificently decorated with antiques. Stefan Gagg is the proprietor and is to be congratulated on maintaining such a fine establishment.

The restaurant is outstanding and makes use of unusual flavours such as verveine and anise to present really different versions of what might be routine dishes. Menus are 220-300f. There is a long wine list but you will have to choose carefully for even the local wines are expensive.

Arrowed for magnificent building, good food.

Crin Blanc
(HR)M   *90 95 93 17   Route d'Orgon   H cl. 1/11-15/3; R cl. Mon.*

Ten rooms here in a modern structure that fits in with the Provençal landscape. At 350f Paul Bourgue is giving good value for there is a pool, tennis and a nice garden, dense with pine trees. Menus begin at 150f and make use of local produce.

Map 2C   **EYRAGUES** 13630 (Bouches-du-Rhône) 7 km N of Saint Rémy-de-Provence

---

(M) *Mon to Sat*

On the D571 which connects Saint Rémy and Châteaurenard, Eyragues is at the heart of the 'Sacred Triangle' of the Alpilles. Perhaps this accounts for the jealousy of neighbouring villages whose inhabitants have always concocted derisory nicknames for the denizens of Eyragues. 'Cacaiejaire' was one of the less unpleasant such names and it means 'gossips'. Other nicknames were rather more scurrilous, some suggesting that they always carried a sack into which anything portable could be slipped and another which put the name of the village of Eyragues at the head of the list of places to seek your stolen horse.

Don't mention any of this when you're in Eyragues though. Not that you will feel inclined for today it is a quiet village, friendly and peaceful.

Festivals

Outside the village and on the road to Maillane is the Chapel of Notre Dame du Pieux-Zèle. It is of Roman origin and there is a pilgrimage to it every Tuesday after Pentecost. The strange name comes from the Provençal 'Pieusello' meaning Virgin.

The last week-end in June is Eyragues' big day of the year.The Feast of Saint Eloi, the patron saint of blacksmiths and one you will have run across in other parts of Provence, is celebrated starting on the Saturday with decoration of the 'Charrettes', the horse-drawn wagons. There is a judging of these later in the day and a ball at night.

Sunday starts with Mass at the parish church of Saint Maxime then there are parades, banquets, boules contests and spectacles featuring the bull throughout the day and on Monday.

The Feast of Saint Symphorien is held on August 22 with parades and an outdoor meal.

One of the districts of Eyragues is named Queue de Tarascon after the legendary monster which used to eat children and terrify neighbourhoods of Provence. Then there is a building with a famous name which you can visit today – though you will do so mainly for eating purposes.

La Maison du Curé
(R)S-M   *90 94 34 17*   *Rue du Planet*   *Cl. Mon*   *Visa, CB.*

This was an important building when it belonged to the wealthy and influential De Réginel family. They sold it to the de Sambucy family who were even more so but in order to keep it out of the hands of the revolutionaries, they loaned it to the archdiocese. The Abbé Jacquier was installed in it and it became known as 'La Maison du Cure'. The Abbé Bonjean came later when it was falling into disrepair and he enlisted the aid of the villagers to restore it. In 1979, it was bought by Olivier de Lestrade and his family who came from Lyon and it was he who had the idea of turning it into a gourmet restaurant.

Many of the features of the building were retained including the 17th-century staircase and the shaded garden and the place acquired a strong following.

Annick le Brigand and Barbara Heise took it over a year ago and it continues to be a rendezvous for serious eaters. Tucked away in a narrow street, you will have to follow the restaurant's signs to find it but that is an exercise well worth while.

A wide choice of fish, meat and game is featured and the three-course menu at 155f is a meal to remember. The long list of local wines starts at a reasonable 85f.

Map 2B   **FONTAINE-DE-VAUCLUSE** 84800 (Vaucluse) 30 km E of Avignon, 21 km S of Carpentras, 33 km W of Apt

---

One of the strangest natural curiosities in France is here: a spring, a source and – oddly named – a fountain which gives the town its name.

40,000 gallons of water pour every second out of a fissure in the limestone rocks where the river Sorgue surges up from underground caverns. In spring, it is a spectacular sight especially after heavy rainfall or at the time of melting snows.

It is only a few minutes walk from the village and more than a million people come here a year to see it, even though in the summer the water output drops to 5,000 gallons a second, for it is then that the water takes on a deep bottle-green, much darker than normal.

This extraordinary waterfall has attracted writers, poets and artists for centuries. The source of the water is still something of a mystery but it's best just to enjoy it as a very unusual phenomenon and different from similar sights in Switzerland.

Almost everything in Fontaine-de-Vaucluse revolves around the Place de la Colonne. The 50-foot column in its centre looks Romanesque but was, in fact, erected in 1804 to commemorate the birth of Petrarch, Fontaine-de-Vaucluse's other claim to fame.

Parking is not easy and you won't find any opportunities to park on the streets but one of the numerous police will direct you to a municipal lot where you pay 10 francs for a day's parking – and your receipt has a beautiful line drawing of the town.

Despite the column, Petrarch was not born here but spent sixteen of the most poignant years of his life. His work in Italy had marked the beginning of the Renaissance and he was the first humanist to re-discover and re-appreciate the great literary works of ancient times. He was sent to Avignon on a diplomatic mission for the Vatican and while staying at an estate near the village of Fontaine-de-Vaucluse, he met and fell in love with the mysterious – though married – Laura.

Petrarch and Laura became one of the great love stories of all time and the poems and sonnets that he wrote to her are among the finest in literature. The small house, embedded in the rocks where Petrarch lived, looks directly across to a soaring wall of hills, sombre in shadow but serene in sunlight, and the house is now a museum with manuscripts of his poems and pictures of Laura.

The museum is open every day except Tuesday from April 15 to October 15 and on Saturdays and Sundays except January and February.

The image of Laura is difficult to assess today. She had eleven children, which is not the norm for a passionate mistress, though the bas-reliefs sculpted by Simon of Sienna and to be seen in Florence show her as sublimely calm and beautiful. She died of the Black Plague at the age of 40.

From the Place de la Colonne there are extraordinarily beautiful views in every direction: the green water rushing down from the source flows over mossy shallows which make it even more green; the old water-wheel, the low bridge, the massive empty four-storey buildings with their broken windows and empty interiors and, behind them all, the ruined château sitting perched on a small hill with the bare grey mountains rearing high, grottoes like open mouths dotting their slopes.

It would all look like a carefully designed film set but for the rusty machinery which once operated the locks and the crowds in summer which would defy the budget for extras in any modern movie.

Walk up the road – there is no doubt which one – and you will see almost everything. There is the museum with an outstanding collection of the discoveries of Norbert Casteret during his thirty years of speleology. Stalactites, stalagmites, crystals and minerals are well-displayed and other cabinets document the history of the spring since its discovery in 1878.

The museum is open 10-12 and 2-6.30; closed Monday and Tuesday, February to May and closed completely November to January.

The Moulin à Papier Vallis Clausa is a re-creation of a paper mill which was erected on the site in 1522 and uses some of the tremendous power unleashed by the waterfall. The mediaeval methods of paper-making are well-shown and the exhibits include money and printed editions of famous speeches, tracts and poems.

The Moulin is open 9-12.30 and 2-6, Monday through Saturday but in the summer months, the hours are 9-7 during the week and 10.30-12.30 and 2-6 on Sunday.

The Musée de la Résistance is a recent addition that has not yet caught on with visitors although it is in a fine modern, high-ceilinged building. Boutiques, gift shops, ice-cream bars and candy shops, cafés and restaurants line the route as you continue upwards. When the road runs out, it becomes a footpath and when it runs out, the rest of the way is a rocky trail. It takes about 30 minutes to reach the source.

Back down in the village, the quaint Church of Fontaine-de-Vaucluse contains several fine architectural features including a nave with vaulted arches and some beautifully fluted columns. The tomb of Saint Véran can be seen in the crypt – he was bishop of Cavaillon in the 6th century and rid the region of a monstrous dragon-like reptile known as the Couloubre which had lived in one of the caverns cut into the limestone rock.

More caverns run into Mont de la Vache d'Or, the mountain which you see towering above the source of the Sorgue. Legend says that one of them contains a huge quantity of gold bullion, possibly transferred here from the Palace of the Popes in Avignon when it was under threat of confiscation as the power in Avignon waned. Certainly a British company had reason to believe it when they made an offer to buy the whole mountain! The town council of Fontaine refused the offer but be warned of the dangers of cavern-exploring if you too feel the gold lure.

Festivals

The big feast days in Fontaine are on Easter Monday and the second Sunday in July. Midnight mass at Christmas has a picturesque offering of the lamb and in summer, there is a Son et Lumière every evening at the fountain. Plaques on nearby trees tell of Mistral and Petrarch.

With so many visitors coming here every year, accommodation can be hard to find in season unless you have booked ahead. The best recommendations are:

Le Parc
(HR)S-M   *90 20 31 57   Rue des Bourgades   H cl. Weds and Nov 1-Feb 15   R cl. Weds and Jan 2-Feb 15   All CC.*

A very pleasant hostelry right in the centre of the village with 12 small but comfortable rooms and near enough to the cascade to be able to hear it. The price of 240f for a room is very reasonable and breakfast is 35f. Ample parking though it's a fair walk to the lobby.

The restaurant serves meals in summer on the terrace by the river and one of the delights here is Chef Edouard Baffoni's use of fresh trout caught in the river Sorgue that morning. There is a wide choice of other dishes and well-selected meals on menus at 120, 130, 143, 163, 181 and 190f.

Hostellerie du Château

(HR)S-M   *90 20 31 54   Quartier Petite Place   H cl. Tues and Jan 30-Mar 1   R cl. Mon p.m. and Tues   All CC.*

Just across the bridge and on the river's edge, this is primarily known as a restaurant but there are 5 rooms at 150-220f. They look out at the water which may keep you awake if you are a light sleeper. Otherwise they are clean and neat and good value. Demi-pension may be mandatory in season.

Menus at 110 and 130f though the à la carte is perhaps preferable. The speciality is magret de canard avec cèpes.

Mme Douyère

(C)   *90 20 31 93   Bois Court.*

Chambres d'hôtes have been rarely recommended in this book. They are not nearly as commonly found in the south of France as in other regions and those that do occur are often of doubtful quality.

However, Fontaine-de-Vaucluse is woefully provided for in the way of accommodation although this is not a reflection on Mme Douyère's excellent establishment which would deserve to be included even if plenty of hotels existed.

On the edge of the village, there are three rooms of which two have terraces. All have wash-basins and private toilets, are pleasantly furnished and priced at about the same level as the local hotels (200f for a single, 250f for a double). All are on the first floor.

Restaurant Philip

(R)S-M   *90 20 31 81   Cl. Oct 1-Apr 1.*

Located on the water's edge, about two minutes walk on the way towards the source from the Place de la Colonne, this is one of the most popular places to eat in the village. As this is where the road ends and the footpath starts, the climb is getting a little steeper so the cascades are more intense and more frequent, making a table by the water an exciting experience.

Menus are 105 and 145f and both are strong on seafood. There are some good à la carte choices too and the écrevisses à l'Armoricaine can be particularly recommended at 95f. If you prefer something other than fish having watched the water much of the day, the quarter guinea fowl, roasted, at 50f is very good value.

The best choice from the wine list are the local Côtes du Ventoux, red, white or rosé at 60f a bottle.

Restaurant la Vanne Marel

(R) M   *90 20 32 56   Rue des Bourgades   CB, Visa*

There is a choice here of the large enclosed dining room or the extensive open-air terrace and both have a fine view of the waterfalls and the old bridge.

The menu at 95f is very good value. You might start with the caillettes provençales (quails) then the bavette d'aloyau grillé (grilled sirloin of beef with shallots) and a choice of desserts.

There is a four-course meal at 170f but I plumped for the 125f menu, starting with smoked salmon, then the poêlée de gambas Provençale, flambéed (giant shrimp) and selected a superb apple tart for dessert.

Lou Fanau
(R)M

This restaurant is also adjacent to the old bridge and has an excellent view of the château, the mountains and the hordes making their way up to the source.

Indoor or outdoor eating is a choice here too with menus at 85, 125 and 135f. The 85f menu offers marinated salmon then braised beef, cooked in the old traditional manner and served with cèpes. The profiteroles on this menu are irresistible. The 125f menu is all fish while the 135f menu is 4 course.

Restaurant Petrarque et Laure
(R)S-M   *90 20 31 48*   *Place de la Colonne*   *Open every day*   *All CC.*

Conveniently located right on the Place de la Colonne, this restaurant (named after the town's famous lovers) is also by the edge of the rushing green waters coming down from the source. This means that you can dine on the outdoor terrace or in the shady garden.

There are three carefully chosen menus which should satisfy all tastes and all wallets. The 85f menu could consist of feuilleté de fruits de mer followed by filet de loup in tarragon sauce, although I greatly enjoyed the cuisse de lapin with rosemary sauce. The choice of desserts is tempting but the fruit tarts are extremely good.

The menu at 120f offers some slightly more up-market dishes but if you are feeling really hungry, the 150f menu has four courses.

| Map 2C | **FONTVIEILLE** (13990) Bouches-du-Rhône 10 km NE of Arles |

The village gets its name from 'Font vieille', an old fountain which exploited water probably from a Roman well.

Its greatest fame, however, comes from its association with Alphonse Daudet, novelist and short-story writer, who lived much of his life in Provence, coming here to Fontvieille at the age of 20.

It was here that he wrote his drama *L'Arlésienne* which was set to music by Georges Bizet and became not only one of the most tuneful operas ever written but managed to convey the spirit of life and love in Provence. His famous *Letters From My Windmill* was actually

Fontvieille: The Mill of Alphonse Daudet

written mostly in Paris but when the Society of Friends of Daudet was created in 1935, they decided to establish a museum in his honour and had the happy idea of using the windmill Saint Pierre which is just south of the village of Fontvieille.

The mill still possesses its original mechanism and a visit to it and to its adjacent museum are simplified by a parking area and an information bureau. In fact, all of these are made even easier by the 'Promenade d'Alphonse Daudet' which takes in all of these plus a visit to the Château de Montauban which has another exhibit of the writer's correspondence and text and illustrations showing various facets of his work.

The Promenade leaves from the Office of Tourism on Rue Marcel Honorat. It takes 90 minutes and is conducted from 9-7. There is a small charge. On the way, you will see two other photogenic windmills. If you want to visit the museum without taking the promenade, its hours are 9-12 and 2-6.

Festivals

During the summer, there are several fêtes and spectacles, boules tournaments, bull festivals and folklore presentations but dates vary. A village fête is also held on the first Sunday in August.

Hôtel Valmajour
(HR)M   *90 54 62 33   Cl. Nov, Dec, Jan, Feb   Visa, CB.*

Just out of the village on the road to Arles, this is a quiet, comfortable hotel in extensive grounds. There are 32 rooms, gardens, a pool and tennis courts. There is parking in the grounds and a garage. At 300f, this is a lot of hotel value.

Meals are mostly Provençal style and make use of locally available ingredients. The menu at 96f is the one to choose and there are several inexpensive Côtes d'Aix wines on the list.

Hostellerie Saint Victor
(HR)M   *90 54 66 00   Open all year   All CC.*

Outstanding value here too in a hostellerie which is a new building but in a pleasingly Provençal style. It is in a short cul-de-sac just off the road between Arles and Fontvieille and the air is heavy with the smell of lavender.

The ten rooms are priced from 395-595f and those at the higher end of the range are air-conditioned. All are quite large and attractively furnished. There is a pool, tennis, parking and a garage. A restaurant is now being added and meals will be about 100f.

La Peiriero
(H)S-M   *90 54 76 10   Avenue des Baux   Cl. 30/10-20/12; 5/1-1/4   All CC.*

A huge building, recent but in rustic style and in a large park. The 30 rooms are 330-410f but there are also 10 apartments at 480-600f. All are fully equipped even to a mini-bar. There is a pool and a garage. M. Monforte does not offer a restaurant but he does run a fine and deservedly popular hotel.

La Ripaille
(HR)S   *90 54 73 15   Route des Baux   R cl. Tues; Nov-Feb   All CC.*

Completely renovated and now at a high standard despite the very reasonable prices. Raphael Maroto supervises everything here and you will love the Provençal decor of the 20 fully equipped bedrooms. At 200-280f, they are extremely good value. A bar, a terrace and a pool are among the other amenities. Menus are 90, 110 and 150f and there is a varied choice of meat and fish dishes.

Hôtel le St. Victor

Le Patio
(R)M   *90 97 73 10*   *Route du Nord*   *Cl. Tues p.m.; Wed; 2/1-6/2*   *All CC.*

An old Provence farm building with a lot of rustic charm and a strong following in the area. The terrace is the first choice for booking a table in the summer. Mme Rémy takes last orders at 9.30 so don't leave it too late to eat.

Menus are 120, 150 and 190f and you will find such unusual Provençal specialities as 'Aigo Sau', a garlic flavoured soup which is eaten with croutons, rouille and grated cheese just like fish soup. Civet de taureau is another local dish that you won't find on many menus, even here in bull country.

L'Amistadouso
(R)M-S   *90 54 73 17   Route du Nord   Cl. Tues p.m. o.o.s.; Tues lunch from 15/1-15/2   All CC.*

A simple pleasant little Provençal village house – very attractive. Thierry Bounoir uses fresh ingredients from the neighbourhood and cooks cuisses de grenouilles as good as any I have ever tasted. His gratinée de moules is also excellent.

Menus are 90, 130 and 150f and all of them are good value.

Map 4B   **FORCALQUIER** 04300 (Alpes de Haute-Provence) 20 km N of Manosque

---

 Mon

The road from Manosque is the customary approach to Forcalquier and long before you reach it, you see the town ahead of you, built round the lower slopes of a conical hill and capped with a cupola.

From the 10th to the 13th century, Forcalquier was the capital of an important county. In the 14th century, the town was laid waste by mercenaries and then again by the Huguenots in the 16th century. It never regained its former stature.

The cathedral of Notre Dame is right in the centre of town. It is large but plain and severe – very much like some of the great Norman cathedrals in England. The old town spreads south of the cathedral, where some of the streets are 13th century. Two pretty fountains remain. The one in front of the cathedral in the Place Bourget with its stone needle commemorates the marriage in 1235 of Eleanor of Provence to King Henry III of England. The other is on the Rue Mercière and is 15th century. It is surmounted by a statue of St Michael killing the dragon and is said to be the work of a monk, Pierre Garcin.

Going up towards the citadel on the hill is the Convent des Cordeliers on the Boulevard des Martyrs. It was probably the first Franciscan monastery in France and construction was begun in the 13th century. The library ceiling is original and today the room is used for exhibitions and concerts. There is a small museum of early religious art. *Open 10.30-11.15 and 2.30-5.30 from July to mid-September. From mid-September to October, May and June, Sundays and holiday afternoons only. Closed from November to April.*

The 19th-century Chapel of Notre Dame de Provence on the hill is in Roman-Byzantine style and is guarded by eight music-playing angels. Dominating the town, it offers a fine 360 degree panorama and there is an orientation table which identifies for you the directions of Constantinople and St Petersburg. Some of the mountains you can see are identifiable without the help of the table – especially Le Lubéron and La Sainte Baume.

Festivals

The Feast of St Pancrace on April 25 starts off the year's activities in

Forcalquier. Besides the weekly market, there is a fair the first Monday of each month. The Feast of St Marc is celebrated in April and St Pancrace returns for a second feast on May 11. A pilgrimage goes up to the nearby shrine of St Loup in August and midnight mass at Christmas is an affair that brings people from considerable distances.

In July and August, there is a flea market every Sunday and the Festival de Haute Provence runs through the first two weeks of August with exhibits, arts and crafts fairs and local produce.

Forcalquier is an excellent centre for trips into the surrounding countryside where there are several places worth visiting.

About 30 kilometres north along the D12, the winding road finally arrives at a place where you can park then walk about fifteen minutes up to the Signal de Lure. At an altitude of 1,826 metres even the coast is visible and the views in all directions are magnificent.

If you take the D12 east from Forcalquier until it reaches the Durance river and then drive north on the N96 – about 17 km in all – you come to Le Prieuré de Ganagobie. It dates from the 13th century and is a delightful building, partly in ruins; restoration that has been done has been carried out with care. The priory has a poetic grandeur that transcends time and it is a shame that it is little known.

South-west of Forcalquier, take the N100J then the D5 and the D306 to the Observatoire de Haute Provence. On the way you will go through the quaintly-named St Michel l'Observatoire, a blend of religious-ancient with scientific-modern. The site was selected partly because of its position but also because of the purity and clarity of the air which permits better astronomical viewing. Visiting times and days to the obervatory vary so check in Forcalquier first.

→Hostellerie des Deux Lions
(HR)M   92 75 25 30   11 Place du Bourguet   Cl. Sun p.m.; Mon o.o.s.; Jan and Feb All CC.

This is one of those hostelleries that you take an instant liking to just from seeing the façade. It was a popular post house on the long coach trip from the Alps to the Mediterranean coast as far back as the 17th century and it is just as popular today. Its position opposite the cathedral is a landmark in Forcalquier. Careful restoration has maintained the character of the place and the tradition of extending hospitality to the weary traveller is as strong today as it ever was.

The 18 rooms are warmly furnished and priced at 270-360f and the public rooms are reminiscent of the past to the degree that you need very little imagination to hear the clip-clop of horses' hooves as the coach rattled into the courtyard two centuries ago. (Today there is a garage.)

With all this, you could be thinking that good food could hardly be expected too. You would be wrong for proprietor Claude Audier is proud of the reputation of gourmet cooking that Les Deux Lions offers. Any of the locally caught game can be highly recommended (including pigeons) and so can fish from the local rivers. Lamb anywhere in Haute Provence is excellent. Menus are 125, 160 and 190f

and the wine list here is famous. Value in this restaurant is
outstanding for such reasonable prices.

Arrowed for exceptional value in a famous old inn.

Charembeau
(HR)S   *92 75 05 69   Route de Niozelles   Cl. 15/11-15/2   Visa, CB.*

About three kilometres out of Forcalquier, Charembeau is on the
N100. It is a calm, quiet farmhouse converted to have 11 rooms and
these are priced at 210-275f. Demi-pension is obligatory in season at
225-255f. The terrace is very pleasant in summer and the pool and the
tennis courts unusual luxuries for such reasonable pricing. The
cooking is reliable, farm-style but reserved for guests only.

Le Colombier
(HR)S   *92 75 03 71   Les Dragons   Cl. Mon; Feb   Visa, CB.*

A stone farmhouse in a peaceful country setting, four kilometres south
of Forcalquier on the D16. The 14 rooms are well-equipped and cosy.
At 195-240f, they are attractively priced. You are obliged to take demi-
pension in the season at 230-255f but this is not a hardship as the food
is tasty and plentiful. There is private parking.

Map 3B   **GARGAS** 84400 (Vaucluse) 2 km N of Apt

 Wed

The village gets its name from 'Gargassian', referring to the Eocene
epoch, second oldest of the five geological periods. Even the village
coat of arms contains some gypsum crystals, which has caused
neighbouring communities to refer to the denizens of Gargas as
'plasterers'.

Fossilised remains of mammoths have been found near the village
though none of these interesting facts are likely to tempt a passer-by
on the N100 to turn off for a visit. The area though is part of a much
vaster one in which mining of ochres has been carried out for dozens
of centuries. Some of the labyrinthine underground passages left from
the mining operations are today being used for the raising of
mushrooms as the temperature and humidity remain at constant
levels.

Festivals

Gargas' two big feast days of the year are on the first Sunday in
September and October 9. The Mardi Gras Carnival is also celebrated.

Mas de la Tour
(HR)M   *90 74 12 10   Open all year   All CC.*

An old-established and very popular hotel and restaurant, favoured for its warm atmosphere and its convenient location a few minutes off the N100. In fact, it is the Mas de la Tour that brings people rather than the village.

The 33 rooms cost 230-350f. There is a pool and parking.

The restaurant brings in even more people than the hotel and on a summer night there could be well over 200 diners. The terrace is usually filled and so is the garden. The cooking is well above average auberge quality and the loup Provençale is beautifully prepared and served. The magret de canard is served with a pear in wine and the favourite dessert is nougat glacé with raspberry coulis.

Menus are 115f and a meal here is outstanding value for money.

Mme Hélène Guigou
(C)M   *90 04 73 57   Open all Year   No CC.*

The advantage of Hélène Guigou's excellent chambre d'hôte is that there is only one room so you will be sure to be pampered. It is a very large room though, with private bath and toilet and the price is a modest 180f for two people. The room will accommodate up to four people and even then at only 300f total. There is a pool, and Mme Guigou will cook you a dinner for 75f per person.

Naturally, the food is the main feature here. To sharpen your appetite, you should start with the house cocktail, known as Le Potion Magique, at 40f. The menu at 150f might start with the Assiette Saint Pons (cold meats and pâtés), move on to the lapin à l'estragon then fromage du chèvre and dessert. The 165f menu could begin with melon au Rivesaltes et jambon cru, then the magret de canard au miel, then cheese and dessert.

The local Domaine du Boulon wine (red or rosé) is a good choice to accompany it (and only 49f). The Cuvée de Gemenos is even more reasonable at 40f.

Hôtel du Parc
(HR)S-M   *42 32 20 38   Vallée de Saint Pons   Open all year   Visa, CB.*

Sheltered below the mountains and situated in a lovely wooded area, the Hôtel du Parc is just outside the town as the road enters the valley. Don't expect anything too fancy inside but the prices are reasonable at 220-400f, all rooms equipped with a W.C.

The restaurant offers good meals and the civet de marcassin is a favourite whenever it is available . Menus are 90, 140 and 220f.

Le Fer à Cheval
(R)S-M   *42 82 21 19   Place de la Mairie   Open all year   Visa, CB.*

One of the best restaurants for miles around and very well-known, so be sure to book. René Alloin and his pupil Eric Giraud have a fine reputation in the kitchen and continue to live up to it.

The building was a blacksmith's forge in the 17th century and was converted into a restaurant twenty years ago. Dominique Corvi took over in 1988 and though the choice of dishes is a little routine, everything is expertly done. There is a menu at 100f but you might prefer to go à la carte. The coquilles St Jacques aux agrumes et estragon at 90f is a real treat. The tournedos Rossini may not be unique but you won't taste better and the price of 140f is not at all exorbitant.

Le Moulin de Gemenos

(R)M   *42 82 24 48   Vallée de Saint Pons   Open all year   Visa, CB.*

At the foot of the hills on the edge of town, le Moulin is another valuable contribution to the eating scene around Gemenos.

The 150f menu is the best one to choose. You could start with the terrine campagnard au cognac and then have the fillet de rascasse avec crème de basilic, plus dessert.

Map 3D   **GEMENOS** 13420 (Bouches-du-Rhône) 3 km E of Aubagne, 35 km SE of Aix-en-Provence

---

The old château has now become the Mairie and the beautiful building with its classic lines and four towers is a functional part of Gemenos. The old origins of the town are quite obvious but every structure seems to have been so well preserved or maintained or renovated that you have the feeling of a film set just waiting for the cameras to roll.

The rue des Artistes contains the house where Maurice Chevalier spent many years of his childhood with his grandfather and many other artists of one kind or another have lived in or around Gemenos, including Victor Hugo, Lamartine, Mistral, Balzac, Flaubert and Châteaubriand.

The town's name derives from 'gemme' meaning gem and the whole surrounding area has an archaeological/industrial background. Remnants of saw mills, paper mills, forges, glass-works as well as olive oil mills and flour mills dot the valley. The 'Vieux Moulin' has been restored and is now used for banquets and receptions. The water-powered wheel which provided the energy still turns and the reddish-brown chimney you see was once known as 'Le Paradou'. This was not a reference to Paradise in Provence but a treadmill which rolled paper for cigarettes. At the entrance to this valley is the natural amphitheatre where Bizet's masterpiece *L'Arlésienne* is still performed annually.

Festivals

The Fête de Saint Jean is held every summer and so is the Fête de Saint Eloi, the patron saint of blacksmiths, complete with its 'carreto ramado', the parade of gaily decorated horse-drawn wagons.

Le Relais de la Magdeleine

(HR)   *42 82 20 05   Cl. Oct 1-Jan 15, Mar 15-May 1   R – Sun p.m. and Mon   All CC.*

A 17th-century mansion, four storeys and covered with ivy – a wonderfully welcoming old place where you feel at home as soon as you drive into the grounds. It has all the attributes of a really expensive Relais yet it is easy-going and modestly casual. The grounds around it are delightfully simple, not over-pruned but not neglected. There is a swimming pool and even a library.

M et Mme Marignane spare no effort to make the hotel comfortable. The 24 rooms are exquisitely furnished with antiques and are good sized, priced at 420-700f. Demi-pension is obligatory in season at 545-775f. The menu is 240f and the food is well-prepared and uses all local ingredients.

Le Saint Pons
(HR)S-M   *42 82 24 08   Vallée de Saint Pons   Cl. Sun p.m.; Mon (R only)   All CC.*

Really a restaurant with seven rooms. It is a popular eating spot for the local residents. The rooms all have a bathroom and are nicely furnished, while being attractively priced at 215-370f.

Map 2B   **GIGONDAS** 84190 (Vaucluse) 18 km E of Orange, 39 km NE of Avignon

---

Here is another name which is familiar to every wine drinker. Gigondas is best known as a rich, full-bodied red wine (crimson, the French say) which may be slightly rough when young but attains maturity in as little as two years.

Gigondas suffers by comparison with its more snooty neighbouring wine – Châteauneuf-du-Pape. Certainly Gigondas is considered more earthy and commands a lower price but its heritage is at least as long. It has been grown in these vineyards for around two thousand years and its popularity has grown in recent times as its character and its reliability make it a very good buy at more reasonable price levels than its up-market neighbour. You may want to taste some of the whites but they are unremarkable. The rosés are delicate and fruity but are only really drinkable when young.

Dry soil and lots of sunshine are the two climatic conditions which make Gigondas such a good wine and the same two make the village area popular, lying as it does between Orange and the 2,000 metre Mont Ventoux. The nearby Dentelles de Montmirail, a strange ridge of limestone peaks which reach, claw-like, into the azure sky, are another reason for Gigondas' attraction as the village makes a good base for exploration.

It is a charming little village but with only just over 600 inhabitants, it does not have much to offer the tourist beyond its wine and places to stay. But then when both are this good, how much more does it need?

Within a few kilometres of Gigondas are a dozen ruined chapels. Whichever direction you head, you will see one or two of them – Notre Dame des Pallières, Sainte Anne, Notre Dame du Bon Secours, Notre Dame de Pitié ... the only one which is not a ruin is the chapel of Saint Comé – Saint Damien which comes into its own every year on

December 24 when the traditional Provençal Midnight Mass brings worshippers and sightseers from great distances. The Monastery of Prébayon is also worth a visit though it too is now a ruin. Built in 611 on the banks of the Trignon, it was sacked by the Saracens, re-built and destroyed several times so that now only the base of the walls remain.

The wine though is the principal attraction and there are over 40 caves where you can taste it and see if you do not agree that it is one of Europe's finest reds. The principal grapes in Gigondas are Grenache and Cinsault while the addition of Syrah and Mourvèdre are considered to add flair, style and longer life. The Domaine des Pallières, the Domaine du Pesquier, the Caveau du Gigondas and the Moulin de la Gardette are but four of the caves where you can taste as many wines as you wish and where you may expect to buy a very good 3-year-old Côtes du Rhône for not more than 40f a bottle.

In the village itself, much revolves around the Place de la Mairie where a Caveau des Vignerons offers most of the wines from the surrounding vineyards. You can taste and also buy at the same prices.

The Côtes du Rhône wine region has several 'wine routes' which thread their way through the finest vineyards in the region and also link the principal villages. Following such a route enables you to taste wines on frequent occasions, stop in delightful villages, enjoy fine regional food and see historic remains and buildings. One of the most scenic (and tasty) routes is known as 'The Lavender Road'. It covers 70 kilometres and Beaumes-de-Venise lies at one end and Bollene at the other end. Between them are some of the prettiest villages and the best wines in the region. Gigondas is on this route and so are Sablet, Cairanne and Vacqueyras.

Festivals

Gigondas has a liking for art and there are several major art exhibitions during the year. The first is at Easter and there are others in June, July and August – dates vary. In September, there is a great Aïöli feast on the first Sunday.

Les Florets

(HR)S-M   90 65 85 01   Route des Dentelles   Cl. Weds all year; also Tues o.o.s.; all Jan and Feb   All CC.

Of the numerous places to stay around Gigondas, Les Florets probably wins out by a short head. It is small and beautifully kept, the kind of establishment that is really inviting. In the middle of a pine forest, it consists of an old farmhouse and several bungalows. There is a tree-shaded terrace and a lovely garden which Madames Bernard and Germano keep looking in perfect condition.

It's secluded and quiet. There are 15 rooms and 12 of them have private toilet and bath or shower. Prices run from 260-355f. Breakfast is 35f.

The extensive seating in the restaurant and outside tell you that local residents too come here to eat, attracted by both the food and the value. Noisettes d'agneau à la crème d'ail is one of the popular specialities and for lovers of them, the pieds et paquets are outstanding. Menus are 140 and 190f and some excellent examples of Gigondas wine are on the wine list.

Hôtel de Montmirail
(HR)M   *90 65 84 01   Cl. Sun; Mon o.o.s.; Jan 1-Feb 15, Nov 5-Dec 31   Visa, CB, E, MC.*

There are 46 simple but practical rooms here and priced at 260-450f. Many have terraces and the building is in a large park in a tranquil forest. It's located outside Gigondas, about 6 km on the D7 heading for Vacqueyras. There is a pool and the atmosphere is extremely serene.

Menus are 130 and 160f. You will find several unusual items on them and may have to seek assistance in translation from the helpful staff.

Map 2C   **GLANUM** 13210 (Bouches-du-Rhône) 2 km S of Saint Rémy

Take the D5 south out of Saint Rémy and you come to Glanum, one of the finest collections of Roman ruins in Europe.

A Neolithic settlement was originally established here, then in the second century BC the Gallo-Greeks came, probably spreading out from Marseille. This was never a Greek colony although the construction of the buildings was along Greek lines. It was the Romans, arriving about a hundred years later, who built the town whose ruins you can see today. It was a station for the Roman army and an important spa town.

Driving from Saint Rémy though, the first sights you see are known as Les Antiques. They are right at the edge of the D5 and you can park alongside them and examine them freely.

The triumphal arch was built to celebrate the conquest of the Gauls by Caesar. It is sculpted with fruit and flowers and chained Gallic prisoners, both men and women. Next to it is the 60 foot high tower, long known as the Mausoleum. This is one of the finest Roman structures remaining anywhere. Long believed to have been a mausoleum, it is now established that it was in fact a monument to the grandsons of Augustus Caesar, Lucius and Caius who were known as 'the princes of youth'.

Cross the road to the entrance to the city of Glanum, built during the same period. A large hall contains beautifully constructed models which show the town layout, individual buildings and even the interiors of rooms. Detailed explanations with sketches and drawings accompany the models making it all very clear. The importance of Glanum at that time is stressed – it was at the crossroads of the two major routes between Italy and Spain, one over the Alps and the other along the coast.

Walking through the ruined city you pass temples and houses, the Forum, altars dedicated to Hercules, a swimming pool, gates and monuments – and most important, the thermal baths. These come

The ruins at Glanum

from the same springs that the Neolithic forerunners had used. The Romans considered the water sacred and capable of effecting cures so Glanum soon acquired the status of a Lourdes.

A brief last stop in the entrance hall will help to seal in your mind the picture of a living city. It lived only until AD 270 when the Barbarian hordes destroyed it. Fortunately though the bases of the buildings remain and from these the city layout can be reconstructed.

Villa Glanum
(HR)S-M   *90 92 03 59   46 Avenue van Gogh   Cl. 15/10-15/3   All CC.*

Literally next to the ruins of Glanum and still only 2 kilometres out of Saint Rémy. Should you prefer to explore that town from a country location the Villa Glanum is unexcelled value for money.

M et Mme Vincent are warm and welcoming hosts and the atmosphere is relaxing and friendly. The pool is surrounded by trees and bushes and you can stroll at leisure through the gardens. The tower of the Roman Mausoleum can be seen in the adjacent grounds while the jagged teeth of the Alpilles range cross the horizon to the north.

The 23 rooms are pleasantly furnished and priced at 220-365f. There is a bar and a salon de thé. The restaurant is Provençal style with beamed ceilings and a huge fireplace. Cooking is Provençal too and menus start at 59f.

Map 3B   **GORDES** 84220 (Vaucluse) 38 km E of Avignon, 17 km NE of Cavaillon, 20 km W of Apt

---

(M) *Tues*

It's the price that has to be paid.

Gordes is one of the biggest and best-known of all the Provençal perched villages, it has not declined the title of the resort capital of Vaucluse and it has so much to offer the visitor. Little wonder then that it is inundated in the summer season.

In the 1930s, the Cubist painter André Lhote discovered Gordes. Other artists followed and many established homes here. It was badly damaged in 1944 when the retreating German army blew up much of the village in retaliation for raids by the French Resistance but restoration after the war was speeded by an influx of film people, musicians and artists – many of them foreign – who bought or built second homes.

On top of the piled cluster of houses and narrow streets which make Gordes a hill-top village, perches a huge Renaissance château, erected on the site of a 12th-century fort. The heart of the village is around the château.

The gateway is impressive and so is the Great Hall. Especially notable is the fireplace which is so large that a whole steer can be spit-roasted. The lintel is richly decorated and contains a dozen niches intended to hold a dozen coats-of-arms. It is said to represent the twelve apostles and remind those present of absent lords. The dining room is on the right when entering the château and contains a 40 foot deep well which has proved its value in many times of siege.

Among the artists who came to Gordes were Marc Chagall and Victor Vasarely. It was the latter who was instrumental in the restoration of the château and in 1970 Vasarely opened his Didactic Museum in the château. In Aix-en-Provence can be seen the Fondation Vasarely and according to the personal views of the Hungarian scientist, the Fondation presents art as related to science, architecture and technology whereas the Didactic Museum here at Gordes considers art in terms of the artist's creative development.

There is a similarity between the two museums in the means of their presentation. Both use automatic sliding panels to explain Vasarely's theories and if you have seen and enjoyed the Fondation at Aix, you will likewise enjoy this museum. Mosaics and tapestries are used to display brightly coloured geometric designs which have much of the technique of the optical illusion. It is all more attractive than it might sound and you cannot fail to be impressed by the dazzling kaleidoscopic effects. *The museum is open 10-12 and 2-6, closed on Tuesdays except in July and August.*

In violent contrast to Vasarely's scientific approach to art is the Village des Bories. It is 3 kilometres east of Gordes and just off the D2 heading for Cavaillon. Bories are stone huts, some pyramid-shaped, some conical and others various combinations. They are built of rough-cut stone slabs, no mortar or bonding of any kind has been used and they look like giant beehives.

They have a strongly prehistoric look but were in fact built during the same period as the château (12th to 18th century). It is remarkable to learn that these were inhabited until about a century ago. There are about a dozen of them and served as houses, workshops, storage rooms and bakery. They have been restored so as to highlight displays of hunting relics and communal ovens containing cooking pots, roasting spits and other domestic items. If you have been in Sardinia, you will immediately note the resemblance to the 'nuraghi' there though the structures on Sardinia are far more numerous and most are larger. The shape and construction method however are the same.

The nuraghi on Sardinia are of Bronze Age origin so it is not surprising that historians are still debating why the Provençal inhabitants put up similar dwellings so many years later. It is known though that they lived a sedentary agricultural life, raising grain, catching game and making wine and olive oil. Fragments of leather have been found suggesting that they made leather garments.

As you enter Gordes coming from Cavaillon along the D2, you will see, opposite the Hôtel Gordos, a Roman villa. It is called Insula Maria and it has a date on it – 1965. The villa was built entirely with his own hands by André Argentais, a former railway worker from Brittany. André had a fetish about Ancient Rome and was determined to be able to claim that he was the only Frenchman living in a Roman villa. Roman scholars have pronounced it to be an extremely faithful replica. *It is open to the public every day.*

Three kilometres to the north-west of Gordes can be found the Abbey of Sénanque. It is one of the 'Three Sistercian Sisters', Sylvacane and Le Thoronet being the other two. It is a pale grey building, huge and somewhat forbidding though its austere appearance is mellowed by the masses of lavender around it.

Sénanque is considered to be the purest example of 12th century Cistercian architecture. Purity is carried over to the interior of the building too as lack of adornment was one of the intentions of the Cistercian order. This ban extended to paintings, sculpture and stained glass. The monks left Sénanque over a century ago to revive the old Benedictine monastery on the Island of St Honorat, just off Cannes. Now they have returned and the part of Sénanque which is open to the public was built entirely in the 12th century.

Around the château are clustered boutiques, artists and artisans selling their wares from Provençal cotton prints, ceramics and honey to candles, soaps, vinegars and hand-made jewellery. L'Atelier Alain Dubert offers gems and gold and silver articles. Peyron Georges et Fils sells royal jelly and honey while Boucherie Rambaud has mouth-watering displays of pâtés and charcuterie.

Festivals

Gordes holds a big wine festival which features the wines of Côtes du Ventoux on July 13 and 14. The Festival de Gordes is held from the last week-end in July to the first week-end in August. There are concerts of classical music and of jazz as well as dramatic performances, usually of an historical nature. All these are at the Théâtre des Terrasses.

A village fête is featured on the first Sunday after October 11 and a votive feast falls on the the third Sunday in September.

There are lots of places to stay in and around Gordes though sadly the fame of the village has pushed prices skyward. La Bastide de Gordes in the village and the Domaine de l'Enclos on the Route de Sénanque both offer top-class comfort and service, a swimming pool and haute cuisine. Both charge up to l000f a night for a single. For more reasonable accommodation you should try:

La Mayanelle

(HR)S-M   90 72 00 28   6 Rue de la Colombe   H cl. Jan, Feb   R cl. Tues   All CC.

Eugène Mayard has been the owner/chef here for many years and has an enviable reputation. The ten bedrooms are all decorated differently and are fully equipped with modern comforts. At 250-360f, they are excellent value while breakfast is an additional 44f.

However, it is the restaurant here which is the main attraction. M. Mayard is a traditionalist and his cooking is classic Provençal. Diners are mostly locals and regulars and one of the specialities you will enjoy here are the tiny puff-pastries stuffed with a mixture of sausage meat, olives and anchovies – and that's just to tickle your palate for the meal itself. The truite aux almondes is perfectly done but then the canard aux olives is just as good.

Expect to pay around 200f for a meal.

You will probably select a Gigondas or a Côtes du Rhône to accompany your meal and the rosés in both cases are far above most Provençal rosés.

In summer, you will want to enjoy the terrace with its sweeping panoramic views.

La Ferme de la Huppe
(HR)M   *90 72 12 25   Cl. Mon lunch, Tues in season.*

The building that houses the six bedrooms dates back to the 18th century but all the comforts of the 20th century can be found in the rooms. This was originally a farm and the old farm implements hung on the walls and the wood manger filled with dried plants remind you of this. Rooms are 400f for a single and 490f for a double, but breakfast is included. There is a pool.

M et Mme Konings are from Holland and speak excellent English. Their son, Gerald, is the chef and the dining room overlooks the terrace where breakfast and lunch are served. Food emphasis is strictly traditional Provençal and so you will find most of the diners to be locals. Gerald is particularly proud of gnocchi parisienne which is served as a dish with most main courses. The rouget (red mullet) in puff pastry with basil sauce is highly recommended, as is caille au chou and pintádi aux olives. The raspberry bavarois aux flamboises is a succulent dessert.

The cost of a three-course meal will be 180-200f but there are few places where you can eat better.

➤ Auberge de Carcarille
(HR)M   *90 72 02 63   Les Gervais   Cl. Fri; 20/11-30/12   Visa, CB, EC.*

There are few hotels in Vaucluse more recommendable than this one and I have been disappointed more than once when unable to get a room here. It is on the D2 just south of Gordes so you are out of the crowds which fill the town in summer. The setting is peaceful and the masses of sunflowers in the adjoining fields add to the rustic Provençal scene. The long stone building with its red-tiled roofs looks out on to the pool, the grassy gardens and the nearby hills. There are 11 rooms and all have either a terrace or a balcony with views. The rooms are delightfully decorated, good-sized and bright. At 290-330f, the value easily deserves an arrow.

In the dining room, a big fire blazes in winter but at any time of year, the beamed ceilings and the bright red table decor harmonise with the Provençal furniture and decorations. Demi-pension is obligatory in season at 300-335f but Francis Rambaud, chef de cuisine, will make you glad you chose it. Fish and game are the specialities and menus are 100-170f.

Arrowed for good value in delightful building.

Chez Tante Yvonne
(R)S-M   *90 72 02 54   Cl. Sun; Mon p.m.   Visa, CB.*

You'll find praiseworthy attempts at original cooking here not perhaps always 100% successful but never a complete failure and such ambition deserves support. The terrine d'épinards is one such example while another starter, the tarte de roquefort was so good I wouldn't have believed it. Filet de sole garni avec pamplemousse was far better than it sounds. Menus are 110 and 150f.

Auberge de Carcarille

Map 3C   **GRAMBOIS** 84240 (Vaucluse) 12 km NE of Pertuis, 21 km SW
of Manosque

The unusual name has an unusual meaning. Grambois comes from a
Provençal word 'garamboi' which means lop-sided. It was given the
name in the 13th century and the village is considered to look that way
as it sits almost on a hilltop.

Châteaux are ten-a-penny in Provence but Grambois goes one
better and has two of them. The older was built in the 17th century
and received many famous guests, including Madame de Sévigny and
Mirabeau.

The Château de Pradines is of 19th-century construction and its
story has been peaceful – in contrast to most castles. It was acquired
by a rich poet, Joseph Autran. His wealth came from inheritance, not
poetry, and he put his home at the disposal of painters, sculptors and

poets. It was here that Mistral gave the first performance of his *Reine Jeanne.*

The village itself is a scaled-down version of a perched village even though it is only minutes from the D956 which runs right through the Regional Park of the Lubéron. The narrow alleys snake in and out among the ancient walls which are part of the older château but it hasn't yet been touristified so don't expect any boutiques or artisans manufacturing antiques. In fact, there are hardly any people at all and not that many visitors.

Festivals

Grambois celebrates the Feast of Saint Pancrace at the beginning of May and the Feast of Saint Francis of Assisi on October 4.

Hostellerie les Tilleuls
(HR)S-M   *90 77 93 11   Cl. Tues; Wed o.o.s. and June 19-July 7   No CC.*

This is really a restaurant and just barely qualifies as a hotel with its four rooms. These are priced at 120-185f though demi-pension is required in season.

The cooking is Bourgogne-style and menus start at 80f with some good, inexpensive Lubéron wines on the list.

Map 2C   **GRANS** 13450 (Bouches-du-Rhône) 6 km SW of Salon-de-Provence

---

If you want to see a completely unspoiled, natural, Provençal village, still untouched by tourists, you can't do better than head for Grans. It's conveniently located just off the N113 between Salon-de-Provence and Arles and it's really surprising that it should have remained isolated for so long with flows of tourists passing in several directions.

The centre of the village consists of a double ring of houses, curving in protective fashion around the church which is mentioned in the archives of the Archbishopric of Arles in a document dated 1207. The first counts of Provence lived here including Alphonse, King of Aragon, but the quiet, modest village of today shows no signs of an illustrious past.

Three kilometres to the west of the village is the Chapel of Saint George which probably dates from the 12th century. The romantic site of the 'Fontaine Mary-Rose' has given rise to legends recalling the charming love story of Auguste Saurel, a local poet, and Marie-Rose Carias who lived in Grans. Saurel was a member of the 'Felibrige' movement and a friend of Frédéric Mistral and declared his undying love for Marie-Rose in poems in the Provençal language. She was 14 and Saurel 17 when they met and after Saurel discovered the 'fountain' (actually a spring), it became their trysting place. She died at the age of 16 leaving Saurel inconsolable until his death at the age of 84.

It is the narrow, quiet village streets though that are the most captivating feature of Grans and they have a timeless quality which is rarely found even in Provence. Every corner brings another scene to photograph, every alley is a new delight.

The tiny centre of the village contains a small market, a bakery, a fruit shop and a casual bar-café-pizzeria – 'La Touloubre'. The Touloubre runs by, no longer a river but just a stream as it trickles through the square.

M et Mme Richard
(C)M   *90 55 82 98   Domaine du Bois Vert   Open all year.*

A beautiful, traditional old house with pale green shutters setting off the red-tiled roof where Veronique and Jean-Pierre Richard offer two fine chambres d'hôte on the banks of the Touloubre river, surrounded by pines and oak trees. There is a separate entrance for guests, TV, table tennis, a lounge with a fireplace and a private terrace. The host and hostess speak English. Both rooms have bathroom and private toilet and are priced at 180-250f.

L'Auberge des Eyssauts
(R)S-M   *90 55 93 24   Route de Saint Chamas   Visa, CB.*

Shady trees grow all around this gourmand restaurant where regional products are used with skill and imagination. The big dining room seats 200 and is air-conditioned though in summer, you will want to eat out under the trees. Fish is the main speciality and the other is meats grilled over wood fire. Menus are 95, 155 and 210f.

Map 2C   **GRAVESON** 13690 (Bouches-du-Rhône) 11 km S of Avignon

(M) *Fri*

It was the monks from the monastery of Montmajour who were responsible for the establishment and growth of Graveson. They drained the marshy land and then turned the soil over to the Benedictines to cultivate.

Graveson was often described in the past as being at the heart of the 'holy triangle' of Provence due to its inhabitants being particularly devoted to religious traditions and practices. Mistral refers to their fondness for wood-carving and many churches in the region have examples of their work. One of the nicknames given to the people of Graveson was 'mange crapauds' (toad eaters) because of their predilection for catching and eating the frogs that abound in the swamp locality.

In times of drought, pilgrimages were made from Graveson to the church of St Michel-de-Frigolet carrying the bust of their patron saint Saint Anthime.

Just south of Graveson on the D80 is the Musée des Aromes where Nelly Grosjean has converted a 19th-century farmhouse into a museum. Here, you can see the production of essential oils and watch how the plants of Provence are treated in order to extract from them their health-giving constituents. The ancient equipment is still used and there are diffusers, extractors, jars and flagons of old and fascinating designs. *The museum is free and open 10-12 and 2-6 every day. Light meals are obtainable of fruit and health foods.*

Festivals

Graveson celebrates the Feast of Saint Eloi on the last Sunday in July and there is a 'Carreto Ramado' featuring brilliantly decorated horse-drawn wagons. On July 14, Bastille Day, there is a big aïoli and a running of the young bulls. The second Sunday in September sees a local fête.

Mas des Amandiers
(H)S   *90 95 81 76   Route d'Avignon   Cl. 1/11-3/1   All CC.*

Several old farm buildings have been renovated and surround a pool. The 26 rooms are decorated in attractive Provençal style and priced at a reasonable 220-290f. Besides the garden, there is also a garage and a gymnasium – a rare extra.

Jean-Louis Bayol offers Provençal cooking, starting with an 85f menu.

Hôtel du Moulin d'Aure
(H)S   *90 95 84 05   Cl. 1/11-15/3   All CC.*

What a pity the Moulin does not have a restaurant! If it did, though, the room prices of the 14 rooms (240-290F) would surely double so perhaps you should be satisfied to have all the luxury of a place which has all the earmarks of a Relais et Châteaux but at a fraction of the price.

It is a two-storey building of fairly recent construction but in perfect Provençal style. Only 12 kilometres from the autoroute exit (Avignon Sud), the Moulin is among the pines and olive trees of a beautiful park, calm and quiet.

Madame Aurelio is herself a calm and quiet person who will ensure that you are well taken care of. The public rooms are particularly spacious and have a restrained elegance. There is a beautiful pool.

Map 4C   **GREOUX-LES-BAINS** 04800 (Alpes de Haute-Provence)
         50 km NE of Aix, 15 km SW of Manosque

 Thur

As you might suppose from its name, there are thermal baths here and have been since Roman times. A date of 176 can just be distinguished on one of the stones. In those times, it was believed that sunlight reduced the efficacy of the spa baths and so these were taken only at night. Some authentic and convincing reconstruction has

Graveson: Hôtel du Moulin d'Aure

made it possible to see what the baths were really like. Now they are within a park.

The popularity of Gréoux as a spa town faded with the decline of the Roman Empire and it was not until the 12th century that it recovered. This was due to members of the Order of the Knights Templar establishing themselves here, having been converted to the Saracen idea of bathing. They built an enormous château, in the form of a square with a vast interior courtyard. It passed subsequently into the hands of the Knights of Saint John and underwent some structural changes. Its ruin remains.

Villa Borghese

(HR)M   *92 78 00 91*   *Avenue des Thermes*   *Cl. 1/12-1/3*   *All CC.*

Named after the Princess Pauline Borghese who stayed often in
Gréoux, this long four-storey building has delightful balconies covered
in vines. Most look out over the umbrella-decked patio and the flower
gardens.

Jean-Claude Redolfi performs marvels here, as the villa is a fine
hotel, a gastronomic restaurant, a health and beauty centre and a spa,
all at the same time. There are even hair-dressing salons, a sauna and
a bridge club in addition to a pool, tennis courts, a park and the
garden. Golf is adjacent.

The 70 rooms are beautifully furnished and air-conditioned. They
are priced at 330-560f and demi-pension is also available at 370-690f.

You can have a complete vacation here with dietetic food if desired.
Otherwise enjoy the gastronomic restaurant. Menus are 150, 195 and
260f. The bourride uses lotte and is strong on garlic in authentic
Provençal style. The filet de boeuf aux morilles is similarly delicious.

La Crémaillère

(HR)M   *92 74 22 29*   *Route de Riez*   *Cl. Dec-Mar*   *All CC.*

A fine hotel with a pool, tennis, a garden and a patio. The 54 rooms
are modern almost to the point of being stark but they are calm and
relaxing. They are 350-380f and all have TV.

The restaurant is renowned. The ballotine of pigeon with just a little
walnut oil is excellent and the filet de Saint Pierre is pan-fried with
white wine to perfection. Menus are 200-390f.

Grand Hôtel des Colonnes

(HR)S   *92 78 00 04*   *8 Avenue des Marroniers*   *Cl. Dec-Mar*   *Visa, Cb, EC.*

François Angelini has 35 rooms, not fancy but more than adequate
and they are priced at a reasonable level of 250-300f; in season, full
pension at 250-300f is probably the best bet.

The hotel is near the baths and the restaurant is really for residents.
The vaulted archways, the beamed ceilings and the chandeliers give it
an opulent atmosphere.

Map 4D   **HYERES** 83400 (Var)

Napoleon and Tolstoy were among those who appreciated the mild
climate of Hyères and then a strong English influence was established
in the late 19th century when London specialists recommended it to
their tuberculosis patients. Tea-rooms, English libraries and churches
sprang up and, of course, a golf club was established.

Robert Louis Stevenson was one of those who came for health
reasons and he wrote *Treasure Island* while living here. Among royal
visitors, Queen Victoria and the Empress Josephine were prominent.
Unfortunateiy for those who came hoping that the air would be

bracing and beneficial, Hyères is five kilometres from the sea and the surrounding land is marshy.

Still, it did become the first resort on the Côte d'Azur and the wide boulevards you see today were built at that time while the many palm-trees provided that touch of tropical glamour that the visitors were looking for. The old mediaeval town on the hill-slope above has a ruined castle and you should also visit the 12th-century Collégiale de Saint Paul, the 13th-century Church of Saint Louis, formerly a monastery on Place de la République and the Tour Saint Blaise, the tower being the only remaining part of a Knights Templar lodge of the 12th century.

In the modern town the Municipal Museum recalls the Greek and Roman past of Hyères. It is on the Place Th.-Lefèbvre and has natural history and archaeology exhibits as well as weapons, sculpture, paintings, cloth and underwater finds. *Open 10-12 and 3-6 Monday to Friday, 10-12 only on Saturday and Sunday, closed on Tuesday and holidays.*

A six-acre natural park on the Route de Valcros, just south of Hyères, houses an exceptional collection of tropical birds. Many are rare species and seldom seen. The park is filled with pine trees, cork-oaks and eucalyptus. *Open every day of the year.*

There is tasting and touring at La Cave Gasperini in adjacent La Crau. They produce a pleasant Côtes de Provence A.O.C. wine. *The cave is open every day from 8-2 and 2-7.30.*

The pleasure port and Hyères-Plage are south-east of the town and as you continue along this road, you are on a narrow spit of land with extensive salt pans on your right. These were created in the 15th century by the Jesuits who also established a very profitable trade in the commodity.

On the left are miles of caravan and trailer camps with multi-coloured tents and even more miles of washing on the line. These are mixed in with older houses and some newer beach homes. You can drive in between these – the roads are not paved – to the shingle beaches. These are not the Riviera's finest but they are popular in the summer when the still water may be almost too warm.

Continuing along this road brings you to the Presqu'Ile de Giens – well-named for it used to become an island when violent storms isolated it from the mainland. You're not likely to be marooned though as the last time it was cut off was nearly 200 years ago.

Giens is only about five kilometres long and barely one kilometre wide and the western end is military property. At the eastern end though, La Tour Fondue was built in 1630 and completed the defensive fortifications of the off-shore islands, Les Iles d'Or. There is a ruined castle on a hill in the centre of the island but most of the 'island's' perimeter consists of steep cliffs. There is a hotel though if you want to stay overnight (see below).

Les Iles d'Or are also known as the Iles d'Hyères and all three are fascinating to visit. They are called, individually, Porquerolles, Port-Cros and the Ile du Levant. Rabelais wrote rapturously of them when he was at college in Montpellier and was writing when he should have been studying medicine. All three islands have been occupied and used by pirates for centuries and you can almost see the thoughts going through Robert Louis Stevenson's mind as, living in Hyères, he heard about the islands, visited them and conceived the idea for his famous novel. The islands are so-named because of the way the cliffs look golden coloured on the southern side especially in the evening sun.

Porquerolles is the largest and is rich with exotic vegetation for the climate is sub-tropical. Greeks, Romans and Turks have had garrisons here and the island saw British occupation during the Napoleonic Wars.

The finest building remaining is the Tour de Sainte Agathe, a formidable circular stronghold with powerful walls and around it several outbuildings including a small museum. Francois I built it in 1531 and Napoleon erected the village below the fort three hundred years later to provide housing for army veterans. The lighthouse on the south side of the village is worth a visit and the only beaches are in the village vicinity, the rest of the coast being too rocky.

The Fort of Alicastre was built by the military-minded Cardinal Richelieu in 1633. Its name comes from a monster which ravaged the island – the description tallies with that of the 'tarasque', the legendary beast that 'a dozen lions could not kill' and gave its name to Tarascon but might have been a giant alligator. The Man in the Iron Mask was, for a time, in one of the cells in Alicastre. The Fort de la Répentance on the south coast of the island is of more recent construction, late 19th century.

Porquerolles is great for walking and you can cover the island quite easily. Pine trees, eucalyptus and heather cover the island – you can also rent bicycles. The landscapes are beautiful and mostly empty.

The second island, Port-Cros, is hilly with dense vegetation which makes it harder to get around though it is smaller than Porquerolles. There is a small village around the boat landing but the only other sights are the forts. A marked path leads to the Fort of Moulin. Construction was begun in the 16th century but work continued until the early 1900s. Next to it is the Fort d'Estissac (1633) then the Fort de Port Man (also 1633). On the south coast of Port-Cros is the Fort of La Vigie and west of the village the Fort de Bagaud, both put up in the first part of the 19th century.

Port-Cros is where D. H. Lawrence lived for a short time with a titled Englishwoman. In an intimate moment, she told him of her affair with a gardener and Lawrence, always avid for a plot, wrote *Lady Chatterley's Lover* around the episode.

The smallest island, Bagaud, is not inhabited so that leaves the Ile du Levant, the easternmost of the group. If the name strikes a chord of memory, it is because it became famous in the 1930s when it was the first nudist colony. It still is, though all the rest of the island is a naval base.

The sun and the humidity have resulted in a riot of vegetation where everything grows to huge sizes – yucca, agave, eucalyptus. It is also a paradise for mineralogists and finds are still being made of tourmaline, garnet, mica and quartz.

How to get to the islands ... There is a boat service from the port of

Hyères which leaves approximately every hour from 8.15 to 2.15. You can go to any of the three islands or you can take a circuit of Port-Cros and Ile du Levant. The direct trip takes about an hour and costs 75f round trip. A circuit of all three is available too at 95f which makes a full if exhausting day.

There is a trip from La Tour Fondue on Giens to Porquerolles which takes 20 minutes. Boats leave continuously from 7 a.m. to 8 p.m. From La Tour Fondue, there is also a catamaran with underwater vision which takes 40 minutes and costs 65f. It makes four trips a day from 9 to 2 30.

Festivals

In March, Hyères has a 'Corso Fleuri', a parade of wagons decorated with flowers. There is a festival in April and a Provençal Festival in June. Summer jazz concerts prevail through July with many big-name performers participating and another festival is in September.

Many towns celebrate onion and garlic fêtes and in August, Hyères does both, usually around the 24th of the month.

Also in August – the 15th – pilgrimages go to the churches of Notre Dame-de-Consolation and Notre Dame-du-Fenouillet.

You may see some of the local specialities in the confiseries of Hyères. These are known as 'Massillons' and are petit-fours made from almonds.

Hôtel Mozart
(H)S-M   94 65 09 45   26 Rue Alfonse Denis   Open all year   All CC.

It's not the biggest or the most luxurious hotel in Hyères but for comfort, convenience and value, the Mozart is hard to beat.

The front looks smart and inviting with its red awnings against the clean white walls and the delicate wrought-iron balconies lend a touch of nostalgia.

It's in the centre of town but just far enough away from the busy heart to be reasonably quiet. A few streets above it and towards the old castle on the hill are many of the spectacular old villas from the halcyon days of Hyères.

The 13 rooms are sound-proofed anyway and all have bath or shower and TV. There is parking nearby and at 245-300f, the rooms are very good value. The only criticism is the busy wallpaper. There is no restaurant but breakfast is served as a fine buffet.

Le Ceinturon
(HR)S-M   94 66 33 63   12 Boulevard du Front de Mer   Cl. Nov   All CC.

On the popular L'Ayguade beach and barely two kilometres from the centre of town, the Ceinturon looks out to sea. The 15 rooms are 200-350f and 12 of them have bath or shower. M. Hocquellet also offers demi-pension at 260-300f.

La Méditerranée
(HR)S-M   *94 58 03 89   Avenue de la Méditerranée   Open all year   All CC.*

> On the other hand, if you'd rather be near the port, just by the
> Hippodrome is the Méditerranée, only about 50 metres from the
> water's edge but still a good combination of port, beach and town.
>   Its 13 rooms all have bath or shower and cost 250-330f. The
> restaurant serves reasonable food at 90-130f.

Hôtel Provençale
(HR)M   *94 58 20 09   Place St Pierre on Presqu'Ile de Giens   Cl. Nov-Mar   All CC.*

> This is one of the four hotels on the 'almost an island' of Giens. It is
> fairly modern and has beautiful views of the islands of Hyères. All 45
> rooms are nicely decorated and furnished and all have either a terrace
> or a balcony. There is a pool, tennis and a solarium. The park in front
> has a grill and a bar for summer relaxation.
>   Prices are 180-570f. One disadvantage is the limited parking in the
> garage. Demi-pension is available at 360-1050f and in view of the
> shortage of restaurants on the 'almost an island' is not a bad idea.

Le Delfin's
(R)S-M   *94 65 04 28   Place Clémenceau   Open every day and all year   All CC.*

> Renowned for its excellent fish cuisine and yet not at all expensive. It's
> right in the centre of town and Denis and Françoise Ohl (she does the
> cooking) present the traditional seafood dishes cooked in traditional
> style. The bourride is exceptionally enjoyable (I prefer it to
> bouillabaisse) and so are all the grilled fish – loup, pageot, rouget. If
> you are a real seafood fanatic, you'll love the seafood platter with
> something of everything. Menus range from around 90f to 180f.
>   The best way to enjoy the islands is by taking day trips. The ride is
> short enough and you can stay long enough to see as much as you
> want to see. There are hotels out there but as they know you are a
> captive audience, their prices are unreasonably high. Full board is
> required. They usually book up months in advance despite this,
> though mostly with groups from clubs and factories and unions.
> Should you be determined to sleep on an island regardless, the
> following are available:

Porquerolles	Le Mas du Langoustier	94 58 30 09
	(at the western end of Porquerolles)	
	Hôtel Sainte Anne	94 58 30 04
	Les Glycines	94 58 30 36
	Auberge de l'Arche de Noë	94 58 30 74
	Relais de la Poste	94 58 30 26
	(all four in the village)	
Port-Cros	Le Manoir d'Hélène	94 05 90 52

	Levant	Héliotel	94 05 90 63
		La Pomme d'Adam	94 05 90 13
		La Brise Marine	94 05 91 15

Map 2B **L'ISLE-SUR-LA-SORGUE** 84800 (Vaucluse) 17 km S of Carpentras, 10 km N of Cavaillon, 23 km E of Avignon

---

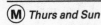 *Thurs and Sun*

The town itself is not perhaps that pretty but the river Sorgue running alongside the old buildings and the frequent tiny foot-bridges across it make it quite unusual. The huge moss-encrusted water-wheel as you enter the town from the south is a very much photographed sight. In earlier days, it and other wheels, provided the power for silk works, tanneries, dyeworks, paper mills and grain and olive oil mills. The river Sorgue divides into five branches here and in the past all of these waters teemed with fish – shrimp, trout, eels – as well as otters and beavers. Herons swooped down to feast on the abundant prey. Today most of these are gone though fishing is still popular and trout are frequently caught – and as large as 10 kgs.

Antiques are one of the principal attractions of L'Isle-sur-la-Sorgue today. The massive warehouse-like building next to the railway station contains over 100 stalls and others are scattered throughout the town. There is a flea market every Sunday at which some antiques and much bric-à-brac are displayed (and sold).

The Church of Notre Dame of the Angels in the central Place de l'Eglise was consecrated in 1672 and is one of the finest in Vaucluse. There are frescoes, ornamentation and drapes in the most luxurious Italian style and 22 statues adorn the nave.

The old Hospital – accessible from the Rue de Roues – was built in the early part of the 18th century and has an exceptional wrought-iron gate. Here too is the old pharmacy, with porcelain vases and painted jars containing cures and poisons.

Festivals

The festivities in L'Isle-sur-la-Sorgue include the Fair of St Laurent which is held the last Thursday in October and the Festival of La Sorgue which comes at the end of July. This includes music, drama and dance in addition to the crowning of the King of the Sorgue which follows a jousting contest from boats with the contestants in full costume and a fair number being knocked into the river.

Mas de Cure Bourse
(HR)M   *90 38 16 58   R cl. Sun p.m.; Mon; Oct   All CC.*

An old relais of the 18th century, simple but warm and inviting and full of Provençal welcome. There are 10 sizeable rooms, a pool and a large terrace. Rooms are 250-420f .

Jean-François and Françoise Donze are hard-working and efficient proprietors and this extends to the kitchen too. Menus are 154, 188, 210 and 248f. The food is without pretension or frills but is tasty and imaginative. Mignons du porc au thyme, filet de rascasse, coulis de la crabe are good examples.

Pricing of meals is perhaps marginally above budget levels but justified by the care and integrity in their selection and preparation.

Le Pescador
(HR)S-M   *90 38 09 69   Cl. Mon o.o.s.; 1/1-15/3; 15/11-31/12   Visa, CB, AE.*

Just over a kilometre out of l'Isle-sur-la-Sorgue is Partage des Eaux, truly a parting of the waters and where the two main branches of the river Sorgue separate. Local poet René Char described the spot with great delicacy and it is an inspired location for this simple hostellery.

The 8 rooms are a reasonable 210f and though far from luxurious they are adequate for an overnight stay. There is parking and a garden.

If all the seating accommodation for dining – indoor, outdoor and the garden – were to be filled, there would be 400 people so it is evident that the emphasis at Le Pescador is on the restaurant. Trout from the river is, of course, the main attraction and you won't find better within a day's drive. Menus are 100f and the service is willing if sometimes over-taxed.

Map 2C   **ISTRES** 13800 (Bouches-du-Rhône) 60 km NW of Marseille, 21 km SW of Salon

---

 Tues

This unusually named town derives from 'ostrea' meaning oysters and its history goes back through Greek times to prehistoric days.

It is between the tiny Etang d'Olivier and the much larger Etang de Berre. As the latter has on its shores the huge oil refineries, the water is much more polluted and the Etang d'Olivier has always been a prized breeding ground for oysters, mussels, mullet, carp and perch. These latter fish are still caught by the ancient method using a light to lure them to the surface and then spearing them with a trident. It is the mullet which is known as 'muge' locally and its eggs are used in the popular local dish 'poutargue' which you will see on many a menu.

If you want to explore the region around the Etang, Istres is probably the best place to use as a base. You may catch the occasional whiff of sulphur from the oil refineries to the east but otherwise it is a pleasant town, not too touristy and with an every day sort of life that gives you a good picture of the region.

Its museum, the Musée du Vieil Istres, is one of the best around. Archaeology, mineralogy, palaeontology, ornithology, history and folklore are well-displayed all the way from Neolithic times. *It is open from May 1 to October 1 every day from 2-7 except Tuesday.*

Festivals

There are numerous local festivities and all of traditional origin. There is the Fête de Saint Jean on June 24 which includes the sale of the work of local artisans while the hamlets of Entressen and Rassuen have their own fêtes in July. At the beginning of August, there is the Fête de Saint Etienne and midnight mass is celebrated in the old style at Christmas but December also has the biggest fête of all. This celebrates the herding of the sheep through the streets in memory of the times when this was the big annual event, bringing the sheep back from their summer pastures. This culminates in a shepherds' mass at the Church of Notre Dame de Beauvoir.

Le Castellan
(H)S-M   *42 55 13 09*   *Place Sainte Cathérine*   *Open all year*   *Visa, CB.*

This has long been the leading hotel in Istres. It is of modern design and is ideally situated near the park and with views across the Etang.
The 17 rooms are large and priced at only 225f. There is a nice garden and parking is available. None of the accommodation in Istres is expensive but Le Castellan has been good value for a long time. There is no restaurant.

L'Escale
(H)S   *42 55 01 88*   *Boulevard Edouard Guizonnier*   *Open all year*   *Visa, CB.*

A good standard of comfort here at only 130-160f for the 20 rooms. There is a garden and parking but no restaurant.

Aystria-Tartugues
(H)S   *42 56 44 55*   *Chemin de Tartugues*   *Open all year*   *Visa, CB.*

With a number of restaurants and cafés on Avenue Jean-Jaurès and the adjoining Boulevard Aristide-Briand, you can see why there are so many establishments in Istres which offer hotel facilities only.
The Hôtel Aystria-Tartugues is another of these. There are 10 rooms at a very modest 215-245f. The garden is very pleasant in the summer and there is parking.

Le Mazet de Pepi
(R)M   *42 55 42 43*   *Rue des Baumes*   *Cl. Sun p.m.; Mon; Jan 2-9 and July 24-Aug 14   All CC.*

The atmosphere is sophisticated in this 19th-century shepherd's cottage brought up to date as a very warm and welcoming restaurant.
Xavier Hoffalt gives a personal touch to everything especially the cuisine which is traditional and yet manages to be classical in execution too. The tête de veau with herbs and vinegar are an

example of the traditional while the seafood tray with three sauces suggests the more classical.

Prices for such cooking are not cheap – menus start at 150f but the quality and the style justify.

La Jasse

(R)M   *42 56 41 86   Quartier des Craux de Boisgelin   Cl. Sun p.m.; Mon; Aug 1-15 and at Christmas   All CC.*

This building is also converted from an old shepherd's cottage – they seem to have made very good restaurants from them.

You'd never know it though – the atmosphere is quite refined with elegant furniture, beamed ceilings and a huge fireplace.

Seafood is always on the menu in various forms and there is usually a filet de boeuf and a dish based on lamb. Menus range from 150-250f and the meal is never disappointing.

Map 3B   JOUCAS 84220 (Vaucluse) 15 km NW of Apt

Ravaged by religious wars, persecutions and invasions, Joucas is down to about 200 people today. Its main sight is the Commanderie of the Knights Hospitallers of the Order of St John of Jerusalem. This famous order of warrior-monks was installed here in the 12th century; a fine job of restoration has been done though unfortunately the building is now in the hands of private owners.

Local legends say that a monster called the 'Mandragoule' still lives in the tunnels and grottoes underneath the Commanderie but it has not been observed for many years and you need not avoid Joucas on its account.

Roman remains are still being found in the area. To the east is a plain which is called 'Caesar's Camp' and near it was found a temple dedicated to the god Mars. Statues and heads were unearthed including a colossal statue of Mars and another of Juno.

Joucas' location makes it a good centre for touring the area and there are a number of good hotels. Le Phébus and Le Mas des Herbes Blanches are both four-star and run to nearly 1000f a night. There are some reasonably priced places though.

Hostellerie des Commandeurs

(HR)M   *90 05 78 01   Cl. Wed; Jan   CB, Visa, MC and EC.*

A simple hotel at the foot of the village, with fine views of the Lubéron mountains to the south. There are 14 simple but adequate rooms at 270f and there is a nice garden, a pool and parking.

Cooking is Provençal. The daube is very good and the cuisses des grenouilles avec sauce provençale is another speciality. The desserts are especially irresistible. Menus are 90-150f and you can eat in the garden in the summer.

Two disadvantages – the bar at the road entrance can be a bit noisy in the evening but the other disadvantage is more serious. Mme

Michot will take your reservation for one night but if someone comes along afterwards and wants to book for a longer period, she has been known to give them the room and make up a story about yours having been cancelled. In season, when other accommodation is not available, this can be disastrous. Acknowledgement of reservation in writing would seem to be the antidote.

La Pinède
(HR)M   *90 05 78 54   Route de Murs   R cl. Mon   H cl. 15/1-5/2; 15/11-30/11   CB, Visa and EC.*

Just outside the village and another good bet for reasonable and pleasing accommodation. The pool is very welcome in the summer and not crowded as there are only seven rooms. These are 310f for a single and 310-420f for a double. Breakfast is 60f. Ample parking in country surroundings.

For outdoor dining there is a shaded garden and a terrace and this makes La Pinède more of a restaurant with rooms. The specialities of the kitchen are fish and meat grilled over a wood fire and menus range from 95 to 150f.

Guy Herbst
(C)M   *90 05 78 26   Cl. 1/1-1/3.*

With all this hotel competition, it is surprising that the chambre d'hôte thrives in Joucas. This is a decidedly superior one – a country-house built in the 18th century. There is a lounge, a living room, TV, a dining room, a shady garden – and even a library. The four rooms have shower and wash-basin – the only bad news is that they have to share one toilet. At 180f for a single and 250f for a double, this is really good value. Dinner is 90f but if you pay 140f, wine is included.

Map 3C   **JOUQUES** 13490 (Bouches-du-Rhône) 28 km NE of Aix

---

The Chapel of Notre Dame de la Roque dominates the village. It has long been called locally the Château d'If but not because of any connection with the prison for five years of Alexandre Dumas' *Count of Monte Cristo*. The name was a corruption of Château des Juifs, 'Castle of the Jews', because it was believed to have once been a synagogue.

On the road to Saint Paul, the D11, and about 4 kilometres from Jouques, you will find the Chapel of Notre Dame de Consolation, built in the 12th century. It has a statue of a Black Virgin of undetermined date and several other relics though these latter date only from the 17th century. A pilgrimage to the chapel is held every year on September 8.

Just outside Jouques too is the Chapel of St Bacque. Some say it is so named because a Roman temple dedicated to the god Bacchus once existed on the site but a more likely explanation seems to be that it was named for St Bacque, a hermit who lived in a hut near the chapel. The Feast of St Bacque is held every year on the first Sunday in October.

Several vineyards in the vicinity of Jouques produce Côteaux d'Aix wines of quite good quality.

Auberge le Réal
(HR)S   *42 67 60 85   1 Boulevard du Réal   Open all year   Visa, CB.*

M. Scandolera's smart brown-and-white hotel on two storeys is simple in the extreme. 10 rooms cost 120-200f and they are adequately equipped for a short stay. Parking is on the street only. Meals are also simple but they are satisfying and priced at 80 to 150f.

Map 3C   LACOSTE 84480 (Vaucluse) 14 km SW of Apt

A charming hilltop village but it's never going to live down its heritage. The ruined castle that dominates it was built in the 11th century but the only important factor in its history seems to be that it was occupied for thirty years by the infamous Marquis de Sade. He lived here in between serving his numerous prison sentences. The orgies that are described in his own books and those of his various biographers took place here and the children who were sexually tortured and then murdered were all abducted from the surrounding countryside.

The castle's earlier history was just as blood-stained however and during the Wars of the Huguenots, Catholic troops attacked it as a stronghold of the 'heretics'. The castle surrendered to the overwhelming strength of the besieging army when Balthazar de Simiane gave his word that the garrison would be spared. Instead, every man, woman and child was massacred.

Lacoste is really two villages. One is virtually a ghost village, huddled around the château and in the slow and laborious process of being restored. Hopefully, by the time this appears in print, enough of this work will have been completed that tours of the château will be possible. Included in the restoration are several of the houses built into the walls of the château. If you're interested and not afraid of ghosts, there is even one with the date 1634 carved in the stone lintel and for sale.

Even those who are not of a superstitious nature admit that there is a gloomy and mysterious aura here and it seems that it is due to other influences than the knowledge of the association of the château with the sinister Marquis.

The other village is at a lower level and is a delightfully mediaeval place with a snack bar next to the old Café de France where you can sip a cool drink and gaze out over the extensive valley.

To the west of Lacoste and on the plateau of Hauts-Artemes can be seen the strangest of all the 'bories' in Provence. These are beehive-shaped structures, built of flat stones but without using any mortar or bonding material. In some parts of the Vaucluse, there are many of these and there is a strong resemblance to the 'nuraghi' to be found in Sardinia.

You can see a whole village of 'bories' just outside Gordes but the one here near Lacoste is unusual because it has a door which leads in spiral fashion through four rooms, all different sizes and shapes. Being built on a plateau and near the edge of a cliff, it would seem to have some defensive purpose. Like the bories near Gordes, this one was probably built about the same time as the château even though the design and construction originates from the Stone Age. It all remains a mystery.

Festivals

Lacoste has a Mardi Gras carnival. In August, there is a local fête and on the 25th of the month a big local fair with products of the region and an aïöli.

Restaurant du Marquis de Sade
(R)M   *90 75 83 21   Cl. Wed and Thurs lunch; Dec 20-31 and Jan 1-April 4   No CC.*

It's inevitable that the restaurant here should be so named and it doesn't seem to hurt business. The cooking shows more originality than many – the slices of gigot are served with a garlic and tomato cream sauce and the lavender flavoured ice-cream is the first I've tasted. It's surprisingly delicious.

There is only one menu and its 138f but there is a good à la carte selection too.

Map 3B   **LAGARDE D'APT** 84400 (Vaucluse) 18 km NE of Apt

This small hamlet of less than a hundred people on the D34 leaving Apt is the highest point of the Monts de Vaucluse and 1085 metres altitude.

It doesn't get many visitors. The slopes around it are perfect sheep grazing land and even the lavender distillery of Maurice Fra seems surprised to see people. It welcomes them though and besides sheep and lavender, the other two products of the neighbourhood are cheese and honey. You see beehives on all of the hills round Lagarde.

The Chapel of Notre Dame de l'Amarron is still a pilgrimage destination but has little of importance to the visitor.

M. Chassillan
(C)S   *90 75 01 04   Les Esfourniaux   Open all year   No CC.*

The above information will suggest that this is not ideal hotel territory and indeed it isn't. Apt is not far away if you want a hotel and there are numerous others within a short drive.

Still, if you want to stay in Lagarde and if you want a friendly and very inexpensive chambre d'hôte, you need go no further than M.

Chassillan's. There are four rooms in an old farm building in an idyllic country setting. All the rooms have a shower and wash-basin and cost only 150f; demi-pension is offered at 270f. There is swimming and fishing in the lake only 10 kilometres away.

Map 2B   **LAGNES** 84800 (Vaucluse) 14 km NE of Cavaillon

 Fri

The name of the village probably comes from 'laine' (wool), the working of which was the principal occupation of the local inhabitants in earlier days. Village rivalry is very keen in Provence and sarcastic wit is one means of expressing it – which is why other communities maintain that the name of Lagnes comes from the Provençal word 'Lagnous', meaning surly or sullen.

It has been a fortified village since the 12th century and had not one but two baronial manors, both enclosed by a massive circular wall with only two entrances. From the north, entry could be gained only through a heavily fortified gate and from the south only up a staircase covered on each side by walls perforated with slits for archers.

Eventually the owner of the manor to the north (Cambis) bought the manor to the south (Fortia) and today they are in final stages of restoration.

Hôtel le Mas des Grès
(H)M   *90 20 32 85   Route Nationale 100   Cl. Jan and Feb, Nov and Dec   Visa, CB.*

A very comfortable hotel with a charming garden and a pool in a quiet country setting. The 12 fully equipped rooms are all doubles and priced at 280-500f.

Mme Martine Delorme
(C)   *90 20 36 29   Route de l'Isle   Cl. Sept 15-June 15   No CC.*

This chambre d'hôte is in a new building but if you don't mind forsaking rustic charm, here is quality of room you won't find anywhere around at this price. There are two rooms with toilet and bath and one room with toilet and shower and they cost 250f for a single and 350f for a double. There is a nice lounge, television, a closed garden and a private pool.

Map 3C   **LAMBESC** 13410 (Bouches-du-Rhône) 20 km NW of Aix, 15 km E of Salon de Provence

 Fri

A pleasant quiet town with a long past. Today, it sits on the N7 as it goes north-west from Aix but in earlier days it was in a commanding position in the Valley of Concernade. Celts, Greeks, Romans were all

here and in the Middle Ages many of the noble families of Provence had homes here.

Lambesc has been besieged, sacked, pillaged, destroyed and rebuilt several times. In 1909, it was levelled by an earthquake and in 1944, a German ammunition train was blown up in the railway station causing much damage to the town.

It's still here though and when you stop, you should see the 300-year-old Church of Notre Dame de la Rose which retains a 14th-century clocktower. North of Lambesc about five kilometres is the Chapel of Sainte Anne de Goiron, founded in 1040 by monks from the abbey of Silvacane. It is flanked by two Gothic chapels and pilgrimages still go there in times of drought. The town has clearly learned this lesson, for there are twenty fountains in the streets, all picturesque and photographable, in addition to numerous public wash-basins.

The Museum of Vieux Lambesc has displays of archaeological interest, local history, prehistory and folklore. It is open the last two Sundays in each month from 3 to 6.

Lambesc is in a district heavily endowed with vineyards. Its Côteaux d'Aix wines are very drinkable and quite inexpensive. Several caves will welcome you for a wine-tasting session and some of the names to watch for are: Cave Sainte Cathérine (on Route de Pelissane), Cave la Baraque and Clos St Eldrad (both on Route de Caire Val), Domaine de Calavon (on Avenue Badonviller) and Les Vignerons du Roy René (on the N7).

Festivals

The local saint, Saint Eldrad, has a feast day in May with a big funfair, a mass and folklore singing and dancing. A horse fair and an antique fair are also held in May. In June, there are concerts and fêtes and in July, the Fête of Lambesc with games, parades and a funfair. There is a local fête on September 16.

Château Montplaisir
(HR)S-M   *42 57 01 64   Cl. Oct 16-Mar 15   R cl. lunch Wed and Sun   All CC.*

A long established and popular inn, handily situated on the N7 just a few minutes north of Lambesc. There are 12 rooms at a very reasonable 180-260f and demi-pension is an alternative worth considering, at 220-270f per person. The restaurant serves good, local products and menus are 120-160f.

Moulin de Tante Yvonne
(R)M-L   *42 92 72 46   Cl. Tues, Wed and Thurs in Feb and Oct   No CC.*

This charming place, under the vaulted arches of the old olive oil mill, will soon be celebrating its hundredth birthday and owes most of its success and fame to Tante Yvonne herself.

In the restaurant, the emphasis is on seafood. The crème de poissons de roche and the flan de langouste are renowned The aïöli is exceptional and the daube is true Provençal. It will probably cost you about 300f here but it will be a memorable meal. The wines from the vineyards of Visan are the ones to select from the wine list.

Map 2C | **LANCON-DE-PROVENCE** 13680 (Bouches-du-Rhône)
11 km S of Salon

South of Lançon, a vast deserted plain littered with bleached white rocks is all that remains of a Celtic encampment which covered nearly 20 acres and was probably the largest in all Provence. It is not easy of access today but can best be reached on foot from the D10 which runs along the coast of the Etang de Berre and even then it is over difficult terrain, part of which is an army gunnery range and a restricted area.

Two caves can be found here, one of them horseshoe-shaped and fifty feet in diameter. According to local history, massive solid gold statues of the Emperor Constantine, his wife Helen and their daughter still stood here in the 16th century. Expeditions mounted in the 17th century met with disaster and the ensuing years saw more efforts to find the statues with equally tragic results. One of these expeditions claimed to have been attacked by hordes of gigantic insects and it was not until 1946 that the answer was found. One of the caves led to a tunnel which contained an underground lake of deadly carbon monoxide gas. The expedition members had walked through the invisible gas which is an intoxicant and hallucinogenic. So be careful.

The ruins of a 6th-century chapel have been identified and near it are the bases of the old city walls which are more than ten feet thick. So far, 18 towers have been uncovered and an unknown number of others remain to be discovered.

Lançon itself has many ancient buildings clustered around the 12th-century château constructed by the Lords of Baux. Several vineyards in the region produce very drinkable Côteaux d'Aix wines. One of the best is the Château de Calissane.

With a population of 4,000 people, you would expect Lançon to have a few recommendable hotels and restaurants but it seems to rely on Salon-de-Provence which is less than ten minutes away to the north.

Map 3C | **LAURIS** 84630 (Vaucluse) 20 km S of Apt, 6 km W of Cadenet

---

 Mon

Approaching the village from Cavaillon along the banks of the Durance river, the château is particularly striking. When you get closer, it appears less so. Its terraces are beautifully arranged though – a tribute to the missionary order of monks to whom the château was bequeathed. Potatoes and olive oil are two of the most prolific crops in the area and you will be reminded that these often constituted the sole diet of the monks.

Festivals

From September 15 to November 15, there is a fête for the local table grape. There is a fair on the first Sunday in February and a feast of the local Saint-Roch on the first Sunday in August.

Pilgrimages are still made to the Chapel of St Roch to plead for rain if it is a dry year.

La Chaumière
(HR)M   *90 08 20 05*   *Cl. Nov 15-Dec 15*   *R also cl. Tues; Wed lunch*   *All CC.*

An old house which has been brought up to extremely high standards. It is in a beautiful location and is famous regionally for its food.

There are 15 rooms at 400-750f and, of course, they are fully equipped and magnificently furnished. You should specify when booking if you want to be in the main building which is preferable. Seven of the rooms are there and the others in an adjoining building.

The chef is Julien Corcinos, a pupil of Alain Chapel and Roger Vergé so you know the cooking is gastronomic. There is a menu at 198f and one of the dishes might be canard sauvage farci avec foie gras.

Map 3C   **LOURMARIN** 84160 (Vaucluse), 5 km N of Cadenet

 Fri

This must be the Beverley Hills of Provence villages. Even the public toilets in the parking area are sparkling clean. When you pop into the leading hotel – Le Moulin – and see that the best rooms are 2500f, you'll agree with the comparison.

It is an extremely attractive village and should be seen – although you will inevitably say that it's a far cry from a typical Provence village. It has been restored and rebuilt more thoroughly than anywhere else in the South of France.

But the streets are still narrow and picturesque, with the occasional tinkling fountain and numerous boutiques and gift shops.

The Renaissance château sits up on a grassy slope across from the hotels, the restaurants and the parking area. It looks as if it would be more in place in England than here, having once been fortified but modified so that it now looks much more like a home. It belongs to the University of Aix who run summer courses for artists, scientists and philosophers but it is open for tours. Disregard all other information – it provides guided tours only at 2.30, 3.30 and 4.30 every afternoon. In July and August, there are musical concerts every Saturday night.

The prices of the hotels indicate staying in another village but eating is a different matter. There are several reasonable restaurants.

Le Bistrot
(R)S-M   *90 68 29 74*   *2 Ave Philllipe de Girard   Cl. 10/12-31/12; 10/3-20/3   Visa, CB.*

On the corner looking across the meadow at the château, Le Bistrot has dining inside on two levels and a pleasant shady terrace in front.

The young staff is smiling and helpful and the cooking is thoughtful. There are menus at 78, 98 and 118f but the à la carte choice is my preference. The coquilles de St Jacques with a small patty of baked, shredded aubergine and a mixture of mushrooms, carrots and zucchini is delicious and different.

La Récréation
(R)S-M   *90 68 23 73   15 Ave Phillipe de Girard   Cl. Jan; Feb   Visa, CB.*

A large open area out in front is popular in summer and the three-course menu is 85f. One special is râble de lièvre avec amandes. Known locally as 'La Récré'.Excellent.

Map 2C   **MAILLANE** 13910 (Bouches-du-Rhône) 7 km NW of St Rémy-de-Provence, 13 km E of Tarascon

Maillane's main claim to fame is that it was the birthplace of Frédéric Mistral, the poet-troubador who almost single-handed put the Provençal traditions and way of life on the literary map.

He also won the Nobel Prize for Literature and you can learn all about him at the Musée Mistral, installed in the villa which he built as his home, which has been preserved almost intact. *Open 10-12 and 2-5 in summer, 10-12 and 2-4 in winter, closed on Mondays.*

The village cemetery contains Mistral's tomb which is a duplicate of the Pavillon de la Reine Jeanne at Les Baux. Giant bones have been unearthed at Maillane and were first thought to be those of mammoths but that belief has now been demolished and the bones have been confirmed as those of African elephants, probably some of the animals which Hannibal brought with him for his attack on Rome.

Four people died of cholera in Maillane on August 13, 1854. The next day, six more died and within two weeks the death toll was sixty. Panic spread and many villagers fled into the country. On August 28, a group of villagers came to the Curé and suggested that a penitential procession be held.

An ancient wooden statue was kept at Maillane and known as Notre Dame de Grace. It was to the statue and the traditional devotion to Our Lady that the attention of the villagers turned now. The church bells were rung. A handful of people brought the statue and carried it through the silent streets. In ones and twos, others came out of their houses and joined in the procession. At the church, a petition for the intervention of the Virgin was sung.

Among those gathered was an elderly lady who was not expected to survive the night. During the service, she felt progessively better and at the end of it, declared herself cured. The bells were pealed and there were no more deaths in Maillane. In the ensuing years, cholera swept through Provence on more than one occasion but no villager of Maillane was affected.

The village church is named for Notre Dame de Grace and there is a feast of the saint every year on August 28. This is marked by a procession and a re-enactment of the events of 1854. If you are in Maillane on this date, it is a sincerely moving event and still with all the simplicity that must have accompanied the original.

The statue is draped in purple. The bearers are called 'priors' for the occasion and are appointed by the Curé. They wear smart black suits and white buttonholes. Their wives follow, wearing white hats. The clergy walk behind the statue, then the men then the women. Along the streets, small shrines are decorated with white flowers. In front of the church, the same petition is sung and the names of the cholera victims are read out. The church is not large enough to hold everyone and many squeeze into the doorways.

Stands and stalls have been erected and a brisk trade in food and drink is carried on when the congregation leaves the church. Later in the day, there are fireworks displays and a torchlight procession. At 3 o'clock in the morning, the first Mass of the 29th is said. This is followed by other masses until 'La Gran Messe' and then Vespers.

Finally everyone sits down to a a big meal of cold meat and vegetables then a massive aiöli with fish, then veal followed by roast mutton and green beans and ending with fruit and ice-cream. That is the traditional meal which marks the miracle of Maillane.

Festivals

A folk festival and Provençal mass is held on the anniversary of Mistral's birth (September 8, the Feast of the Virgin Mary).

The Feast of Saint Eloi, the patron saint of blacksmiths, is held throughout the last week-end but one in July and is a great event. On the Friday evening, there is a big variety show at the municipal stadium. Saturday begins at noon with a salvo of artillery and a parade through the village followed by a meal for the 'charretiers', the drivers of the horse-wagons. There are more festivities in the evening culminating in a ball.

Sunday begins with mass at 10 and immediately afterwards, there is blessing of the horses and the wagons. The wagons are paraded through the streets and there is a banquet luncheon at 1. A boules contest in the afternoon is followed by various other events which vary a little year to year but always ending with a ball.

On Monday, there are children's events, more boules contests and another ball in the evening. On Tuesday, for those with the stamina to have survived this far, there is a big traditional 'aiöli' at lunch, events featuring young bulls, more boules contests and any still standing can go to yet another ball that night.

On September 8, the Feast of the Virgin Mary, there is a folk festival and Provençal mass which also celebrates the anniversary of Mistral's birth.

Frédéric Mistral is not a character well-known outside of France (though you can read more about him elsewhere in this book). Consequently, foreign visitors don't flock to Maillane and though you would expect French tourists to revere such a romantic figure, the village remains remarkably untouristic and not endowed with good places to stay or eat. However, Graveson and Saint Rémy-de-Provence are both quite close by and have very good accommodation at reasonable prices.

Map 2B   **MALAUCENE** 84340 (Vaucluse) 18 km N of Carpentras, 42 km NE of Avignon

(M) *Wed*

As you drive through Malaucène, it seems an ordinary little place strung along the N538 between Carpentras and Vaison-la-Romaine. In fact, it has several minor claims to fame.

The most minor is probably Malaucène's claim that the first potato was planted here. It is true that the potato is known locally by the name of 'tartifle' and that this is probably the origin of the German word 'Kartoffel'. Arguments exist that there was confusion in mediaeval days between the potato and the truffle but then the locals call the truffle 'rabasso'.

This is however the heart of truffle country and the market in Carpentras is the biggest in the region. Malaucène's title of 'the cherry capital' is without argument and if you are there in the season, you will be able to participate in the festivities and the enjoyment in a host of dishes.

Firmly established too is Malaucène's position as the best starting place for expeditions up to the top of Mont Ventoux. It was from Malaucène that Petrarch set out with his brother in 1336 to be the first to climb the almost 2,000 metre summit of 'the magic mountain'. Mont Ventoux, a solitary peak, stands like a strange pyramid rearing straight up from the plain of the Comtat, covered with snow in winter and spring. Its bald limestone top sometimes looks like snow in the summer when the sun sparkles on it. Despite such inhospitable ground, alpine plants grow in profusion and even Greenland lichens. The lavender is believed to have magical properties which makes it much sought after and preferable to other Provençal varieties.

It is an easy drive today from Malaucène along the N574 up to the top of the mountain where there is a spectacular view. On a clear day you can see the Alps, the Pyrenees, the Cévennes and the Mediterranean. An observatory and a few snack bars are near the chapel of the Holy Cross built by Bishop Pierre de Valetariis in the early 15th century. It is still a destination of pilgrimages and a fragment of the True Cross is said to have been buried beneath it.

On the drive up to the summit, just after leaving Malaucène, you will pass the Chapel of Groseau which contains frescoes made by Pope Clement V who stayed here from 1308 to 1314. A path runs from the chapel to the spring of Groseau, a place of devotion even before Roman days for the name derives from Groselos, a Celtic god. One of the first actions of the Romans upon arriving here was to build an aqueduct to carry water from the spring to Vaison-la-Romaine which they were developing as a city to house retired politicians and Legion officers. Traces of this aqueduct can still be seen through the countryside.

Because of the position of Malaucène, it is a very convenient place to stay and there are a number of inexpensive but quite satisfactory hostelleries here.

Hôtel Origan
(HR)S   *90 65 27 08   H cl. Oct; R cl. Nov-Mar   Visa, CB, EC, MC.*

Right in the middle of the main street, which runs right through Malaucène – the only drawback is the street carnival right in front of the hotel which may bother you if you want an early night.

Otherwise, this is a clean and pleasant place, with 23 rooms equipped in spartan fashion but, at 190-225f, ideal for a budget stay. There is parking.

Choose between dining room, terrace and garden for eating. Cuisine is Provençal and portions are hearty. Menus start from 78f.

➤La Chevalerie
(HR)S   *90 65 11 19   Cl. Tues   Visa, CB, EC, MC.*

This is a really special place to stay – if you can get in. It's in the ramparts of the old town, on the south side of Malaucène as you head for Carpentras. The mediaeval setting is delightful and the large garden in front is casual enough to lend an air of relaxation to the entire establishment.

There are only five rooms but they're good sized, appropriately furnished and a bargain at 150-230f. There is parking and a garage.

The restaurant caters to the locals and it's not unusual to have over a hundred diners on a summer night, inside and out. The menu at 85f is the attraction and it varies frequently according to whatever is in season.

Arrowed for good value and charming setting.

Le Siècle
(R)S   *90 65 11 37   Cl. 11/11-Easter   Visa, AE.*

On the main street and very popular with the residents. There is a terrace and a garden and a wide choice to satisfy most tastes. Menus are from 65f.

Restaurant de Grozen
(R)S   *90 65 21 83   Route du Mont Ventoux   Cl. Mon. o.o.s.   Visa, CB.*

If you take the N574 in the direction of the towering Mont Ventoux, you pass the restaurant which is near the Chapel of Groseau. Don't let the change in spelling bother you – there is still local argument about which is correct, so they use both.

This is a popular camp-ground and picnic spot so it's always busy in season, but the restaurant is popular too and the villagers come from Malaucène when they want the calm of the countryside and the trickle of running water.

Fresh trout is the most popular dish, pulled right out of the stream.
Menus are from 65f and there are plenty of other dishes besides fish.

Map 2C   **MALLEMORT-EN-PROVENCE** 13370 (Bouches-du-Rhône)
         18 km SE of Cavaillon, 17 km NE of Salon-de-Provence

---

 Fri

Not to be confused with the other – Malemort-du-Comtat – which is in
Vaucluse. It is a lIttle confusing though because both villages take
their name from the same Latin words 'Ortus a Morte'. This means
something like 'death gives birth to life' and refers to the devastation
of both towns by the Barbarian hordes from North Africa and their
subsequent renaissance.

This one, Mallemort, is a quiet, picturesque village in the middle of a
rich agricultural plain on the south bank of the Durance river.

Festivals

There is a fair every spring and every autumn and a community fair at
the end of June. The Feast of St Michael is held in September.

Moulin de Vernegues
(HR)M-L   *90 59 12 00*   *Just off N7 (Senas)*   *Open all year*   *All CC.*

The Marquis de Sade lived here in the 16th century and you can stay
here today, but don't worry – the treatment is much gentler now.

In 1560, the Marquis married Anne de Damian, daughter of the Lord
of Vernegues, and it was then that he came here and refurbished this
lovely building.

It was a corn-mill when it was built originally in the 13th century but
has now become one of the most charming hotels in France. The 36
bedrooms have massive timbered ceilings, flowered wallpaper and
are lavishly furnished with antiques and original oil-paintings.

Kings of France have been entertained here and you too will find
luxury, comfort and relaxation in a setting that is rare.

You can ride through the 1200 acres of land surrounding the Moulin
and hunts are frequently organised. Three tennis courts adjoin the
building and there is a large, heated swimming pool. There are
pleasant walks along the secluded lanes through the vineyards which
also belong to the Moulin.

I have stayed here numerous times during the past three decades
and have thoroughly enjoyed every visit – until the last. The facilities
have now been extended to accommodate seminars and business
conferences. The management say that this is essential in order to
survive.

Rooms are 700-1000f. The menu is 300f minimum and the food is
exquisitely prepared. Red and rosé wines from the Moulin's own
vineyards are the ones to select. They are raised by natural methods
only.

You will dine by candlelight under the stone arches of the old wine-cellar or out on the terrace by the pool in moonlight and will find it an unforgettable experience (if you can avoid the groups).

| Map 4B | **MANE** 04300 (Alpes de Haute-Provence) 4 km S of Forcalquier, 20 km N of Manosque |

South-west of the village on the road to Apt, you will see Notre-Dame de Salagon, an ancient Benedictine priory. One of the most remarkable buildings in Haute Provence, it was originally a 12th-century fortified Roman church. Massive to begin with, it was enlarged in the 16th century and converted into more of a castle with courtyards, stables and barns.

It is now run as a conservation centre and is open for visits every day from 2-6. There is a permanent museum and various exhibitions are held during the year.

On the N100 and going south from Mâne, after the priory you see a magnificent mansion, the Château de Sauvan, that looks as if it has been transplanted from the Loire valley. The setting is extraordinary for the territory around Mâne does not look in the least appropriate for such a sumptuous residence. The lake and the gardens are very impressive and the strutting peacocks add further to the atmosphere. *Open every day except Saturday from 2-6 for guided tours.*

| Map 3D | **MARIGNANE** 13700 (Bouches-du-Rhône) 28 km NW of Marseille, 27 km SE of Aix |

The name is best-known as the site of Marseille's busy international airport and, as you can see from its position, it is equidistant from both Marseille and Aix. It has a fine location for an airport – on the Berre d'Etang – so that much of the engine noise is carried away over the water and causes minimum population distress.

If you recall newspaper headlines of the early 1950s, you may remember that Marignane was one of the places visited on several occasions by flying saucers. Whether distress was caused on those occasions may be doubted but certainly thousands of people saw the visitors (if that is what they were). These instances prompted historians to produce files that showed Marignane as having being visited on numerous occasions in the 17th century by objects in the sky. Sketches made at the time resemble huge flaming coffins.

A third aerial connection is that Marignane is the home of one of Aerospatiale's largest plants, producing helicopters and Exocet missiles.

Many prehistoric finds have been made in the region and there are indications of habitation long before the Greeks and the Romans arrived. Nothing remains of these, but Marignane remains a pleasant Provençal town and the Cours Mirabeau and the Avenue Jean-Jaurès are the centres of activity if you have some time to spare before a flight. Many of the chains are represented – Sofitel, Novotel, Campanile, Ibis, Primotel.

Buses to the airport are frequent and take ten minutes. At the airport itself, Le Clipper and Le Romarin are good modern restaurants with snacks or full meals, interesting menus and not expensive.

Festivals

A recent event is the annual International Music Festival with top musicians coming from all over the world to perform. This is held in the first half of July in the Château des Covet. Tickets are considerably cheaper than you will pay at most other places – only 70-150f.

Map 3D   **MARSEILLE** 13000 (Bouches-du-Rhône) 64 km W of Toulon

(M) Sat, Sun, Mon

Nobody considers Marseille a tourist attraction but as a major airport, a major seaport, a bigger population than any French city after Paris and 2,500 years of history – who can ignore it? Besides all this, it invented bouillabaisse.

Greek merchants founded it in 600 BC and it was later partly destroyed by Caesar in reprisals when it backed Pompey, his former co-ruler-become-enemy. The thousand-strong Marseille battalion sang the battle hymn for Napoleon composed in one night by the young engineer, Rouget de Lisle, when they went to storm the Tuileries during the Revolution and *La Marseillaise* went into the language. With the opening of the Suez Canal and French colonisation in North Africa, Marseille became an important port. It is today an industrial centre and a big producer of food and drink.

So a tourist town it isn't but, if you should be here by either accident or design, there are things to see and lots of good restaurants.

You will have heard of La Canebière, one of the great thoroughfares of Europe. It's only about 12 blocks long and runs east–west, ending at the old port. North of it is mainly Arab, south of it is the principal shopping area along three streets, Rue de Rome, Rue St Ferréol and Rue Paradis.

Notre Dame-de-la-Garde is a 19th-century cathedral famous only for its enormous size, surmounted by its statue of the Virgin which can be seen far out to sea and the view from the top. Marseille's 'other cathedral' is much more pleasing architecturally. The Abbaye Saint Victor was built in the 5th century on the site of a Greek cemetery which has been dated at 200 BC by remains found in recent years. Saracen raiders destroyed the abbey and when re-built it was much more fortified, which is why it stands today in much the same form.

Notre Dame is open from 9-12 and 2.30-6 every day except Monday from May to September and 9- 12 and 2-5 the rest of the year. Abbaye Saint Victor is open 10-11.15 and 3-6 every day, closed Sunday morning. Be sure to visit the crypts.

Le Château d'If, Marseille

The Château d'If is most famous as the fortress in which Edmond Dantès, the Count of Monte Cristo, was incarcerated for five years. It occupies much of the six-acre island which is only a 15 minute boat ride from the Quai des Belges on the old port.

The château was built by François I in 1524 to defend the approach to Marseille harbour but it was used mainly as a prison. Besides Alexandre Dumas' creation (whose cell is identified!), most of the occupants were political prisoners, Huguenots and defeated revolutionaries. You can see engraved markings on the walls of many of the windowless cells where survival was short.

Marseille has a dozen museums. The Musée des Beaux Arts is the first you should see. It is on the Boulevard Longchamp and about two kilometres east of the old port. It has a fine collection of paintings by French and foreign artists.

In the same building is the Museum d'Histoire Naturelle. Both are open 10-12 and 2-6.30, closed Tuesday and Wednesday morning.

Almost opposite is the Musée Grobet-Labadie. This was a private home in the 19th century and was the home of a lover of art and music who left it to the city. It is sumptuously furnished with porcelain, tapestries, paintings, sculpture and musical instruments. It has the feeling of a personal and private collection rather than that of a museum. It has the same opening hours.

The Musée d'Histoire de Marseille relates the history of the city from its earliest days using models, mosaics and items of daily usage, but the most interesting is an actual Roman merchant vessel which was found intact recently. *Hours are 10-7, closed Sunday and Monday.* Adjacent is the Jardin des Vestiges, a garden laid out to show the original Greek port with the ruins of the fortifications and the quays.

Along similar lines is the Musée de Vieux Marseille on the Rue de la Prison. It has something of everything, the most interesting exhibits being the models of the city in earlier times. There are tableaux with hundreds of small santons, paintings, furniture and moving photographs. *Open 10-12 and 2-6.30, closed Tuesday and Wednesday morning.*

La Vieille Charité was built in 1640 as an alms-house and has been restored to a really magnificent structure with extraordinary tiered galleries. The archaeological museum is now here but the emphasis is still on Marseille and its Greek, Roman and Arab origins. There are temporary exhibitions too with cleverly-organised demonstrations of themes in art using painting, photography and other media. *Open 12-7 every day.*

Entertainment of every kind can be found in Marseille. There is an opera house, a philharmonic orchestra and the Roland Petit Ballet is based here. There are cafés with shows, especially jazz – the Quai de Rive-Neuve has several of these. Restaurants which put on shows are on the Quai de Rive-Neuve too and also on the Cours d'Estienne d'Orves and the Rue de Chantier. In these, you can choose between various cuisines and show styles – Rustic French, Brazilian, Russian, Gypsy, African, Provençal or Antilles. Meals are around 100f. Discos are everywhere and most charge 70-80f admission.

There are café-theatres and café-art galleries. There is even a restaurant dedicated to Elvis which plays his music non-stop (Le King at 12 Rue des Trois Rois, meals 120f). If you want English pubs, Lyonnaise bistros, Paris 'zincs', German beer cellars, gay clubs, billiard rooms, Armenian restaurants, 'Western' saloons, curry restaurants, Mexican cantinas, piano bars, dance halls, Creole clubs or Hamburger palaces – Marseille has them all and lots more. Prices are much lower than along the Côte d'Azur. An occasional dive may be a bit risky but most of Marseille's 'waterfront' reputation is now in the past.

Having said that Marseille Is not expensive, I will have to point out that with more than a million population it classes as a big city and all big cities have a range of hotel prices, those at the high end being really high.

The Petit Nice offers luxury in a 19th-century villa at well in excess of 1,200f for a room and around 700f for a meal. The Concorde-Palm Beach with built-in mineral springs feeding the pool, the Sofitel on the old port, the Pullman-Beauvau which has hosted Hemingway and Chopin, and the Concorde-Prado, a modern palace with shopping galleries – all are only just on the right side of 1,000f.

For more modest prices, these offer good value, in a choice of locations –

Grand Hôtel de Genève
(H)M *91 90 51 42   3b Rue Reine-Elisabeth   Open all year   All CC.*

Completely refurbished recently and on a pedestrian zone only a couple of minutes from the old port and the Quai des Belges. The 33 rooms are fully-equipped. They cost 320-460f. Parking adjacent. Although there is no restaurant, snacks and small meals are available up to 100f and there is room service.

New Hôtel Bompard
(H)M *91 52 10 93   2 Rue des Flots Bleus   Open all year   All CC.*

Modern, quiet, and just behind the Corniche JFK, less than two kilometres east of the old port. It sits high on a hill in its own extensive park-like grounds and the 47 large cheerful rooms are fully-equipped. Most have a balcony or a terrace. Some of the rooms are in bungalows in the grounds, some have kitchenettes. Prices run from 340-430f. No restaurant but there is private parking.

Hôtel du Petit-Louvre
(HR)S-M *91 90 13 78   19 La Canebière Open all year but R closed Sunday All CC.*

An old favourite hotel on the old port. The rooms on La Canebière side are sound-proofed and this accounts for the spread in the prices of the 31 rooms from 200-380f.

Menus are 85-190f and you can be sure of a satisfying meal, especially, of course, seafood.

New Hôtel Select
(H)S-M *91 50 65 50   4 Allée Léon-Gambetta   Open all year   All CC.*

Fully modernised when it added the 'New' part of the name, this is right in the very heart of Marseille. The 60 rooms are air-conditioned and sound-proofed at 300-360f. Parking adjacent.

Marseille has no shortage of restaurants and seafood is the main dish. The famous 'bouillabaisse' originated here and, not surprisingly, the city claims that its version is the best.

Basically, it is a stew made from shellfish, rockfish and white fish, heavily flavoured with garlic and saffron. It is best ordered in advance, for one of the secrets in its preparation, so say the Marseillais, is rapid boiling over a high heat (the name comes from 'bouillon à baisse', bouillon boiled down).

The dish was becoming too much of a catch-all, with some unscrupulous restaurateurs putting into it whatever was left over from other fish dishes. Consequently, if you are looking for the authentic bouillabaisse, one precaution you should take is make sure that you order it in a restaurant which carries the sign 'Charte de la Bouillabaisse Marseillaise'.

Les Arcenaulx
(R)M   *91 54 39 37   25 Cours d'Estienne d'Orves   Cl. Mon p.m.; Sun   All CC.*

A wonderfully atmospheric restaurant with huge beams and walls of massive stone, it was once an arsenal. Now it is one of the best restaurants on the coast and unique in that the walls are lined with books. Why? you ask. Well, it's because Jeanne, one of the two Lafitte sisters who run Les Arcenaulx, has a bookshop adjoining the restaurant.

A meal will cost 180-250f but it will be an experience to remember. Fish, of course, is prominent but so are Provençal dishes such as daube and barigoules. Gigot aux artichauts may be on the card. Wine by the glass can be had – a rarity in Provence.

Le Chaudron Provençal
(R)M   *91 91 02 37   48 Rue Caisserie   Cl. Sat lunch; Sun   All CC.*

Seafood specialities – everything from bouillabaisse and bourride to langouste and homand and including all shellfish and other fish. Chapon de mer à la Provençal is often featured and so is supions sautés. A meal will probably cost 250f but you won't grudge a centime of it. A good selection of wines can be had at very reasonable prices.

Mme Paul is the efficient and attentive proprietor while Jean-Marie and Gérard are the chefs.

La Flamiche
(R)S   *91 33 00 74   16 Rue de la Paix   Cl. Sat lunch; Sun   All CC.*

Another great place for seafood and at affordable prices. The assiette du pêcheur or the soupe de poisson are the best choice for starters although smoked salmon and other more commonly served plates may be had too. There is baudroie à la crème de safran and tuna either Catalan style or with green pepper.

A brasserie style dish of the day is 60f and there are several menus starting at 80f.

La Dent Creuse
(R)S   *91 42 05 67   14 Rue Senac   Cl. Sat lunch; Sun lunch   All CC.*

The big, self-service salads are a popular way to start a meal here. Not just seafood but plenty of other choices of which I like the bocconcini.

Meals from 60-130f and it's just off La Canebière, only five minutes from the old port.

| Map 2D | **MARTIGUES** 13500 (Bouches-du-Rhône) 40 km W of Marseille |

Martigues sits on the shore of the Etang de Berre, a small inland sea, where the Caronte channel runs out to the Mediterranean.

It is known as the Venice of Provence and with some justification. Until April 1581, it consisted of three separate villages and there were a great many waterways cutting across the three-kilometre-wide strip of land.

Only three of these remain; one is the St Sebastien canal which goes through the middle of L'Isle Brescon, the middle of the three original villages where there are lots of photogenic fishing boats and houses. From the bridge over the canal, the view is known as the Miroir des Oiseaux and it has been painted by Corot, Augustus John and many others.

The Esplanade des Belges and the Cours du 4 septembre are the centre of the area containing most of the restaurants and bars. This is on Jonquières, the southern of the three sections of Martigues. There are several churches of interest. The 17th-century Church of Sainte Madeleine has a magnificently ornamented façade, the Church of St Louis is 14th century, the Church of Saint Génies is 14th century and the Chapel de l'Annonciade has an unusual statue of Sainte Anne.

Those churches which have a midnight mass at Christmas have replaced the traditional lamb with a basket of seafood in the centre of which is loup de mer, 'the king of fish'.

The Museum Ziem is based around the paintings of Felix Ziem, a landscape artist who did most of his work here in Martigues. Other Provençal artists of the 19th and 20th century are represented as well as contemporary artists. There are also sections of the museum dedicated to archaeology and ethnology. It is on Rue Colonel-Denfert on Ferrières, the northern of the Martigues three portions and just over the bridge from L'Isle Brescon. *Open in July and August from 10-12 and 2.30-6.30 except Tuesday. Rest of the year, 2.30-6.30 only except Monday and Tuesday.*

Look out for two of Martigues' food specialities. 'Poutargue' is a pâté made from mullets' roes which are blended with a salt and then baked in the sun. These are formed into small balls and cooked in oil. 'Melets', a fry of small fish, is cooked in a closed pot with a little olive oil, allowed to ferment for a month and then roasted. One more unusual eating custom of the district is that of eating oven-roasted eel as a traditional Christmas dish.

Festivals

A custom known as the Sardinades is worth your participation if you are in Martigues during the months of July and August. 20,000 plates of grilled sardines are distributed every evening and tourists can enjoy them as much as the locals. There are fireworks to celebrate the Feast of St Jean at the beginning of June and in July, and a Venetian festival with brightly-lit boats. In the first week in August, there is a world folklore festival.

For a town of such size it is remarkable that Martigues does not have any recommendable, old and picturesque hotels. There is a large selection of modern ones and all are in the low-to-medium price category but if you are seeking something traditional, then you will have to go further afield – perhaps as far as Salon.

Saint Roch
(HR)M   *42 80 19 73   Ancienne Route de Port-de-Bouc   Open all year   All CC.*

Although it's modern, the Saint Roch is a calm and quiet hotel in park-like surroundings. There is a pool, a solarium and a bar. Parking is available and the garden contains an old olive-oil mill.

The 39 rooms are functional but very pleasant and priced at 300-450f. The two ladies who run the place, Mmes Ferrer and Chabert, make sure it is kept spic-and-span and operates efficiently.

The restaurant does a serviceable job of providing satisfying meals – menus are 100 and 140f.

La Gousse d'Ail
(R)S-M,   *42 07 13 26   42 Quai de Gen. Leclerc   Cl. Sun   All CC.*

Locally very popular and with a strong reputation for quality and reliability. The brochettes de fruits de mer are very good and the filet de boeuf with cèpes is carefully prepared and presented. Many of the other items on the menu are ones you will often see but here they are cooked with all the care of a rare dish – magret de canard is a good example.

The view out over the Etang de Berre is pleasant and menus are fairly priced at 100 and 170f.

Restaurant Pascal
(R)S-M   *42 42 16 89   3 Quai Lucien Toulmond   Open every day   All CC.*

Views over the port and excellent seafood at reasonable prices – a fine combination. Bouillabaisse and bourride are two of the specialities and sardine beignets are a less common offering. There is always a wide selection of grilled fish and you don't have to pay more than 120f.

Auberge le Mirabeau
(R)M   *42 80 52 38   Place Mirabeau   Cl. Sat lunch; Sun   Visa, CB.*

If you want to get away from the seafront (not an easy thing to do in a town split by three waterways), you will enjoy the Mirabeau and its quiet position on a pedestrian-only square.

The decor is rustic but low-key and the emphasis is on seafood. Try palourdes (clams) with spinach and there are all the other shellfish available. It's rather pricier than most restaurants here and a meal will cost around 200f.

Map 2C   **MAUBEC** 84660 (Vaucluse) 8 km E of Cavaillon

The inhabitants of Maubec will understand your French well enough but don't be surprised if you have trouble understanding theirs. It is remarkable that a village of less than a thousand people should have a difficult tongue almost of its own but it is true that the villagers speak as incomprehensibly as the people of Marseilles. The name of the village comes from 'mau-parlant' – those who speak badly – and you will find that they do indeed.

If you should be here when a marriage is taking place, take the chance to observe one of the curious traditions of Provence. As they leave the Mairie, the newly-married couple have to jump over a wooden beam decorated with leaves and flowers. The act has additional significance when one of the couple is a villager and has married someone from outside the village as it symbolises their determination to surmount all obstacles to their married life.

Festivals

During the season of April to June, there are cherry markets selling the produce of the local farms. In February, Maubec holds a fair with agricultural products, horses, antiques and the works of local artisans. There is a festival in honour of St Jean at the end of June and a local fête on the last Sunday in July. From May to September, a peasant market is held every Sunday in the hamlet of Coustellet.

Max Vialis
(C)S   *90 76 90 62   Les Biguières, Route d'Oppède   Open all year.*

Maubec doesn't try to compete hotel-wise with neighbouring Menerbes, Oppède or Les Beaumettes but it does have a chambre d'hôte, with one room at 140-155f. It's just out of the village in a quiet country atmosphere. The room is large and has a bathroom and private toilet.

Map 2C   **MAUSSANE-LES-ALPILLES** 13520 (Bouches-du-Rhône)
20 km E of Arles

One of the prettiest villages in the Bouches-du-Rhône, unpretentious but with an air of affluence about it; even its oldest walls and buildings look clean and cared for.

North of the village, the range of Les Alpilles stretches from horizon to horizon, like a colossal barrier of jagged limestone teeth.

To the south, the Plaine de la Crau sweeps down to the Camargue and the irrigation that this provides to the sub-soil has made the orchards around Maussane hugely productive. Cherries, apples and apricots are the principal fruit while thyme and rosemary grow in abundance. The closeness of the Camargue has meant that the lore of the bull is in evidence here too. You will see 'Taureau' on many a menu – here, it is marinated in olive-oil rich with thyme and rosemary.

Maussane owes its early history to the olive. The old mill can still be seen – once a producer of 80,000 litres of oil a year. The shops sell green olives, black olives, olives packed in dry salt or pickled in brine and olives flavoured with any of a dozen herbs of which fennel is the most popular.

Festivals

The big event of the year is held on August 15 with a 'Running of the Bulls' followed by a big aïoli for everyone. A festival of the bull is also held on July 14 and the horse is not forgotten – herding of the bulls would be impossible without it and so there is a horse fête on the first Sunday in October.

The weekend in the middle of June is another big day in Maussane when the Feast of Saint Eloi is celebrated. He is the patron saint of blacksmiths and any village which fêtes horses is going to pay homage to the saint. There are aïolis, wine-tastings, sale of local fruit and herbs and other produce, folklore dancing and a parade of 'Charettes', gaily decorated horse-drawn carts.

Maussane has a number of good places to stay. This is partly due to its proximity to Les Baux, a 'must' on everybody's list of places to visit but so popular that its hotel prices are 'elevated' to put it mildly.

Val Baussenc
(HR)M   *90 54 38 90   Open all year   All CC.*

A large two-storey Provençal building, recent but authentic in appearance, with beautiful grounds and a large pool overlooked by the dining room.

It is on the D17 going east out of Maussane two or three minutes. The 21 rooms are sparkling white and maybe could stand a touch more colour but the stone slabs which form shelves and benches are a nice idea and come from the quarry down the road. All rooms face due south.

The dining room is candle-lit and welcoming. From the 170f menu you might select les foies du poulet, coulis de tomate, followed by the roulade d'agneau in a delicious sauce tasting like a blend of tomato sauce with tapenade (yet another use for the olive). A plate of three cheeses and finally a rich chocolate gâteau filled with mousse. The wine list is not long but carefully chosen and the waiter will probably recommend the Mas de Sainte Berthe, a full-bodied red and really excellent. It comes from the local vineyard and is the cheapest wine on the list at 85f.

L'Oustaloun

(H)S-M   *90 54 32 19   Place de l'Eglise   H open all year; R cl. Wed; 2/1-mid March*
All CC.

Pleasingly old fashioned in style, L'Oustaoun is on the old square and was the village chapel in the 16th century. The 10 rooms are 250-350f and are fully equipped. There is a garage.

Roberto Bartoli puts his native Italian talent to work in his kitchen where the emphasis is divided between Italian and Provençal. Menus are 140 and 160f.

Hostellerie les Magnanarelles

(HR)S-M   *90 97 30 25   Cl. 5/1-10/2   Visa, CB.*

Right in the centre of the village, on the road to Les Baux and opposite the large statue in the shrine. The 18 rooms are small and adequately

Maussane-Les-Alpilles: Les Magnanarelles

furnished, all but one having a bath and toilet. The pricing at 220-280f is good value for there is also a pool. Demi-pension is obligatory in season at 200-215f.

Regional produce is featured in the restaurant, where menus start at 90f.

Hôtel du Touret
(H)S-M   *90 97 31 93   Open all year.*

A recently built hotel in Provençal style, just west of the village. There is a pool but no restaurant. The 16 rooms are good value at 270f and the surrounding olive trees and pines lend an atmosphere of calm.

Ou Ravi Provençal
(R)S-M   *90 97 31 11   Cl. Mon p.m.; Tues   All CC.*

Little wonder that there are several establishments around Maussane which are hotels only – Ou Ravi Provençal is such a renowned restaurant that you need look no further for an outstanding place to eat.

M and Mme Richard Daura have a deserved reputation at this small place opposite the Mairie. The decor is cosy and inviting and there are more paintings on the walls than many art galleries can boast. Menus are 110, 140 and 230f and you will be tempted by such specialities as pigeon rôti au miel de la lavande.

Map 2B   **MAZAN** 84380 (Vaucluse) 7 km E of Carpentras, 34 km N of Cavaillon

---

 Mon

On a hill near the village stands the cemetery with sixty Gallic-Roman sarcophagi. In the middle of the cemetery is the strangely named Chapel of Notre Dame de Pareloup. According to local belief, the chapel was built to keep away the wolves (or werewolves?) which were said to come here to eat the buried corpses.

The museum in the village tells the history of the region. *Open every day in July and August, Sunday afternoon and holidays in June and September.*

Festivals

The last Sunday in July is the local fête and there is a pilgrimage on the second Sunday after Easter to the Church of Notre Dame la Brune (a Black Virgin). On the last Sunday in March, there is a horse fair and antiques market.

Le Secret des Malauques
(HR)M   *90 69 86 12   R cl. Sun p.m.; Mon from 1/10-30/4   Visa, CB, EC.*

Five fully-equipped, cheerful rooms in an old fortified farm-house building in the middle of a vineyard. Priced at 350-500f each, these are good value as breakfast is included and there are *two* pools and mini-golf for recreation.

There is a shady terrace and a garden and the restaurant specialises in seafood. Menus start at 130f.

Hôtel Le Siècle
(H)S-M   *90 69 75 70*   *Cl. Sun o.o.s.*   *Visa, CB.*

Located right in the village, a long-established hotel of deserved popularity. The 12 rooms are comfortable and good-sized and the price of 120-250f fits most pockets. There is a garden and parking.

Map 4B   **LES MEES** 04190 (Alpes de Haute-Provence) 23 km NE of Forcalquier

---

(M) *Tues and Fri*

The village owes its name to the string of extraordinary rocks known as 'the Petrified Monks' which dominate the Durance river valley.

The rocks were called 'metae' in Latin, 'meo' in the Provençal language and are tapered cones coming to a pointed top. They stretch for more than two kilometres and the local story of their origin is ...well, it's different.

It seems that when the fortress of Forcalquier was under siege by the Saracens, the Seigneur de Bevon commanding the garrison succeeded in defeating the Arabs and capturing large numbers of them. Among the captives were many women who were taken at first as hostages but were then used for the pleasure of the Christian knights.

Father Donat (later to become a saint) was the abbot of the nearby monastery in the Montagne de Lure. He strongly disapproved of such activities and threatened excommunication. When this was ineffective, he ordered the women to be sent back to their homes and arranged for boats to take them. To ensure no further hanky-panky, a number of monks were assigned to stand guard during the boarding. As the women were walking along the banks of the Durance towards the boats, their beauty proved irresistible to the monks. So Donat (who had already performed several miracles) performed another and turned all the monks into stone.

Or so they say.

Auberge des Pénitents
(HR)S   *92 34 03 64*   *8 Boulevard de la République*   *Open all year*   *Visa, CB.*

A very pleasant little auberge with eleven rooms at 150-180f for a double. Considering that there is a pool and tennis, this is remarkably good value and the simple country cooking uses local produce, particularly trout. Eugene Vincent runs an efficient operation and can arrange hiking trips, bicycling and fishing. Menus are inexpensive too at 70f but if you are feeling really hungry and affluent, you can go for the one at 195f.

Map 3C   **MENERBES** 184560 (Vaucluse) 15 km E of Cavaillon

Mainly famous today as a popular place to live for writers, actors and politicians, Ménerbes has had more publicity in the last few years than any French city outside of Paris. President Mitterand has a home nearby and so does Jack Lang, the highly controversial Minister of Culture. Christine Ockrent, France's best-known television interviewer, Emmanuelle Beart and Jane Birkin from filmland are here too and the television series based on Peter Mayle's *A Year in Provence* will doubtless raise property values even higher and bring more residents and visitors.

You might think that the locals would object to this disruption of their serenity but at least, up to now, the attitude is that it's all good for business so let the good times roll. You will want to see Ménerbes, of course, but be prepared to be a little disappointed because, in the village itself, there is little sign of any effect resulting from the media attention and, in fact, the village seems surprisingly understated and many streets are almost deserted. You see the occasional village house which has been restored almost completely but many, many others that are still virtual ruins, waiting for a developer to come along.

Ménerbes lies on a promontory with fine views of the Lubéron mountains to the south. The 16th-century fortress has been restored so as to remove most of the traces of the siege by six thousand soldiers and numerous heavy artillery weapons commanded by the Grand Prior of France. There are many picturesque sights – old stone towers, crumbling walls, solitary columns and delightfully inviting, flowered courtyards behind formidable iron gates.

The church is exceptionally beautiful and manages to combine ornate decoration with a feeling of genuine welcome. The low arched ceilings preserve an intimate atmosphere. An earlier church had existed in the 12th century when there was also a priory belonging to the Benedictine Order on the same site. Church and priory were both destroyed by plague and stray groups of soldiers disbanded after the Hundred Years' War. The present church structure was erected about 1520 though it was soon damaged by Protestant soldiers and a siege which lasted fifteen months. Nevertheless, it is still referred to locally as 'the brand-new church'.

Le Roy Soleil
HR(M-L)   *90 72 25 61   On the D103   R cl. Wed lunch; 15/11-15/3   Visa, CB.*

Calm, quiet and very eye-appealing, this 17th-century fortified farm-house has been restored to a very high quality hotel. It is on the road out of Ménerbes towards Les Beaumettes.

It sits serenely in a large park and there is a pool and a tennis court. The 14 rooms are classically furnished, good-sized and comfortable bordering on elegance. Their price of 400-750f is just within the range which can be considered as reasonable for this level of excellence. There is enclosed parking.

The dining room is mediaevally attractive with its vaulted ceilings and the food matches the surroundings. Cooking is classical but with a light touch and makes good use of locally available ingredients. Menus are around 200f.

Clémentine
(R)M   *90 72 32 81   Place Albert Roux   Visa, CB.*

The terrace with panoramic views and musical soirées in the evenings is very popular. The menu at 88f might be soupe de poissons followed by daube Provençale and then cheese or dessert, while the 138f menu could start with smoked salmon salad with a main course of fricassée de rognons de veau then cheese and dessert. On the à la carte list, truite pochée à la menthe at 62f is in strong demand.

Map 3B   **METHAMIS** 84570 (Vaucluse) 17 km E of Carpentras

Provence has an extraordinary number of extraordinary sights. One of these is around the little village of Méthamis which is on a back road, the D5 and in the wooded valley of the Gorges de la Nesque.

Many terrible plagues have swept through Provence and one of the worst was that of 1720. Nothing was known of how the plague was spread but it was killing up to one out of every three people.

All other means of prevention having failed, the villagers around Méthamis built a massive wall to keep strangers out. You can trace its remains today. It spreads in an arc from Pouraque and La Corneirette to the south-west then goes east past Murs then swings north to Sainte Foi and Saint Hubert.

It was a colossal undertaking and even its ruins are impressive. Sentry boxes were located at intervals but it was a vain enterprise, for the wall did not protect Méthamis.

Festivals

May 3 is an important day for the village. It is then that the inhabitants make a pilgrimage to the Chapel of Notre Dame de Vie of Venasque to pray before the statue of the Virgin and thank her for delivering their ancestors from a dragon which used to crawl out of the Gorges of the Nesque and devour the children.

Whit Monday is another day of pilgrimage for the villagers. This time it is to the Chapel of Sainte Foi, about 8 kilometres east of Méthamis, where the saint was beheaded.

The immediate area is not well endowed with places to stay though there are several good gîtes in Méthamis. The Château Unang at nearby Malemort is very popular and Venasque has a choice of several recommended hotels.

| Map 3C | **MIMET** 13120 (Bouches-du-Rhône) 30 km NE of Marseille |

Half-way between the two autoroutes which run north and south, both approaching Marseille, Mimet is not on any beaten path. It is a modest village of about 2,000 people but, sitting on the flank of the Chaîne d'Etoile at 510 metres, it has a spectacular view of the gulf of Marseille.

Above the village can be seen the mouths of numerous grottoes which have had various inhabitants since prehistoric times. The largest of these, known to the Provençals as the 'Baumo Vidalo', was later used as a hermitage for solitary monks. The sanctuary of Notre Dame des Anges was built in it in the 13th century and expanded in the 17th. The first known Provençal crèche was established here, consisting of figures carved in wood of the Virgin Mary, Joseph, the infant Jesus, a donkey and an ox. Only the first two remain and these can be seen in the church at Mimet.

Festival

The village fête is held every year during June.

Hostellerie du Puech
(HR)S   *42 58 91 06   Cl. Wed lunch from 23/2-13/3; 20/9-11/10   Visa, CB.*

A little auberge, simple and unassuming but very quiet and picturesque with fine views out over the countryside north towards Aix. It is a popular place for hikers and campers to use as a base before setting out on their exploration.

The eight rooms are 140-230f or you may prefer demi-pension at 160-200f per person. Meals are simple country fare and 75-220f.

| Map 2C | **MIRAMAS-LE-VIEUX** 13410 (Bouches-du-Rhône) 11 km SW of Salon, 60 km W of Marseille |

This old part of Miramas looks like a typical Provence perched village and it is hard to believe that it is only 50 metres altitude. It sits on a rock just off the D10 and south of Miramas itself which has little to offer except hotels.

The ruins of the 13th-century château are well-maintained and so is the 15th-century church of Saint Vincent. The narrow, winding streets have numerous boutiques and shops, pizzerias and ice-cream parlours but the total effect has not been spoilt.

Varly
(HR)S   *90 58 21 01   10 Avenue Charles de Gaulle   Open all year   Visa, CB.*

South of the railway station and in the modern part of town, the Varly is a family hotel with 15 rooms at an unbeatable 150f. Nothing fancy but quite serviceable – with a garage.

Menus begin at 55f which offers a limited choice but, for a budget stay, the Varly is good value.

Map 2B **MONDRAGON** 84430 (Vaucluse) 7 km S of Bollène

 Tues

Mons Draconis, the mountain of the dragon, is the dramatic name in Latin. It may, in fact, owe more to the great aristocratic families of Dragonet and Mondragon who have lived here for a thousand years but legend dies hard and even Mistral has pointed out that the coat of arms of the town depicts a golden dragon with a human face.

Festivals

Whether history or legend dominates Mondragon, on May 14 every year the Fête du Drac holds sway. And sway is the right word for at night a long procession of dancers weaves through the town. Most are dressed as knights or mediaeval serfs. The next day, a tournament involving armoured knights on horseback takes place and then there is a big feast on the grass.

Those are Mondragon's big feast days but there are others during the year. In March, there is a local fair, in July there is a wine festival and at Christmas, there is a living crêche.

If you are unfortunate enough to be here at other times, the feudal castle is a very imposing collection of ruins while the Chapel of Notre Dame des Plans dates from the 12th century when it was a part of a Cistercian abbey. It was badly damaged and then re-built in the 18th century. Since then it has been restored but not too noticeably. The statue of the Madonna at the entrance is credited with a number of local miracles.

Hôtel du Sommeil du Roi
(H)S   *90 40 81 58   Open all year   All CC.*

Madames Vallat and Roch confine themselves to hotel-keeping so there is no restaurant.

The 10 rooms are sparkling neat and clean and a bargain at 105-225f. There is parking and a garage.

Auberge de la Table Ronde
(HR)S-M   *90 40 93 21   Open all year   Visa, CB.*

Like many auberges, this is a restaurant with rooms. There are five of them costing 80-260f.

Seafood is the emphasis in the restaurant. The bouillabaisse is ambitious but there are plenty of shellfish and fresh fish. Menus are 98f.

Map 3B **MONIEUX** 84370 (Vaucluse) 6 km SW of Sault, 32 km E of Carpentras

At the eastern entrance to the fabulous gorges of the Nesque Valley, Monieux has been an archaeologist's dream. Bones of prehistoric

animals have been found in profusion – bears, wolves, bison, foxes –
and mostly of species long extinct. In the canyon walls of the Nesque
can be seen the grottoes that were the homes of the prehistoric
inhabitants. Many of them were accessible only by ropes made from
vines.

South of the village on the D942 is the Rocher du Cire which is not
only 872 metres altitude but rises a sheer 200 metres above the gorge.
A 'belvédère' (a look-out point) is close by it and affords some
spectacular views.

Near it and at the foot of the gorge is the 12th-century priory of
Saint Michel. When threatened by Saracen invaders, the monks of the
priory used to hide in the grottoes above.

Monieux celebrates its local feast on the Sunday before July 14 and
every year there is a pilgrimage to the Chapel of St Michel on
September 29

With barely 200 population, Monieux is not the kind of village where
you expect to find a choice of hotels. There is a restaurant though and
there are two good chambres d'hôtes just outside the village.

Bernard Dupasquier
(C) *90 64 06 94   La Tuiliere   Open all year   No CC.*

Less than a kilometre out of Monieux, you will find M. Dupasquier's
chambre d'hôte. There is only one room and it is priced at 150f but
three or even four people can be accommodated in it. The room has a
private toilet and wash-basin. Meals are available if you want them –
at 40f and 70f.

Mme Michèle Picca
(C) *90 64 04 64   Le Moulin   Cl. end Nov to beginning April   No CC.*

A large country house with five attractive rooms, a big lounge and a
garden. There is even a private pool and tennis! At 150f, this is a
bargain. The rooms are all on the second floor and have shower and
common toilets. No meals but you can eat in Monieux.

Les Lavandes
(R) *90 64 05 08   Open all year   Visa, CB.*

You can eat outside or in the garden in summer and Les Lavandes is
always busy. Game is the speciality – whatever the hunters have
caught – but there are other dishes too and the gratin d'agneau is
popular. Prices vary but you can have a good meal for under 100f.

Map 2B   **MONTEUX** 84170 (Vaucluse) 5 km SW of Carpentras

 Sun

The enormous château built in the 11th century is, alas, no more but

there remains one tower, named La Clémentine after Pope Clement V who used to stay here.

Festivals

The Feast of Saint Gens is held every year on the first Sunday after May 16 and there is also a pilgrimage which is led by his statue. The Feast of St Jean is at the end of August and is accompanied by fireworks, as the manufacture of these is a local industry. A fruit and flower market is held every day from May 1 to September 30.

Hostellerie Blason de Provence
(HR)S-M   *90 66 31 34   Route de Carpentras   H cl. Jan; R cl. Sat lunch   All CC.*

A very popular place with visitors and local residents alike. The 20 rooms are attractively furnished and priced at 270-350f. Tennis and a pool are among the amenities and a park surrounds the hotel in its country location.
    This is a hive of activity much of the year. There are gastronomic evenings, folk dancing groups, piano soirées in the winter while in the summer there is outside dining on the terrace and in the garden.
    Menus are 89 and 150f. The speciality recently was charlotte d'agneau à l'aubergine, different and very tasty.

Le Saule Pleureur
(R)M   *90 61 01 35   Quartier Beauregard   Cl. Tues p.m.; Wed also 3 weeks in March and 2 weeks in Nov   All CC.*

A small Provençal farm-house surrounded by trees and especially the weeping willow of the restaurant name.
    Local produce and whatever is in season is the motto here. If it is the truffle season, you can expect a choice of one or two dishes featuring that speciality.
    The cheapest menu is 200f but you will have a memorable meal.

Map 3B   **MORMOIRON** 84570 (Vaucluse) 12 km E of Carpentras

(M) *Tues*

Six hundred years of papal occupation gave the district known as the Comtat de Venaissin its own rituals and customs and a tradition of independence. Mormoiron is at the heart of this small pontifical paradise.
    Barely a thousand people live here today but 40 million years ago giant tapirs ruled the land and their skeletons are still being found embedded in the clay soil.
    On the hill known as the Colline du Boeuf stands the Chapel of Notre Dame-des-Anges with its fortified tower. It was built in the 16th and 17th centuries. Pilgrimages go to it on March 25 and again on

August 2 to pray for rain. On the occasion of the latter, a cake shaped like a crown and called a 'tourtilhado' is traditionally eaten.

The Chapel of Saint Roch (at the western entrance to the village) was built in 1632 to honour the saint whose intervention is said to have protected the villagers from the Black Plague which was ravaging Provence at that time.

Only the keep remains of the 12th-century castle but the Chapel of St Alban and the Chapel of St Martin (which is in the cemetery) are worth seeing. So too is the old house of Hilarion Vilaris in the Plan de Veyrier, the centre of the old town. Only the façade remains but you can also see the monumental door, with a false clock above it – a symbolic reference to eternity.

In the very centre of the old village are the ruins of the Chapel of the White Penitents, a charitable brotherhood comprising mostly craftsmen and peasants who cared for the sick. In other villages, you will see remains of their chapels as well as Chapels of the Black Penitents. These were members of the nobility who cared for the poor, buried the dead and took care of orphans. Gypsum, clay and ochre are still mined in small quantities around the village but today the uses are mainly pharmaceutical.

You will want to visit the beautiful Château Pesquié too – not just for its simple splendour as a building but also because it is a modern winery continuing a wine-making tradition established in 1253. In the heart of the Côtes-du-Ventoux country, high quality wines are aged in stave-wood casks and you can taste their reds and rosés under the coloured arcades with ochre walls. *Open 10-12 and 2-7 every day except Monday.*

Mme Dallara
(C)M   *90 61 91 37   Rue Costefroide   Open all year.*

This chambre d'hôte comprises only one room so it's not easy to book. It is in the village in an old stone house with an open garden and a terrace. There is a large living room with TV. The bedroom has a bathroom and a private toilet. It is priced at 180f, breakfast included.

Mme Mongeois
(C)L   *90 61 95 83   Bastide de Majoulière   Open all year.*

Two rooms in this chambre d'hôte. It is just outside the village and in an 18th-century bastide right in the middle of a park. One room is on the first floor and has a wash-basin and W.C., the other is on the second floor and has a bath and W.C. They are 400f, breakfast included.

There is a large lounge with TV, video and fireplace. You can bathe and fish in the river which is only 500 metres away. A closed garden is around the house.

Map 2B **MORNAS** 84420 (Vaucluse) 11 km N of Orange, 42 km N of Avignon

(M) *Sat*

One of the most extraordinary fortresses in Europe, Mornas has been seen by millions of people. It is visited by very few.

It stands alongside the A7 autoroute and the N7 national route and dominates the Rhône valley. Everyone driving by stares up at the imposing edifice and the next time you do so, stop long enough to scramble up the steep slope to the ruins. They hang on the edge of the cliff, blending into the rocks, sometimes coming magically out of them – presenting an impossible task for a besieging army and there have been plenty of them.

There are few more splendid locations for an impregnable castle in all Europe and it is not surprising that the rock of Mornas has been fortified for nearly two thousand years. Documents from the 11th century refer to a much earlier castle on this site and, in 1274, the Vatican entrusted its defence to the Knights of the Order of St John of Jerusalem, one of the most powerful of all the orders of warrior-monks.

The castle was badly damaged during the wars between the Catholic Union and the Huguenots when the army of the Baron des Adrets swept through the area with fierce reprisal raids. It is remarkable that one of the hotel-restaurants in the village should be named after the man who ravaged the village and the castle.

Festivals

Mornas holds a big Spring Fair over the Pentecost weekend and a religious feast on August 15.

It seems likely that Mornas will remain a sight to be viewed while driving by rather than a place to be visited. The fact that this is so is attested by a scarcity of recommendable hotels and restaurants. Orange is less than ten minutes away to the south while to the east are several villages in the wine region which have a wide choice of accommodation between them, such as Séguret, Gigondas, Vacqueyras and Sainte Cécile-les-Vignes. West of Mornas across the Rhône, the huge sprawling atomic energy power plants and nuclear fuel-processing factories rule out that area for hotel consideration but if you should want to stay in Mornas, there is:

Le Manoir
(HR)S   *90 37 00 79   Cl. Sun p.m.; Mon o.o.s.; 15/11-10/12; 10/1-10/2   All CC.*

At the foot of the soaring cliff with the castle on top and near the church on the N7, Le Manoir is an 18th-century residence with imposing columns and balconies, huge fireplaces and a lovely shady garden.

There is a bar and the 25 good-sized well-equipped rooms. Demi-pension at 270-360f is very reasonable but be warned that seminars in three large rooms are held all the year round. Closed parking is limited.

Map 3B   **MURS** 84220 (Vaucluse) 13 km NW of Apt

At its lofty height of 535 metres, Murs has long been a valuable look-out post on the road between Apt and Carpentras. Neolithic man occupied the site and there remain traces of large grain storage silos and primitive tools.

The massive château you see was built by the Vayson de Pradenne family in the 15th century. Some careful restoration was carried out in the 19th century. The château is now private property. Adjacent, the tiny church dates from the 12th century and contains a fine wooden sculpture of Saint Loup.

About 2 kilometres out of Murs on the D4 which then becomes the D102, you reach the Grottoes of Barigoule. These consist of a maze of underground chambers and passages which are also known locally as the Grottoes of the Vaudois. During the religious wars, a fanatical Catholic, Captain Mormoiron, entombed alive scores of Protestant men, women and children and it is said that their cries can still be heard echoing through the rocks.

Mistral too refers to the 'Matagoun de Varigoulo', supernatural beings who live in underground caverns of the grottoes.

Festivals

The village fête is held on the first Sunday following August 15 and on Ascension Day, a pilgrimage leaves Murs and goes to the Chapel of Notre Dame du Salut (about a kilometre south of the village).

Hôtel Le Crillon
(HR)S-M   *90 72 60 31   Cl. Tues; 15/11-1/12   All CC.*

Right in the village, a restaurant with rooms that has been here as long as anyone can remember and looks like continuing. Rooms cost from 210-260f but it's the food that people come for – game in particular and all from the neighbouring countryside. The tournedos aux morilles are delicious and you can't go wrong with the 60f menu. There are numerous à la carte items too, mostly Provençal specialities. Note that last orders are at 9 o'clock.

➤ Le Mas du Lorlot
(HR)M   *90 72 62 62   Open all year   Visa, CB.*

The restaurant has a nice garden and a terrace for summer eating. There is usually only à la carte choice and it will cost about 150f per person. The choice is wide and there is a good selection of inexpensive wines. Note that last orders are at 9 o'clock.

Map 4D **NANS-LES-PINS** 83860 (Var) 40 km SE of Aix, 36km NW of Toulon

 Sun

Nans-les-Pins was important in earlier days as the village from which pilgrimages left to make the journey up to the Grotto of Mary Magdalene. François I, Henri IV and Louis XIV are among the royals who made the journey which resulted in the route being known as 'Le Chemin des Roys'.

Pilgrims still make the trip up to the grotto which is now known as La Grotte de la Madeleine. Today it is best approached from Plan d'Aups and on arrival you must walk from the parking. You enter the Grotte Obscure then proceed along a tunnel cut out of the rock which leads to the Salle de Chaos. Galleries contain strange rock formations a hundred feet high and though more tunnels continue, they are opened only to professional speleologists. The visit takes about 40 minutes.

The ruins of the 13th-century castle sit on a hill just above the village.

Festivals

The village fête takes place on April 3 and there is a Provençal Fête at the beginning of August. The first week-end in August sees the Fête of Saint Eloi, the patron saint of blacksmiths, and is celebrated with a parade of 'charrettes', the gaily decorated horse-drawn wagons.

Domaine de Châteauneuf
(HR)M-L   *94 78 90 06   Cl. 1/11-1/4   All CC.*

If there were nothing to tell about Nans-les-Pins it would still have to be included here because of the Domaine. I have been staying here over more decades than I care to remember and it remains almost as it was on the occasion of my first visit.

I can recall thinking that here was all the charm and elegance of a château-become-a-hotel and yet there was no pomposity about it. The prices were reasonable and the air was casual.

I said it was almost the same as when I first visited it; the only difference is that now it accommodates seminars, the bane of the private traveller. So far these are not affecting the atmosphere of the Domaine de Châteauneuf – let's all hope it continues that way.

There are six apartments and 26 rooms. All are delightfully furnished and have TV and mini-bar. The rooms are 600f for demi-pension and 790f for full pension. There is a private pool, three tennis courts and golf.

The building is an 18th-century Provençal home inside its own walls and verdant with trees and bushes and flowers. Gilbert Duval is an attentive host and all the staff are friendly and helpful.

Map 2B   **NOVES** 13550 (Bouches-du-Rhône) 13 km SE of Avignon

Once a major stopping place on the Roman road to Spain, where once stood a famous temple to the goddess Hecate, protector of lost travellers.

Today Noves is a quiet market town, mainly famous for its house of 'la Belle Laure'. This is the Laura described in more detail under the heading of 'Fontaine-de-Vaucluse' for it was there that she and the poet Petrarch had their love affair. The house is in the Bourian quarter and near the Porte d'Agel.

The church of Notre Dame-de-Verquières contains a Black Virgin, said to have been unearthed by a grazing cow. The name is strangely Spanish as 'verquiero' is the old Spanish word for a stockade containing cows. Prayers are offered and a pilgrimage made to the church from Noves in time of drought. North of Noves is the church of Notre Dame-de-Pitié to which pilgrimages are also made and have been since the plague in 1720.

Festivals

There is a big aïoli and a running of bulls at the end of August.

Auberge de Noves
(HR)L   *90 94 19 21   H cl. Jan; Feb; R cl. Wed lunch   All CC.*

It no longer enjoys the heady reputation it once had. I can recall staying here many, many years ago when it was one of the top hotels of its kind in France. Nevertheless, it is still an excellent inn and the prices, though high, are justified for a special occasion.

It is an old Provençal manor in a beautiful and serene setting surrounded by 20 acres of park. There is a heated pool, tennis and a garage.

The 21 rooms are furnished with antiques and kept full of flowers. All are air-conditioned and are priced at over 1,000f.

You may feel that this a bit steep but you will change your mind in the case of two of the rooms – the two that are converted from the old chapel. They have a magnificently mediaeval appearance that has been expertly married to modern convenience.

André Lalleman (not Lallemand!) took over this place in 1956 and it is still the food that is the primary attraction. This can still be called one of the great tables of the south. Loup au pistou, caneton en papillote and daube à l'ail are some of the dishes I have enjoyed and the kitchen continues to produce imaginative variations on old favourites as well as be original. I hope the mousse with pralines and raisins soaked in rum is still on the dessert list if you stay here.

A meal will cost 300-400f. There is a good choice of Côtes-du-Rhône wines.

Map 2C   **OPPEDE** 84580 (Vaucluse) 12 km E of Cavaillon

Sometimes known as Oppède-le-Vieux, this is one of the strangest places in Provence. The village of 1,000 people sits perched on top of a 300 metre limestone rock, still largely a ruin despite its population. When you see Oppède from below, it is hard to be sure where the rocks end and the ruins begin.

The castle built in 1209 by the Count of Toulouse has been pillaged. The streets leading up to it pass between piles of stones which were once the houses of the villagers of Oppède who were known as 'teulissie' because their principal occupation was making tiles (tuiles today).

The village thrived until the 15th century, when the activities of various vicious characters like the Marquis de Sade, followed by the massacres of the Protestant Revolution, turned it into a ghost village.

In the 1940s, several architects and artists, including the widow of Antoine de St. Exupéry, began the restoration of a few of the houses. Some of the attempts were over-ambitious but others succeeded and more have followed the idea in recent years as a second home for Parisians and foreigners became the fashion. The result has been an extraordinary mixture of the ancient and the new.

The 12th-century chapel has been restored and is worth a visit. So too is La Chartreuse de Bonpas, a few kilometres west of the village. It is a very ancient chapel where pilgrims and merchants used to stop and pray before crossing the river Durance, a dangerous rushing body of water in those days.

Don't expect a lot of trendy boutiques or gift shops or artisans making their wares – it's not that kind of village. The olive oil from the Moulin Mathieu is prized though.

Festivals

There is a horse fair in April, a wine fair in July, music concerts in August and a market fair of bric-à-brac and antiques in September – so you can tell that the village is slowly coming back into the 20th century.

Mas des Capelans
(HR)M   *90 76 90 29   R cl. Sun; H cl. 15/11-20/2   Visa, CB, AE.*

One of the more highly recommended hotels in the area and an exceptionally charming and welcoming place. The old farm-style buildings used to be the home of a wealthy silkworm breeder and the conversion into a luxury hotel has been carried out with exquisite taste.

There are two apartments and eight rooms, all spacious and beautifully-equipped and furnished. Each is named for the superb views it commands – Roussillon, Gordes, Lubéron ... The pool is heated and there is a billiard room.

Despite all this opulence, prices are less than you might suspect. The rooms are 460-600f per night.

Dining underneath the mulberry trees at the side of the pool is the order of the day in summer and you will be served a complimentary house cocktail before the meal. Phillipe and Jacqueline Poiri pay as much attention to the cooking as they do to the hotel and menus are only 155f, featuring local produce, fresh that day.

Map 2B   **ORANGE** 84100 (Vaucluse) 31 km N of Avignon

 Thur

After the conquest of Gaul by Julius Caesar, suitable sites were chosen as residential areas for the victorious legionaires. One of these was 'Arausio' which is known as Orange today.

When the retirees from the Second Legion arrived here in 35 BC they established a settlement which was laid out in the North-South and East-West style. Most of this disappeared long ago but three structures remain – the great arch, the theatre and the temple.

Orange is known today mainly for its theatre which is the best preserved Roman theatre in existence and the only one which still has its stage façade intact. As many as 10,000 spectators could be accommodated to watch plays, song and dance performances and other entertainment. The acoustics are extraordinarily faithful – so much so that the theatre is used today to host an opera and festival of music every July and August.

In the period intervening the Roman past and the present, the building has seen many uses – a prison, a fortress, a slum dwelling and a beggars' hideout. In the Middle Ages, the religious 'mystery plays' were performed here and, as with so many massive constructions of the past, it has been ruthlessly robbed of its stones for other building work.

The theatre is open to visitors from 9-6.30 April to September and 9-12, 2-5 October to March.

The second outstanding building in Orange is impossible to miss. It is the Arch of Triumph, also built by the Romans and the best-preserved, oldest and largest Roman arch still standing. The N7 route goes right past it – making it easy to see but difficult to examine. You must stop and examine it though as it still preserves sufficient original decoration to make it notable.

The four fluted Corinthian columns flanking each side are beautifully proportioned while the three arches have a facing of fine decoration. At the very top, finishing the mass of the main arch, is a powerful bas-relief depicting a battle between the Romans and the Gauls. It is as magnificent an arch as any in Rome even though the centuries have rubbed away the flutings at the base of the pillars.

Opposite the entrance to the theatre is the Municipal Museum, installed in a old hotel of the 17th century. It contains many Roman remains and fragments from early surveys of the city. There are rooms with items from the 16th and 17th centuries when Orange belonged to the Princes of Nassau. William was the first of these princes and it was he who took the name of Orange for his dynasty – a name to be taken subsequently by the Protestant movement in Ulster, several towns in the U.S.A. and a river and a state in South Africa.

The best view of the town theatre is from the Colline St Eutrope. Here too are the ruins of the castle built by the Princes of Orange but dismantled by King Louis XIV.

The Roman amphitheatre is known as the 'Théâtre Antique' and the summer entertainment is one of the most important events in music in France. Leading opera companies, ballets, musical comedies (*West Side Story* was a big hit) and top artists in popular and classical music can be seen. A performance in this setting on a warm summer night is a memorable experience.

Sporting events from May to September in Orange include chess, petanque, cycle races, drag racing, swimming contests, basketball games and gymnastic tournaments. There's never a dull moment in Orange!

The strategic location of Orange gives it ready access to many vineyards where you may taste and buy. Some of these vineyards are:

Domaine de la Jaufrette, Chemin de la Gironde. A wide choice here – Côtes-du-Rhône red, Côtes-du-Rhône Villages red, Châteauneuf-du-Pape red, Vacqueyras red, Gigondas red. *Open 8-2 and 3-7, closed Sundays and holidays.*

La Fagotière, Domaine Palestor. An opportunity here to taste the rare Châteauneuf-du-Pape white. You can also taste the red and Côtes-du-Rhône red and rosé. *Open 9-12 and 2-7. Closed Sundays and holidays.*

Domaine Roger Perrin, Route de Châteauneuf-du-Pape. Taste the Châteauneuf-du-Pape red (and white!), the Côtes-du-Rhône red and, if you're looking for something inexpensive, their red and rosé table wines are quite good. *Open weekdays 9-12 and 2-7, Sundays and holidays by appointment only.*

All of the above can be visited without appointment except on the days noted. There are other vineyards in the region but check first as many admit visitors by appointment only.

At the end of January, Orange has a wine fair and there is the Fête des Vins late in July. There are seven 'wine routes' which pass through the vineyards of the Côtes-du-Rhône district. Four of these go through Vaucluse and one of them starts (or finishes) in Orange. It is known as 'La Route Orange' and covers 85 km as it passes through several delightful villages – Sérignan du Comtat, Rasteau, Roaix, Villedieu, Buisson and St Maurice-sur-Eygues.

Hôtel Arène
(H)S-M   *90 34 10 95   Place des Langes   Cl. 1/11-15/12   All CC.*

Undisputed number one of the hotels in Orange for longer than anyone can remember and still holding its position run by Gérard Coutel. Provençal style and smart with cherry-red awnings and shades, the Arène has 30 rooms from 300-380f, all pleasant and many looking out to the shady terrace. The location on a pedestrian-only square right in the heart of old Orange and a closed garage are extra bonuses.

Hôtel Louvre-Terminus
(HR)S-M   *90 34 10 08*   *89 Avenue Frédéric Mistral*   *H cl. 20/12-15/1; R cl. Sun; Sat lunch   All CC.*

> Another old favourite, also in the centre of town. Comfortable and classic, it has a garden and a terrace and the pool has now been installed. There is private but limited parking.
> The price is 250-350f in the 32 rooms though they are basic and simple. The restaurant is known as Les Jardins de l'Orangerie and dining is limited to hotel customers only. Menus are 85, 125 and 160f.

Hôtel Le Glacier
(H)S-M   *90 34 02 01*   *46 Cours Aristide Briand*   *Cl. Sun p.m. o.o.s.; 22/12-1/2   All CC.*

> If the Arène has been number one for a long time, Le Glacier has been number two and this looks like continuing. The 28 rooms are in the centre of town and 240-250f. There is parking and a garage. No restaurant.

M. Claude Monnier
(C)M   *90 34 55 96*   *Quartier Bois Feuillet*   *Open all year.*

> If you prefer to be out of town or are looking for inexpensive accommodation, M. Monnier's chambre d'hôte could be just the thing. There are five rooms and it's only about three hundred metres south of Orange on the road to Roquemaure. Unenclosed land surrounds it and there is a large living room. All of the rooms have private toilets and cost 160f for a double, 290f on a demi-pension basis for M. Monnier serves meals too (65f as an individual price).

Le Parvis
(R)S-M   *90 34 82 00*   *3 Cours Pourtoles*   *Cl. Mon (except July, Aug and holidays); 17/11-3/12; 20/1-5/2   All CC.*

> Comfortable and elegant, Le Parvis is under the firm hand of Jean-Michel Bérengier, well-established in the Orange area and strongly-reputed as a chef. Making the best use of local products in season to produce Provençal dishes, he cleverly blends the familiar favourites with original food ideas. His escalope de loup au fenouil is excellent and his oven-roasted carré d'agneau equally so. Menus at 100-180f.

Le Français
(R)S   *90 34 18 30*   *24 Rue des Lilas*   *Open all year   All CC.*

> Check first to see if there's a floor show that night.
> Le Français prides itself on its bouillabaisse, while couscous and paella are always on the menu too. Prices start at 80f and it's a cheerful brasserie-type atmosphere.

Map 2C ORGON 13660 (Bouches-du-Rhône) 8 km S of Cavaillon

The site is no longer as important as it once was, for Orgon sits on the south bank of the Durance river. Many armies found it to be a position commanding the route to Spain as witnessed by the Pierre Plantée, a military milestone dated during the reign of Augustus which can be seen just outside the village.

Festivals

The Church of Notre Dame-de-Beauregard is still the destination of a yearly pilgrimage every September 15 and there is a Provençal Fête around July 20 with torchlight parades and displays of horsemanship by 'gardians' from the Camargue.

Auberge aux Petits Pavès
(HR)S   *90 59 00 22   On the RN7   Open all year   Visa, CB.*

There are 14 rooms, nicely furnished, at 130-200f or full pension at 212-260f which is extraordinarily good value. The reason is that M et Mme Bres and their children run the Auberge primarily as a restaurant. As such, it is known near and far. The heavily beamed ceilings and the red and pink decor make an immediate impression of warm hospitality.

The specialities are bourride at 110f and bouillabaisse at 180f. There are menus at 65 and 85f and Provençal dishes such as pieds et paquets are often featured. The three-course menu at 130f might include truite farcie aux poireaux à la crème while the four-course menu often has bourride as the main course. Aïöli is the speciality every Friday.

Parking and garage.

Map 5C LA PALUD-SUR-VERDON 04120 (Alpes de Haute-Provence) 22 km SW of Castellane

 Tues

A picturesque little hamlet that you pass through between the Gorges du Verdon and Lac St Croix. It was once known as Castrum Novum (in Roman days) and then had other names due to the amalgamation of several hamlets and villages. If you use an old map, you may find La Palud called Châteauneuf – which is now a separate hamlet a few kilometres to the north over the 1,000 metre high col.

The region is even older than the Romans. Troglodyte sites can still be seen in the Mainmorte Ravine just outside the village, pre-Christian remains are around Saint Maurin and at Barris, there are the ruins of an 11th-century château. Another château ruin is at Mayreste, about 9 kilometres west of La Palud.

La Palud has its own château, 17th century and restored in the 18th.

Around it are some of the old houses, many of which date back to the 16th century.

But it is the surrounding area that is the real attraction. Lac St Croix is really a reservoir but it looks more like a lake than most lakes you ever saw. Miles and miles of untouched, unspoiled white beaches seem too good to be true only threequarters of an hour's drive from the busy Riviera coast. Powerboats are not allowed so it is quiet as well as sparsely-visited.

On the other side of La Palud, the drive along the Gorges du Verdon are as hair-raising as you want to make them. You can drive only partway if vertigo gets the upper hand. The sight of climbers dangling from ropes on the sheer cliff faces won't help though. (*French Entrée 10 – the South of France* contains more detailed information on this fascinating and little-known area.)

The Château de Trigance (in Trigance) is only a short drive down the D955 and is a spectacular place to stay. La Palud has alternatives though.

Auberge des Crètes
(HR)S   *92 77 38 47   Cl 1/10-Palm Sunday; R cl. Wed, except July, August and holidays   Visa, CB.*

Twelve simple rooms, three with bath and toilet, the others with shower and toilet, good value at 160-185f. Meals too are simple and the local trout, caught that morning, is the dish to order. Menus at 70 and 95f.

Guided hikes, horse-back riding and rafting on the Verdon are all available.

Hôtel des Gorges du Verdon
(HR)S   *92 77 38 26   Open all year   Visa, CB.*

When you see this beautiful Provençal building, gardens and terraces all around it, a spectacular panoramic view and tennis and a pool, you will refuse to believe that it costs only 330f for demi-pension. The reason is that it holds seminars and conferences – but if these don't bother you or if you catch a time when neither is being held, the host, M. Bogliori-Schaeffer, is giving you unbeatable value.

Map 2B   **PERNES-LES-FONTAINES** 84210 (Vaucluse) 6 km S of Carpentras, 28 km NE of Avignon

In the 16th century, Pernes had 12 fountains, all fed from the same subterranean source and all bearing picturesque names. One of those names was the Fountain of the Moon and neighbouring villagers called the inhabitants of Pernes 'lunatics' because they drank the water from it. During the 18th century, more fountains were built and today Pernes more than justifies its name, with no less than 36. The most interesting is probably the Fountain of the Cormorant near the Porte Notre Dame, adjacent to the old bridge over the river Nesque.

This area is the heart of the village. A few steps away is the keep of the old castle of the Counts of Toulouse and the 17th-century market hall, formerly the home of the Duke of Brancas and Marshal of France and once a slave market. A tiny 16th-century chapel sits on the bridge, while just over the other side is the Church of Our Lady of Nazareth, whose older parts date from the 11th century.

The Tour Ferrand is the most important sight in Pernes. Just south of the river, on the Place du Comtat Venaissin, it was originally a palace erected in the 13th century and it has three storeys, of which the upper storey is decorated with wall-paintings. Some of these are dated 1275 – making them the oldest paintings in France. The Virgin Mary with the infant Christ and other saints, including Sebastian and Christopher, are represented. Worldly personages are depicted too, such as Raymond de Graissac, first Seneschal of the papacy, William of Orange and Charles d'Anjou.

Pernes-les-Fontaine: Porte Diotre Dame

The whole village is historic and delightful to wander around and ramparts, gates, towers and fountains are everywhere. There are several other chapels and those of Our Lady of the Rose and Our Lady of Grace are the more interesting. All of the sights of Pernes are compressed into a small area so it's no problem to see them quite easily.

Festivals

The Taurean Society of Pernes organises a fête every August 25 but the only participation by the bull is to be roasted. It is put on the spit the night before and roasted until the next afternoon.

Hôtel Prato-Plage
(HR)S   *90 61 31 72   Open all year   Visa, CB, DC.*

About 2 km out of the village, this is an unassuming, very down-to-earth hostelry with no frills but out in the quiet countryside and in a huge park. The 'plage' is just outside – it is a small man-made lake or, to be more accurate, a filled-in quarry. But there is a beach all around it and it is extremely popular in the summer heat.

The restaurant is like a very large country kitchen, with tiled floors, a beamed ceiling and a huge fireplace. Vases of dried flowers, copper pots and kettles and paintings of the countryside make it very attractive, though in summer you may want to be out on the shady terrace.

Menus start at 85f and the cooking is regional and Provençal. A high standard is maintained in the quality of the produce and the cooking. Carré d'agneau aux herbes de Provence is a typical main course.

Note: additional rooms are now being built in an annexe building to accommodate the increasing number of travellers who find the hotel a very good and inexpensive place to stop over.

Map 2B   **PIOLENC** 84420 (Vaucluse) 5 km N of Orange

 Mon

A quiet and curiously unsophisticated village of 4,000 people, Piolenc seems to maintain an anonymity throughout most of the year – until the last Sunday in August. If you are anywhere in the neighbourhood on that day, be sure to go to Piolenc.

The place seems to come out of hiding. It is the great garlic festival. Garlic is on sale in every form and hardly anybody even mentions its seemingly unlimited range of health-giving and restorative properties.

There is a Provençal parade with folklore dancing and instruments and at the end, a giant 'aïoli' feast.

Auberge du Bori
(HR)S   *90 37 00 36   Cl. Tues o.o.s.; Jan   All CC.*

255-275f is the price range for the nine rooms in this small auberge in a pine forest. Good value as there is a pool, a garden and parking.

The restaurant serves straightforward Provençal cooking, with an occasional Italian touch. Menus are 98f and summer dining may be on the terrace or in the garden.

Map 2D   **PORT-DE-BOUC** 13500 (Bouches-du-Rhône) 3 km W of Martigues

---

The port itself is of little importance to the visitor but the fort that was built to defend it is one of the most powerful fortifications on the Mediterranean coast and irresistible to any amateur photographer.

The Fort de Bouc was built to prevent enemy ships sailing from the Golfe de Fos and through the Canal de Caronte into the Etang de Berre. A glance at the map makes it clear how a very dangerous situation could develop if this had happened, for an enemy fleet could then take its pick of ports and coves to hide while its crew plundered the region and attacked Aix, Avignon and Salon.

The first fort on the site was built in the 13th century. The massive walls which you see today were first erected in 1607. Three hundred years later, they were still being expanded and enlarged. Even in the 19th and again in the 20th century, this re-fortification went on.

Most of the present fortresses and the huge ramparts were built by the great French military engineer, Vauban, though Napoleon ordered further improved defences to be installed around the port in 1794. Consequently, the present appearance is an amalgam of all this work over the centuries.

It is a most impressive sight and readily accessible, just off the N568. The restaurants at Martigues are only a few minutes away.

Map 3C   **LE PUY-SAINTE-REPARADE** 13610 (Bouches-du-Rhône) 19 km N of Aix-en-Provence

---

The Roman chapel of Sainte Réparade was restored in the 17th century; visitors usually ask about the saint who is not one of the better known names. She was a local woman, prominent in the high society of the time, who decided to give up her shocking love affairs, her frivolous and useless life. She then repented – 'réparant' – hence the name she took. On Ascension Day every year, the inhabitants of Le Puy-Sainte-Réparade make a pilgrimage here.

The Château of Fonscolombe was built in the 18th century and has particularly beautiful, clean lines. In the park around it are numerous rare plants. The nearby Château Lacoste (not to be confused with the one in the village of Lacoste in Vaucluse) was built in 1682 by the Bishop of Digne, the same one mentioned in Dumas' *Les Miserables*.

The vineyards near Le Puy produce Côteaux d'Aix wines, not outstanding but very drinkable.

Festivals

The Feast of Sainte Réparade is held on October 8. Two other neighbouring saints have feast days in Le Puy – Saint Canadet on the first Sunday in August and Saint Michel au Puy on the third Sunday in September.

Domaine de La Cride
(HR)M   *13610 (Bouches-du-Rhône)   42 61 96 96   Cl. Jan; R cl. Wed p.m. o.o.s.*

On the D14 south of Le Puy-Sainte-Réparade, you will find one of the finest and most luxurious country homes in the region. Erik Cavallin virtually opens his home to guests. The six rooms are very comfortably furnished and all have bathroom and toilet. They are priced at 400-650f.

There is a pool, a terrace, an outdoor bar and barbecue. The setting is delightfully rural – in an 8-acre park which has a small river running through it.

The cooking is justifiably described as gastronomic. Menus are only 130f but if you are tempted to go for the à la carte a really sumptuous meal will cost about 250f.

The staff speak English and German.

Map 2B   RASTEAU 84110 (Vaucluse) 19 km NE of Orange

Rasteau is one of the leaders of the 17 villages which produce the famous Côtes du Rhône wines and wine dominates all activities in the district.

Rasteau is a perched village despite its altitude of only 220 metres, with views over the sloping vineyards and with magnificent aspects of the Dentelles de Montmirail, those jagged limestone cliffs that reach up into the blue sky like gigantic teeth, and the Rhône valley.

But wine is the key and you are reminded of this at the Musée du Vigneron on the D975 leaving Rasteau for Roaix. It belongs to the Domaine of Beaurénard and will tell you everything you always wanted to know about wine but were too busy drinking it to ask. Here are displayed in seven rooms all the utensils used in the vineyards for obtaining the grapes and all the equipment that produces wine from those grapes – you will particularly admire the magnificent copper retort.

Paul Coulon and his family have assembled documents and a 30-minute video describing both the history and the legend of wine. In the racks are more than 2,000 bottles. After the tour tasting under the trees is a very agreeable experience. *The museum is open 9.30-12.30 and 1.30-6 from April to October. Other months, hours are 1.30-5.30 during the week and 9.30-12.30, 1.30-6.30 on week-ends. It is closed Tuesdays.*

In addition to the Domaine de Beaurénard, you may want to visit the other vineyards where you are welcome to taste and buy: Domaine

Grand Nicolet; Domaine des Papillons; Domaine des Buisserons; and Domaine de la Girardière. La Cave des Vignerons produces a sweet wine too, a little like the Beaumes de Venise.

One of the great wine routes of the Côtes du Rhône runs through Rasteau and is known as the Route Orange. It runs between Orange and Nyons, passing through Villedieu and St Maurice sur Eygues.

Festivals

The principal village fêtes are the Fête Patronale on the second Sunday in July and the Fête des Côtes du Rhône Villages on August 3.

Hôtel Bellerive
(HR)M   *90 46 14 96   Cl. Jan 2-Mar 16   Visa, CB.*

A pleasing jumble of ochre-coloured buildings looking onto a pool. They are fairly modern but not obtrusive and Michel Petrier has built up the reputation over the years so that the Bellerive can compete for the Vaison-la-Romaine clientele too.

The 20 rooms are good sized and well-furnished and 400-650f or 370-390f for demi-pension. There is a large garden and parking. The restaurant is equally known and the poulet sauté aux écrevisses is, I hope, still on the menu. Meals on a separate basis run 130-300f.

Mme Yvonne Mourgand
(C)M   *90 46 11 12   Route de Cairanne   Open all year.*

With Rasteau having only one recommendable hotel, you might want to consider a chambre d'hôte. You're in luck for Madame Mourgand runs a fine one just a couple of hundred metres out of the village going west on the D69.

There are five rooms at 180f, breakfast included. Three have private bathrooms and a shared W.C. while the other two have showers. There is a large living room and an open garden. Barely a mile away, you can bathe and fish in the river. No meals.

Map 3B   REILLANE 04110 (Alpes de Haute Provence) 26 km E of Apt

Visible for miles around, Reillane sits on its hilltop at 600 metres altitude, with its great belltower climbing up into the sky and the statue of the Virgin on top of it.

In the 13th century, Reillane was a haven for English Jews – all that is left of the synagogue is one room with a panelled ceiling for when the Jews were expelled from Provence by Louis XII in 1501, the synagogue was converted into a church.

The Musée Ethnologique has a good display of local traditions in terms of agriculture, religion and folklore. Open from 3.30-6.00 every afternoon in July and August.

Festivals

The village fête is on the first Sunday in August.

Auberge de Reillane
(HR)S-M *92 76 45 95   Open all year   Visa, CB.*

A simple stone farm-house, ivy-covered and sitting all alone in the countryside about 10 minutes out of the village.

There are 7 rooms, 200f for one person, 300f for two. They are all large, with pastel walls and massive ceiling beams.

A la carte is the way to order in the restaurant and game is the speciality, from the surrounding country. Lapin à l'oseille at 85f is very good and so is the pintade fermière at 90f.

Monte Cinto
(R)M *92 76 41 70   Open only in season   Visa, CB.*

If you're looking for a change of pace, a variant from Provence cooking and some entertainment – this is the place.

It was a hotel and may open as one again very soon. In the meantime, it is a very large building which offers Corsican food and wine, plus Corsican singers and dancers – a seven-course meal including the wine and the entertainment for 250f.

Map 4C   **RIEZ** 04500 (Alpes de Haute Provence) 15 km W of Moustiers

(**M**) *Wed and Sat*

Riez' proudest remnant of its Roman past lies in a field just west of the town. It consists of four beautiful columns of granite, grey at the base and with white marble Corinthian capitals. It dates from the first century BC and in 1641 the town council of Riez offered them to Lyons which, fortunately, refused them. It is firmly believed that many other remains lay buried in the ground nearby – perhaps a temple of Apollo which may have contained these columns and many more.

The next generation may enjoy the thrill of discovering the answer.

Riez was a busy Roman city and it is unusual to find that it also contains one of the oldest Christian buildings in France too. This is a baptistery on the other side of the river, near the D952. It dates from the 4th and 5th centuries. It is in the design of a square in which is inscribed an octagon, four sides of which have a niche. Eight columns of grey-blue granite support semi-circular arches which are surmounted by an octagonal cupola.

The two old fortified city gates survive, the Porte Aiguière and the Porte Saint Sols. The old Hôtel de Mazan with its beautiful staircase should be seen too.

There is a Lapidary Museum and a Natural History Museum.

During the truffle season (November to February), there is a market in truffles on Wednesdays and Saturdays.

Riez has a local fair in mid-May and mid-September. The town does not forget its Roman past entirely and has a celebration of the Roman Columns in August.

Map 2B   **ROAIX** 84110 (Vaucluse) 6 km W of Vaison-la-Romaine

How many fine and yet almost unknown wines there are in this part of the world!

Roaix is a village of 400 inhabitants, perched on top of a hill dominated by a feudal château. Prehistoric remains are still being found in the neighbourhood and the site was later the headquarters of the Knights Templar. Some of the buildings exist still but today Roaix's importance is due to its wine.

The gravelly terraced slopes and the burned red clay soil look inhospitable to any kind of agriculture but the vineyards of Roaix prosper to the extent that well over 80% of the land grows grapes. The red grenache is the dominant variety and to it is added percentages of cinsault and syrah grapes.

The quality of the wine from Roaix was recognised thirty years ago when the right to use the apellation 'Village' was granted. This makes Roaix one of only 17 to have this right. Wine tasting experts will tell you that the Roaix red wines offer the flavours of blackberry, spice and tannin but don't let that put you off! White wines represent only a tiny portion of the total production. The rosé's are fruity and refreshingly light.

Roaix has joined with the neighbouring vineyards of Seguret and between them there are 163 communities in the AOC category. The Réserve St Roch is one to watch for and you will see wine-tasting opportunities on every road and lane around Roaix.

There's more good news – despite its quality, Roaix wine is inexpensive.

Emile Bourdonnas
(C)   *90 46 14 45*   *Route des Princes*   *Open all year.*

With so many vineyards where you will want to stop and taste, the temptation to stay overnight in this region may be strong. Rasteau and Cairanne are only a few kilometres away and they too have some excellent wines. The nearest town of any size is Vaison-la-Romaine but its Roman remains are a very popular tourist attraction and its accommodation is moderately expensive and usually full.

The answer is M. Bourdonnas' chambre d'hôte, a big stone house in an orchard close to the village. There is a garden and you can bathe or fish in the river Ouveze only a hundred metres away.

There is a large lounge, a living room and parking. The three rooms are cosily furnished but have only a wash-basin. One bathroom and toilet is shared by all three rooms. The price is a very modest 165f.

Map 2C   **ROBION** 84440 (Vaucluse) 6 km E of Cavaillon

The men of Robion have worked in the past at the quarries of
neighbouring Les Taillades (which you must see). When they died,
they were buried in the fascinating Robion cemetary.

Robion's quarriers were considered as artists and you will see why.
When they died, they were buried beneath tombstones which
indicated their branch of quarrying specialisation – the tool they used,
be it hammer, axe, chisel, was cut into the tombstone. Men in other
professions felt they were entitled to equal treatment and so you can
see stones engraved with baskets of asparagus (a local product),
knives for cutting grapevines, hoes for the farmers and guns and
powder-horns for the hunters. Even the tombstone of a Robion man
who was murdered in his bed has an engraving of the gory scene.

There isn't much else to see in Robion, which is little more than a
village on the busy D2 coming east out of Cavaillon. An outdoor
theatre is popular entertainment in July and August. This isn't a
village hotel but there is one good restaurant.

Maison de Samantha
(R)S-M   *90 76 55 56   On the D2   Open all year   All CC.*

Jacques-Olivier Roux and his wife keep it simple. Menus at 95, 150
and 180f are limited to two choices for each course but you won't
have any difficulty finding something you like. The fricassée de lapin
is especially good and so are the noisettes d'agneau à l'ail. The wine
list is limited too but the wines are good local ones and quite
inexpensive.

Map 2B   **ROGNONAS** 13870 (Bouches-du-Rhône) 4 km S of Avignon

'If you want to see a proper charrette, come to Rognonas,' say the
villagers. The 'charrette' is a magnificently decorated wagon which is
a vital part of the Feast of Saint Roch which runs from Friday to
Tuesday in the middle of July. It is an intensely Provençal feast and
the 'Ramado', the parade of wagons and horses, is encountered in
many villages in these parts.

Saint Roch and Saint Eloi are both equally venerated and the two
may become intermingled as far as the days celebrating them are
concerned. The Société Confrèrie de Saint Eloi et Saint Roch might be
expected to keep the two separate but they cleverly let the confusion
continue. No-one objects as, this way, both feasts can be enjoyed by
going from village to village.

There are events every day in Rognonas – boules contests,
banquets, Masses, performances of Marcel Pagnol's *Fanny*, concerts,
balls, fireworks and monster aiölis – but the biggest event of all is the
one which features the 'charrettes'.

The horses are harnessed in Saracen-style, collars and bridles richly
ornamented with tufts of dyed wool, multi-coloured ribbons, plumes

and streamers in blue, yellow and red, tiny mirrors, bead-encrusted leather straps and jingling bells.

Each horse is tended by a charioteer, a member of the fraternity dressed in the traditional white shirt and blue pantaloons.

The parade is led by the Harmonie Rognonaise, a band of about thirty musicians but loud enough for a hundred. After them come boys riding ponies and then carts full of younger children who throw coloured confetti into the air. Then come the charrettes.

Twenty horses are considered necessary to constitute a real fête but Rognonas usually musters at least thirty. (The village elders will tell you that their fathers used to relate stories of the memorable year of 1908 when 102 horses participated. They formed a line a third of a mile long and stopped trains at the level crossing.) Many horses are ridden, some by girls in the traditional Arlésienne costumes.

The charrettes are piled high with fruit and vegetables, flags and other decorations just as they have been since the 17th century. Loaves of a sweet bun-like bread are sold everywhere, a commemoration of the bread brought by a dog to the stricken Saint Roch.

The parade goes around the village until finally breaking up in exhaustion with the participants and on-lookers piling into the cafés where pastis and wine flow in copious amounts.

There are variations from village to village in the details of this joyous event but this is the way they do it in Rognonas and the way they have done it for many years.

So if you want to see a proper charrette, come to Rognonas. Mind you, the villagers of Graveson, Maillane, Barbentane and Maussane will give you different advice ...

You may want to stay in the village in order to participate to the full in these festivities or you may be looking for a place to stay which is convenient to Avignon but out of the town.

Auberge Rognonaise
(HR)S   *90 94 88 43   10 Boulevard des Arenes   Open all year   Visa, CB.*

A smart two-storey building with 14 rooms at 160-200f. With a pool in the grounds too – this is good value. 190f for demi-pension is an alternative worth considering or even 225f for full pension.

Proprietor Joseph Graffet works hard to keep the place at a level higher than you would expect for such prices. There is parking and a garage.

Map 3B   ROUSSILLON 84220 (Vaucluse) 12 km W of Apt

 Wed

The name comes from the red coloured rocks which surround the village – seventeen different shades of red were quarried here in the past.

As to why the rock is red, you can take your choice of two versions. One pertains to Raymond of Avignon, the lord of the manor, Sirmonde, his wife and Guillaume de Cabestang, his page and troubador. With a cast like that, you can guess the first part of the story – but not, I guarantee, the latter part.

Raymond went off on a hunting trip and came back earlier than expected – early enough to catch his wife and his troubador in the most embarrassing of positions. Now, it's the rest of story that goes a llttle differently ... Apparently showing admirable restraint, Raymond dismissed the troubador and as a way of making up with his wife, had a magnificent banquet prepared for her. The speciality of the meal was heart of venison and it was not until afterwards that Raymond told his wife that the heart had, in fact, been that of Guillaume.

Sirmonde announced that she had dined well – and, she added, for ever. She went up on to the battlements and threw herself off from the highest point. Her blood, it is said, stained the earth red.

The mineral is known as ochre and when crushed and ground and mixed with linseed oil yields colours from yellow to brownish-red that have been used in painting and staining since prehistoric days. By the 19th century, this had become a major industry in this area but in more recent times, synthetic dyes replaced ochre and production was stopped.

The rocks are startling in their intense colours. You will marvel at the fabulous cliffs of crimson and gold, the deep red and brown gullies and the multi-coloured needles like giant shark-teeth. Many of these have been given fanciful names and from the village you will be able to admire the Giants' Causeway and the Valley of the Fairies, with their breathtaking sheer faces of dazzling hues. You will see, too, grottoes and tunnels that have been used by hermits, bandits and drop-outs for centuries.

Be sure to take the 'Sentier des Aiguilles', a walk through the old quarries. It is only about a kilometre but allow up to an hour to stop and admire the colours and take photographs. The walk is informative too as noticeboards along the way explain the importance of ochre in the Apt region, describe the geological formation of the ore and detail how it was mined and transported.

Even in the village, the colours of ochre are evident. The light in the narrow streets gives off brilliant reflections and the occasional view of a green garden in between provides a brilliant contrast.

The village square is lively and filled with cafés, a popular meeting-place for both locals and visitors. The Town Hall and the house opposite are 18th century. The church was built in the 12th century but significant alterations were made in the 16th. One tower remains of the old ramparts.

If you want to know more detail, the Association Terre d'Ochres on the main street has a gallery describing the geology and history. In the church, the statue of Christ demonstrates the use of many of the colours of ochre while the buildings and the roofs of the once-fortified village are inevitably shades of red.

Mas de Garrigon

(HR)M-L *90 05 63 22   Route de Saint Saturnin d'Apt   H open all year; R cl. Sun p.m.; Mon; 15/11-27/12   All CC.*

It's the best place to stay around Roussillon if you don't mind paying a little extra and want a hotel plus restaurant with a pool, good food and some ambiance.

It really is an old mas, converted into a fine establishment but with only seven rooms priced at 650-850f, which is a bit steep. They also offer horse-back riding, a practice golf range and a garden.

Christiane Rech-Druart knows though that it is the food that is the main attraction and there are several dining rooms. Regional ingredients are used and you may expect to see on the menus those items that are in season – lamb, truffles and asparagus are typical examples. The cooking has a light touch and due care and attention are paid to every dish. Menus are 150f up. The pigéon aux figues is highly recommendable.

Résidence des Ochres

(H)S-M *90 05 60 50   Route de Gordes   Cl. 20/11-20/12; 20/1-28/2   Visa, CB.*

If you don't mind not having a restaurant on the premises, the Résidence has a strong following and is deservedly popular, especially with foreign visitors.

The 16 rooms are air-conditioned, priced at 250-350f.There is a terrace and a garden and some limited parking.

Mme Daniele Giop

(C)L *90 05 60 88   Mas Le Gramenier   Cl. Oct 31-Easter.*

Yet a third alternative is the chambre d'hôte. In a delightfully restored 18th-century mas, Mme Giop has five rooms, all good-sized with various sanitary alternatives. Prices are 350-450f and a meal is available in the evening at 110f.

The array of other facilities is impressive. There is a pool, a music room, a library, a television room, a lounge, a solarium, table-tennis and boules. You can't be bored here!

Restaurant David

(R)S-M *90 05 60 13   Place de la Poste   Cl. Mon; Tues; 3 weeks at end Nov-beginning Dec   All CC.*

Some think it's a bit expensive but it's good value and a meal in the garden in summer is a delight.

It's big and popular with locals, which has to be in its favour. The cooking is Provençal with an occasional imaginative touch such as pintade aux cerises and feuilleté de lotte Cardinale. The cassolette de moules is a favourite starter. Menus are 120f up. The Côtes-du-Ventoux wines at 60f are a bargain.

La Treille
(R)S-M   *90 05 64 47   Rue du Four   Cl. Mon (unless it's a holiday); 12/11-15/12 All CC.*

Small inside but there's a garden and a terrace. The cooking is described as 'Mediterranean' but there's a Middle East influence which shows up in the blinis and the grilled dishes and smoked fish. Menus start at 90f.

La Gourmandine
(R)S   *90 05 68 86   Cl. 15/10-15/3   Visa, CB.*

Right at the lower end of the price scale, La Gourmandine offers a menu at 60f which is simple but satisfying if you haven't brought a big

Saignon: La Pyramide

appetite that day. There are three small courses and the main course varies – it may be crêpes. If you are a little bit hungrier, the 75f menu is more filling. The nice terrace with its panoramic view is an added extra.

Map 3C **SAIGNON** 84400 (Vaucluse) 5 km SE of Apt

'A tiny community of 700 people suspended on the flank of an immense rock like a medallion on the shoulder of a Titan.' That was how the *Lubéron Echo* described Saignon a century ago. It still fits the description and the population has grown very little.

It is indeed a natural fortress, like many Provence villages. Three châteaux dominated the Valley of Apt in ages past – La Roche, Tartamolle and Crugière – but all are in ruins today.

The countryside around is very popular with campers and hikers. Consequently, the chambre d'hôte type of accommodation is very popular and there is a very good one here.

La Pyramide
(C)M   *90 74 46 86   Open all year   No CC.*

Hélène Guillaume is a Provençale herself and she believes in life, peace and serenity. Her approach is a holistic one and if you have any problems, she will be very happy to have you talk them out with her. (There's a service you don't get at a Hilton!)

Her four chambres d'hôtes are modern but in Provençal style and there is a large common area and a big breakfast area. The pool is new and there are panoramic views. Prices are 250f for a double room and 30f for breakfast.

Map 2C **SAINT ANDIOL** 13670 (Bouches-du-Rhône) 10 km W of Cavaillon

On the west bank of the Durance river, almost directly across from Cavaillon – not on the itinerary of too many visitors.

It does have the (almost) obligatory château though, built in the 16th century and since restored. The park around it is pleasant and there is a public walk to facilitate viewing.

Festivals

The local fête celebrates Saint Vincent (I tried to find out why not Saint Andiol but nobody knows). It is on July 14 which is very unoriginal. The 'charrettes' of Saint Eloi is another popular local fête and is in commemoration of the patron saint of blacksmiths. You will run into this saint and his celebrations all over this part of Provence. 'Charrettes' are gaily decorated horse-drawn wagons.

Le Berger des Abeilles
(H)S, (R)S-M   *90 95 01 91   Cl. Sun p.m.; Mon; Dec 2-18 and Feb   All CC.*

> This is really a restaurant with rooms. It is an old farmhouse, a very
> attractive building with six rooms, all fully equipped and only 260-
> 300f.
>   The restaurant is, of course, the principal attraction and brings in
> customers from all around. Nicole Grenier is the welcoming hostess
> and the cooking is original despite limiting its dishes to the produce
> of local farms. The lamb with spices is exceptionally tasty. Menus are
> 130, 180 and 220f; a meal here is a true pleasure.

Map 2B   **SAINTE CECILE-LES-VIGNES** 84290 (Vaucluse) 16 km N of
Orange

 Sat

> This is wine country and the vine dominates every aspect of life here.
>   Before 1789, the normal custom in the neighbouring wine-growing
> areas was that only the Lord of the Manor had the authority to set the
> day when the harvesting of the grapes could begin. Nobody had the
> right to commence picking until most of the grapes in the commune
> were well-matured. That tradition continues to flourish in this region,
> having been brought back by the Commanderie des Côtes du Rhône.
>   Villagers are solemnly reminded of the ban by a proclamation,
> made with full pomp and ceremony, in front of the statue of the Baron
> Le Roy, the first man to convince the local vintners of the need to
> combine their efforts in order to improve yield and quality.
>   Sainte Cécile is justly proud of its grenache noir, rosé and white,
> cinsault, syrah and clairette. You can visit and taste at the following:
>   Château Les Quatre Filles
>   La Grand'Ribe
>   Chantecôtes
>   Les Grands Bois

Festivals

> In July, Sainte Cécile thinks of something else besides wine when it
> puts on an exhibition of art and antiques. The 'Ban des Vendanges'
> proclamation is made in September, the date depending on the
> harvest. In November, there is the wine festival and musical concerts.

Le Relais
(HR)M-L   *90 30 84 39   50 Avenue Jean-Jaurès   R cl. Sun p.m.; Mon; 1/3-15/3;
1/10-15/10   Visa, CB.*

> Success breeds success – well, it certainly has for Edmond Depralon
> who continues to go from strength to strength.
>   The reason the room prices seem high (480-850f) is because of the
> fame of Le Relais, based on its restaurant which has drawn discerning
> diners for years. The exotic plants and flowers add to the elegance of

the dining room but of course it is the food people come for. Menus are 150, 200 and 275f and the emphasis is naturally on dishes cooked in wine. The ravioli au foie gras et au Beaumes-de-Venise makes superb use of one of the region's most renowned wines.

Map 3D   ST CYR-SUR-MER 83270 (Var) 8 km W of Bandol

The old town of St Cyr has a history going back to the great naval battle between Caesar and Pompey here in 49 BC. It was probably called Tauroentum then and the Musée de Tauroentum on the Route de la Madrague is one of St Cyr's most treasured possessions today. The museum is formed from two Roman villas which stood on the site and there are frescoes, vases, tombs, mosaics, lamps and numerous other objects well displayed throughout the three rooms. *The museum is open from the beginning of July to the end of September, from 3-7 every day except Tuesday and the rest of the year Saturday and Sunday only from 2-5.*

An unexpected sight, grabbing the attention, is the Statue of Liberty in front of the town hall on the Place Portalis. Plated in shiny gilt, it glitters in the sun. It is 2.5 metres tall, the same as the length of the forefinger of the original Statue of Liberty in New York harbour and was the work of the same sculptor, Frédéric Auguste Bartholdi.

It is the beaches though that are the big attraction here, just as they are in the neighbouring towns of Six Fours, La Seyne and La Ciotat. The gulf that protects St Cyr contains two kilometres of fine sandy beaches sloping gently into the water. Sailing, wind-surfing, fishing, waterskiing, scuba diving, sailboarding, jet skiing are all on offer. St Cyr is popular but is less frequented than the big name resorts along the Mediterranean coast and not as expensive.

For 26 centuries, the vineyards in St Cyr have been making good wine and they are still doing so. First under the Greeks, then the Romans, then under the patronage of Louis XV and today they have the Apellation d'Origine Controllée of Bandol. The Domaine du Cagueloup has been in the same family for five generations and the Château des Baumelles has a cellar dating from the 15th century. You may taste and buy at both of these (they are open every day) as well as at the Domaine de Frégate, La Bastide Blanche and Domaine des Salettes.

The Chocolaterie de St Cyr at 42 Avenue Jean Jaurès sells some of the best chocolates you have ever tasted.

In addition to the weekly general market, St Cyr has a market selling produce direct from the farms every Tuesday and Friday.

Festivals

The annual fête begins on May 27 and there is a cherry festival on Ascension Day.

Just west of St Cyr is Aqualand with a huge swimming pool with artificial waves and lots of water sports and games.

Grand Hôtel
(HR)M   *94 26 23 0   Les Lecques Plage   Cl. 10/10-10/5   All CC.*

A 58 room hotel in the grand style, about 200 metres from the beach.
Exceptionally beautiful grounds with two tennis courts. The rooms
cost 300-720f depending on the season.
   The restaurant welcomes visitors as well as guests and all can enjoy
the panoramic view. A la carte is the best way to order and will cost
around 150f.

Hôtel Chanteplage
(HR)S-M   *94 26 16 55   Les Lecques Plage H cl. 15/11-1/3; R cl. 15/9-15/6 Visa, CB.*

A more modestly priced alternative to the Grand Hôtel but naturally
more simple accommodation. Mme Marte has 20 rooms at 248-350f,
or demi-pension at 265-295f. Cooking is regional in style and makes
full use of available seafood. Menus are 55-120f. There is a garage.

Map 2B   **SAINT DIDIER** 84210 (Vaucluse) 8 km SE of Carpentras

---

You have probably lost count of the ruined châteaux you have seen in
Provence by now. Saint Didier will prove to be a refreshing change for
its château has not only been restored but it has been serving
humankind for well over a century.
   Built in the 15th century, it was enlarged in the 18th. After being
bought by the Marquis de la Garde in the early 19th century, it was
converted into a hydrotherapy centre and has gone from strength to
strength ever since. It is now well-known throughout France and
brings patients from all over Europe for the treatment of diseases of
the nerves and of the digestive tract.
   If you are careful, you can visit it and admire the purity of its
Renaissance style, although organised visits are not offered. You feel
that the environment could not possibly be improved upon for its
contribution towards recovery.
   Sitting on top of a hill south of the village, the magnificent seminary
of Sainte Garde is visible from afar. The original chapel was built in
1666 and given the name of Notre Dame de Sainte Garde and next to
it was built a retreat home for missionary monks. The Revolution
turned it into a glassworks then, in 1833, it was re-built as a home for
young novices. It now belongs to the church of Notre Dame de Vie in
Venasque.

Festivals

The Cherry Fair is a picturesque fête, held every year from May 15 to
June 15. Throughout September and October there is another daily
fair, this time a grape festival. The village fête of Saint Didier is on the
first Sunday in July.

Les Trois Colombes
(HR)S-M   *90 66 07 01   Avenue des Garrigues   Cl. 15/1-28/2   All CC.*

In farm-house style but not an old building. Nonetheless, Les Trois
Colombes has become a popular, almost renowned, hotel and
restaurant within the past ten years and everybody who stays here
raves about it and comes back.

The 25 rooms are large, nicely furnished and quiet. At 290-360f, they
are extremely good value. In the season, demi-pension is obligatory at
280-315f per person. There is a pool and tennis – rare luxuries at such
a reasonable price.

M. Montorfano keeps up the standards in the restaurant just as he
does in the hotel and in the summer, you can dine in the garden or on
the terrace. Menus are only 90-150f and the l'agneau à la purée d'ail is
delicious. The magret de canard is a dish you see on restaurant menus
throughout the south of France but M. Montorfano had combined
simplicity with ingenuity and serves it with lavender-flavoured honey
– thus utilising two of the region's products.

Map 4D   **SAINT MANDRIER** 83430 (Var) 4 km S of Toulon (by sea)

There aren't many islands you can drive to but Saint Mandrier is one
of them. The saint was formerly a soldier in the army of Alaric the
Goth and when he converted to Christianity in the 6th century, he
came here to the island as a hermit.

In those days, Saint Mandrier was truly an island. It is so close to the
mainland that, bit by bit, it has become joined, first by wooden
causeways and now by a single road. It was in the Middle Ages that
people first came here to settle. Then in the 18th century when the
Hospital of Saint Louis was built to accommodate plague victims,
convicts from the Toulon prison were brought as orderlies. It was
these convicts who built the 'new hospital' and its chapel that you can
see today – they are built too in the form of a Greek temple.

Don't expect too much from Saint Mandrier. The eastern part of the
island is a Franco-Italian air and naval base and there are miles of high
stone walls preventing you from seeing whatever is going on behind
them. Don't get too excited by that either – the answer is probably
'not much'. The occasional helicopter clatters in low across the water
and there are always several warships at anchor and clearly visible
from the restaurants around the bay. There isn't much work going on
though and as a result there are no cranes or high structural
assemblies as at Toulon and most naval bases. Even the warships –
some of them quite large and many quite old – are unadorned so that
they are merely grey shapes against the backdrop of the hills of the
mainland.

About those hills ... with the mainland so close, the effect of an
island is largely lost. The port of Saint Mandrier is the hub of the
island and from it all you can see are hills in all directions. Small
pleasure boats cram the port and it is pleasant to sit by the water in

one of the numerous cafés. The last of the island's hotels has now
closed so that you can only make a day trip here. Six Fours and La
Seyne are both only ten minutes away and both have plenty of
accommodation. There is a frequent boat service to Toulon from the
port if you feel like a short and smooth sight-seeing ride although it
operates strictly as a transport service.

Les Flots Bleus

(R)S   *94 63 97 16   Quai Jean Jaurès   Cl. Tues   Visa, CB.*

The last of Saint Mandrier's hotels to close, Les Flots Bleus is still
operating as a restaurant. Dining is indoors but you have views across
the port. The emphasis is on seafood and, for something unusual, you
should try their calamares à la Romana. Menus at 80 and 115f.

Le Corsaire

(R)S-M   *94 63 97 93   Quai Jean Jaurès   Visa, CB.*

In addition to the dining room which has views across the port, there
is a terrace by the water's edge just a few feet from the boats. Seafood
is the order of the day (every day) and bouillabaisse is the speciality at
200f per person with dessert included in the price. Several interesting
dishes are on the menu such as cuisses de grenouilles, sauce citron
vert at 59f. There are menus at 80, 120 and 160f.

La Presqu'Ile

(R)S   *Quai Jean Jaurès   Visa, CB.*

A smart little place with only a handful of tables but with the walls
covered by large and striking paintings. On the water's edge is a
terrace and a limited menu of light meals. The gratin of mussels at 45f
is highly recommendable. They are served in shell dishes and the
sauce is tangy. There are steaks, cutlets and the most expensive dish
is the flambéed gambas at 110f.

   A disappointment is the absence of white wine from the list – almost
unforgivable in a region of vineyards.

Restaurant Pizza Pacha

(R)S   *Quai Jean Jaurès   Visa, CB.*

A small and cosy place with views across the port and a small terrace
by the water's edge. The spectacularly inexpensive offering here is a
three-course menu at 62f which includes a quarter bottle of wine.
There is also an 82f menu if you feel in a spending mood. An
extensive range of pizzas is also available at 40-50f.

Map 1C **SAINTES-MARIES-DE-LA-MER** 13460 (Bouches-du-Rhône)
38 km S of Arles, 129 km W of Marseille

(M) *Mon and Fri*

Despite its population of only 2,000, this is one of the best-known
names in the South of France – because of an event of 2,000 years
ago which may not have happened at all.

But that's enough of reality – legend and tradition are paramount in
Provence and nowhere more so than here at Saintes-Maries-de-la-
Mer. There were three Marys – the sister of the Virgin Mary, Mary
Magdalene, and the mother of the Apostles James and John. Directly
after the crucifixion, they left Palestine to escape persecution. With
them came Lazarus, his sister Martha, Sarah, a black servant and two
others later to become saints, Maximin and Sidoine. Their small boat
had no oars and no food; they were eventually washed ashore on a
beach on the south coast of France.

The group separated. Martha became the saviour of Tarascon and
vanquished the Tarasque monster, Lazarus went to Marseille,
Maximin and Sidoine to Aix, Mary Magdalene to Sainte Baume. The
other two Marys remained here in the place where they had landed.
When they died, they were buried under the church which was built
on the spot where their boat had beached. This fortress-church stands
today, girt by windowless walls and as formidable now as it must
have appeared to the Saracen invaders it was built to repel.

The tomb rapidly became a venerated place and a cult developed
which has persisted through twenty centuries. Known locally as 'The
Saints', this small town is the destination of a remarkable number of
pilgrims who come here twice a year, on May 21 and 22 for the feast
of Marie, the sister of the Virgin Mary, and on the Sunday in October
which falls nearest to the 22nd.

One of the remarkable features of the first of these pilgrimages, the
one in May, is that gypsies from all over Europe attend it. This makes
it particularly colourful and unusual. The gypsies come to worship in
the crypt the relics of their own saint, Sarah, the black maidservant of
the two Marys. The statues of the saints and their bones are carried in
triumphant procession out of the sea by a group of 'gardians', the
cowboys of the Camargue who guard their herds of tough, half-wild
cattle which roam the swampy marshlands of the Rhône delta.
Arlésiennes are there too in dainty lace caps. There are processions in
the streets, Provençal bullfights, displays of horseback riding and
dancing in gay farandoles to gypsy music.

This is one of the most colourful festivals in the South of France and
one which seems to attract more and more visitors every year. The
authorities have had to adopt strict measures to prevent it getting out
of hand. At present, these appear to be effective.

From the practical point of the view of the normal visitor though,
Saintes-Maries-de-la-Mer is a holiday resort and has everything to
offer that that expression implies – including beaches. There are
streets of white holiday houses and scores of stands and stalls selling

souvenirs – nothing very different except perhaps the cowboy hats. Gypsy music is played in many restaurants and bars and flamenco dancing and guitars abound. Stars come from Spain to perform and Manitas de Plata and Jose Reyes have appeared here.

There is a small bullring and next to the church is the Musée Baroncelli, put together by a local Marquis and an ardent admirer of Mistral. As a poet in Avignon, he became enamoured of the life of the 'Gardians' and eventually went and lived as one. The museum is devoted to Camargue folklore, with Arlésienne costumes, photographs of the earlier gypsy festivals and the flora and fauna of the region. *Open 9-12 and 2-5, closed on Wednesday and all October.*

The drive to Saintes-Maries-de-la-Mer is about 40 kilometres from Arles across the sandy flats of the Camargue, a salty wasteland of lagoons and marshy plains, tufted with rough spiky grass and cut through with shallow canals and streams. It is flat to the horizon in all directions and part of the Parc Naturel Régional de Camargue, one of the largest wildlife preserves in Europe. To the south, the Etang de Vaccarès contains many unusual birds and rare plants and flowers. The only buildings to be seen are the occasional thatched cottages of the gardians and the odd ranch with the small half-wild horses, used to running in water and the black fighting bulls.

If you are sensitive to mosquito bites, be warned that this area is lethal. Near the coast and in Les Saintes-Maries itself you are safe, for these insects don't like salt air, but the Camargue is a vast breeding ground for mosquitoes which may well be more ferocious than any you have ever encountered before.

The *Tiki III* is a paddle steamer carrying 200 passengers which runs all the year round. It leaves every 1½ hours in the summer months and the trip goes up-river from the mouth of the Petit Rhône, on the Route d'Aigues Mortes about two kilometres west of Les Saintes-Maries. The steamer costs 60f and takes an hour and twenty minutes. Smaller boats leave from the Port Gardian just west of the bullring and offer similar trips.

Riding is offered at many of the ranches and you can hire a horse by the hour or all day. Gardians lead parties on rides through the marshes.

Festivals

With all this emphasis on tourist attractions, it is not surprising that here are a considerable number of festivals throughout the year. There are bullfights at Easter and Pentecost (the bull is not killed in this Provençal bullfight), horse parades on the third Sunday in June, at the end of July a fête of Mistral inspiration, a fair on August 15 and midnight mass at Christmas brings in gardians and shepherds.

The slightly tacky seaside atmosphere of Les Saintes-Maries-de-la-Mer has not prevented some hotels from charging 1,000f or more for a room. The Mas de la Fouque, Le Pont des Bannes and Le Mas du Tadorne are all in this category but they do offer every luxury. For more down-to-earth prices, the choice depends on where you want to be located. You can be on the seafront, in the town or out of town.

On the sea-front

Le Clamador
(H)S-M   *90 97 84 26   Route de l'Amarée   Cl. 10/10-1/4   Visa, CB.*

A simple and quiet hotel with views over the port and across the Etang – not an easy combination of features to find here. There is a bar, a patio and a garden. The 20 rooms are fully equipped and modern in comfort, 270-320f. There is parking and a garage. No restaurant but plenty of places to eat close by.

Le Galoubet
(H)M   *90 97 82 17   Route de Cacharel   Open all year   Visa, CB.*

A nice, seaside-type hotel, close to beaches and the port. There are 20 rooms at 280-380f and the style is Camargue-rustic. There is a pool and a bar and parking.

Amphores
(H)S   *90 97 80 31   1 Avenue Gilbert Leroy   Open all year   Visa, CB.*

A neat white hotel with 16 rooms and views out to sea. At 200f, the rooms are very good value. Parking but no garage and no restaurant.

Le Bord de Mer
(HR)S-M   *90 97 89 56   19 Avenue de la Plage   Cl. 30/10-15/3   Visa, CB.*

A smart place right on the sea front. There is a garden and this one has a restaurant. The 22 rooms are 280f and menus start at 70f, with a good range of choices.

In the town

Méditerranée
(H)S   *90 97 82 09   4 Blvd Frédéric Mistral   Cl. 31/12-1/3   No CC.*

Centrally located and reasonably priced with 14 rooms at 160-220f. There is a garden but no parking and no restaurant.

Le Brûleur de Loups
(R)M   *Avenue Gilbert Leroy   Cl. Tues p.m.; Wed except Aug and Sept; 15/11-15/3 All CC.*

There are dozens of small restaurants and cafés, pizzerias and hamburger places but not many good restaurants. This is one of the better choices, with a terrace looking to the beaches. Regional seafood is the style here, with oysters, langoustines and daurade almost always on the menu. A la carte is a good way to order and you figure on paying 150-200f for a very enjoyable meal.

Out of town

Mas des Riegès,
(H)M   *90 97 85 07   Route de Cacharel   Cl. 7/11-19/3   Visa, CB.*

Barely a kilometre out of town, the mas is truly an old farm-house now renovated, with a pool and garden. The 16 rooms are 390f and are well furnished. There is parking but no restaurant.

Etrier Camarguais
(HR)M   *90 97 81 14   Chemin Bas des Launes   Cl. 15/11-1/4   All CC.*

One of the best-known and most popular hostelleries in the Saintes-Maries area. The 27 rooms are in several buildings scattered around a pool and tennis courts. There is a large terrace, a sauna and a discotheque.

François and Françoise Brouzet try very hard to offer their guests all they might want. Horse-back riding can be organised and seminars are held.

Mangio Fango
(HR)M   *90 97 80 56   Route d'Arles   Cl. 4/11-21/3   All CC.*

A delightful small hotel with only 10 rooms, all charmingly decorated with their own patio. There is a garden, a pool and a parking area. Rooms are 320-450f and in the small restaurant meals are served to residents only at 150-190f.

Le Boumian
(HR)M   *90 97 81 15   Route d'Arles   Open all year   Visa, CB, Diners.*

An unusual place as it is a conversion from an old cabana used by 'gardians'. The extra atmosphere justifies the 490-550f price of the 28 rooms furnished in Provençal style. In the summer season, demi-pension is obligatory at 450-650f.

The rooms here are around a patio overlooking the pool. Horse-back riding is available by the hour. Food in the restaurant is Camarguais style and this means that rice is a common accompaniment, as it grows readily in the swampy surroundings. The local asparagus is excellent. Menus start at 75f but à la carte you could spend up to 200f.

There are several chambres d'hôte, especially in Place Portalet near the church, but most do not accept bookings for one night only. An exception is Paulette Roux at 16 Rue Georges Bizet, who has only one room with toilet and shower at 180f.

Map 3B   **SAINT MARTIN-DE-CASTILLON** 84750 (Vaucluse) 12 km E
of Apt

Ⓜ *Wed*

This area is rich in Roman and mediaeval remains. Coins and medals
are still found from time to time, particularly after heavy rains. On
some is the head of Apollo and some have been dated as belonging to
the second century BC.

The old Domitian road ran right through here and this ancient
highway later became the pilgrim route to Compostela. Between the
highway and the spur of the hill is the ruined Priory of Saint Pierre de
Castillon. Many famous personages stopped at the priory, including
Saint Francis of Assisi and Martin Luther. The cemetery of the priory is
a ruin too but some of the gravestones have decipherable words.

Still standing though is the Chapel of Nosto Damo de Coureno
(Notre Dame de Courennes), just north of Saint Martin. It has a
particularly beautiful cloister and restoration has been done with taste
and care. The chapel is still a destination for pilgrimages in time of
drought.

Festivals

This is a village where you may still see the 'fieloas', a local equivalent
of the traditional Provençal fête of the 'fielouso' as it is called in
Mistral-influenced areas. Some other villages have their own versions,
often differing in detail but essentially it is a fête in which the boys of
the village dress in girls' clothing, usually long white robes and
bonnets, then sing and dance through the village streets waving
coloured paper stringers and lanterns. The most likely time to see the
fieloas is on the occasion of the village fête on August 15.

Lou Caleu
(HR)S   *90 75 28 88   Open every day and all year   All CC.*

Tucked away in 16 acres of woods, this is a simple and inexpensive
stopover in a quiet and pastoral environment.

M et Mme Rondard have 16 rooms at 240-300f. Demi-pension per
person is 250-300f. There is a pool and tennis and private parking.
Meals are good local fare and generous portions. Menus are 75-150f.
Watch out for seminars though.

Les Quatres Saisons
(R)S   *90 75 22 39   On RN 100   Cl. 3/1-15/2   All CC.*

A large terrace and further seating in a shady park provides the setting
for a grill where various meats, chicken and fish are cooked over wood
and expertly seasoned. There is parking in the shade and menus start
at 70f.

Map 2B   ST MICHEL-DE-FRIGOLET 13690 (Bouches-du-Rhône)
7 km N of Tarascon, 18 km S of Avignon

 Fri

Between the Durance and the Rhône rivers, St Michel-de-Frigolet is like a small island surrounded by fields of thyme and lavender. Its name comes from 'ferigoulo', the Provence word for thyme.

Half a day's march to the south is the Monastery of Montmajour and it was from there that the Benedictine monks came in the 10th century to found a monastic centre to serve as a stopping place for the pilgrims on their way to Santiago de Compostela.

In the 12th century, St Michel declined and fell into ruins, remaining that way until the 18th century when it was re-built as a school.

Many well-known personages attended it but the most famous was probably Frédéric Mistral. It was then bought and re-built as a monastery by an order known as 'Prémontrés'.

It can be visited today and you will see that little of the mediaeval appearance remains but the effect is not displeasing. There is the cloister, the restored 12th-century church and the sanctuary of Notre Dame-du-Bon-Rémède. There is a Black Virgin dating from the 12th century and carved from fruit wood which has been credited with stopping the spread of cholera, and a small museum with a collection of pharmacy jars from the 18th century.

Festivals

The Feast of Saint Eloi is held on the last Sunday in July and there is a local fête on the second Sunday in September. On Bastille Day, July 14, there is a running of the bulls, although small cows are really used. At Christmas, Midnight Mass is accompanied by the presentation of a baby lamb in a beribboned cart and attended by girls in Arlésienne costumes and 'gardians' (Camargue cowboys). Easter Sunday also has a folkloric festival with songs and dances and blessing of the horses.

Nearby Graveson is the best place to go for hotels and restaurants.

Map 2C   ST. REMY-DE-PROVENCE 13210 (Bouches-du-Rhône)
18 km W of Cavaillon

 Wed

If I were pressed to name one town as my favourite in Provence, it would have to be Saint Rémy. It would be difficult to leave out a few others but Saint Rémy is unsurpassed for natural charm and an unspoiled air of mediaeval grace. It is one of those few places which can successfully combine attractions for the tourist and still be a living, everyday community.

Strolling through the narrow streets that lead off the boulevard shaded by plane trees, chestnut trees and African lotus is a joy in itself and you can follow the traces of the old ramparts. The old town is concentrated in a small circle, making it easy to see on foot. This is not entirely from choice as parking is very difficult – it's best to accept it and leave your car in the first street parking you see.

Nostradamus, the famous prophet, was born here in 1503 in a house on the Rue Hoche. It is currently being renovated and should be open to visits soon. Certainly, it should be open before 1999 which is the year forecast by Nostradamus as seeing 'the king of terror come down from the sky' – believed by some to indicate an invasion of earth by extra-terrestrials.

The former Hôtel Mistral de Mondragon on Place Favier now houses the Musée des Alpilles and has some well-presented displays of folklore, folk art, geology, lapidary and palaeontology. A separate room shows the equipment used in the manufacture of wool, the industry which made many of Saint Rémy's citizens rich. *The museum is open every day 10-12 and 2-6 in April, May, June, September and October; every day from 10-12 and 3-8 in July and August; and every day from 10-12 and 2-5 in November and December. It is closed on May 1, December 25 and all January, February and March.*

Other famous names are associated with Saint Rémy. Gounod lived in the Hôtel de la Ville Verte while writing his opera Mireille. Gertrude Stein lived here for more than a year while writing Capital Capitals, Saints and Singing and Lend a Hand. Joseph Roumanille, 19th-century Provençal poet and founder of the 'Felibrige' movement, was born here.

The archaeological museum is in the Hôtel de Sade and on the Place Favier near the Musée des Alpilles. (The same ticket admits to both.) It contains exhibits excavated in the nearby ruins of Glanum (see the separate entry under 'Glanum'). *Open every day from March 31 to December 31, the hours vary daily.*

The great white classical church of Saint Martin stands on the Place de la République. It has been reconstructed several times and the only part remaining of interest is the steeple which was built by Pope John XXII in 1330.

On Rue Estrine is Hôtel Estrine, Centre d'Art. The attractive 18th-century building is worth seeing for itself alone but it also contains an exhibition of contemporary artists. There is a permanent exhibition of the works of another famous resident of Saint Rémy – Vincent van Gogh. *Open every day from 10-12 and 3-7 in summer, 2-6 in winter.*

Few who visit Saint Rémy will not want to go to the old priory of Saint Paul-du-Mausolée, built in the 12th century but used as an insane asylum since 1605. It is the one in which Van Gogh had himself put away in 1889 while living in Arles. Room number 13 which he occupied has a magnificent view across the fields towards the Alpilles but the sympathetic Doctor Peyron allowed him to go outside the grounds to paint.

Don't be alarmed when you first glimpse bearded, beret-wearing painters busy at canvases in the grounds around the grim grey walls. They are painting exactly the same scenes that van Gogh painted. He produced over 150 paintings and drawings in barely a year here including many well-known works such as *The Iris, Starry Night* and *Wheatfield with Cypress*. His *Corridor of the St. Paul Hospital* depicts a row of receding arches which suggest the serenity and security he found in the shelter of the asylum despite his mental suffering. The building is still a psychiatric clinic today. *The church and cloisters can be visited 9-12 and 2-6, entry free.*

Festivals

Several traditional fêtes are held in Saint Rémy. On May 1, is the 'Carreto dis Ase' in which folklore groups accompany a 'Charrette', a gaily decorated wagon pulled by twenty mules. On Pentecost Monday, the biggest festival of the year sees the 'Fête de la Transhumance'. In this vivid ceremony, the shepherds who were about to take their flocks north for the summer would parade their entire troup of animals – horses, donkeys, mules, deer as well as their wagons. Today, with a declining necessity to go to the Alpine foothills, they cross the town several times instead to simulate departure.

On August 15 there is a 'Carreto Ramado'. Wagons are brilliantly decorated with wheat, straw, fruit and vegetables and drawn by thirty or forty horses and mules in ornate collars and festoons and garlands made of coloured paper. Riders on horseback accompany them – and so do scores of amateur photographers.

The last Sunday in September brings the bull to Saint Rémy and there are bullfights and running of the bulls through the streets, the day ending with a fireworks display.

Throughout the summer season, there are folk dance groups and bullfights. At the end of July there are wine festivals and display and sale of the products of local artisans.

Whether you buy at such displays or at the local markets and stores or even if you are in a restaurant in Saint Rémy, you will want to sample the local wines, the Côteaux d'Aix-en-Provence. Watch out for the Domaine des Terres Blanches which is a fine white and very inexpensive. The Mas de la Tuilière Vieille and the Mas Hauvette are also extremely drinkable.

Celebrities are just beginning to move into Saint Rémy. Princess Caroline has recently bought a 99- year lease on a farm-house nearby. Jacques Grange, decorator to the stars and Pierre Berge, head of the Paris Opera, are two more recent arrivals. It is still too early to say 'There goes the neighbourhood' for this handful of big buyers can't affect such an area but it is an indication of the charm of Saint Rémy and it is a town you must visit.

Le Castellet des Alpilles
(HR)S-M   *90 92 07 21   6 Place Mireille   H cl. 31/10-Palm Sunday; R cl. Mon; Tues lunch; 25/10-Palm Sunday   All CC.*

Just out of the busy heart of town and on the Avenue Pasteur going south towards the ruins of Glanum. This is a serene three-storey hotel,

St Rémy: Le Castellet des Alpilles

casual, not fussy; it has an enclosed garden in front, a garage and parking. All very convenient. Smallish bedrooms cost 300-405f.

The restaurant is deservedly popular. There are menus at 115 and 165f and you might select as the main course either the mignons de porcelet or selle d'agneau au thym et l'ail. If you feel hungry and expansive, there is a five-course gastronomic menu at 225f with dishes like medaillons of lotte as the fish course and filet de boeuf as the meat course.

Les Antiques
(H)M   *90 92 03 02   15 Avenue Pasteur   Cl. 20/10-12/4   Visa, CB.*

Just on the edge of the town centre and heading south to the ruins of Glanum is this very pleasant hotel with a garden and a pool. There is parking and a garage and the 27 rooms are good-sized and nicely furnished in soothing colours. Most look out on to the garden. Prices are 330-450f.

Château de Roussan

(H)M   *90 92 11 63   Route de Tarascon   H cl. 30/10-15/3; R (dinners only) cl. Wed
Visa, CB.*

I wouldn't have included the Château de Roussan in this book a year ago as it didn't have a restaurant and when a hotel is two kilometres out of town, many guests consider it just too inconvenient to go out to eat. Now that one has been added after numerous visitors have made the point, this is a highly recommendable stop.

About three hundred years old, the château is the type built for living rather than fighting. It is one of the finest châteaux-hotels in the south of France and its setting amid 15 acres of flower gardens, pools and antique statues is superb. The strutting peacocks add a mediaeval touch and so does the knowledge that Nostradamus once lived in the old farm-house in the grounds.

The 12 bedrooms are spacious and furnished beautifully with antiques but with, of course, completely modernised bathrooms. They are priced at 360-850f but the demi-pension is a better bet at 545-935f. The food is typically Provençal with such dishes as soupe de poissons and escalope à la basilic.

Auberge de la Reine Jeanne

(HR)S   *90 92 15 33   12 Boulevard Mirabeau   Cl. 22/12-15/3   Visa, CB.*

Easy to miss – right in the heart of town but tucked away at an angle with the entrance behind iron gates. It's worth finding though and you cross the stone-flagged courtyard covered by an archway of vines.

The 11 rooms are only 250f because the emphasis is on the restaurant where over a hundred people can (and do) eat in the summer, half of them on the shady terrace. In the dining room, the old stone wall and the black-beamed fireplace give an authentic air that goes well with the Provençal cooking. Menus are 120 and 175f (there is also one at 65f at lunch). The Tournedos Wellington is an unusual and enjoyable dish.

Hôtel du Cheval Blanc

(H)S   *90 92 09 28   6 Avenue Fauconnet   Open all year   Visa, CB.*

A smart, three-storey, green-shuttered building just as you enter the heart of Saint Rémy. It sits back from the road with a cinema next door, a few local shops across the street and the restaurant La France next to the cinema.

There is parking in front and a garage. The 22 rooms all have TV and are priced at a modest 200-250f. There is a garden but no restaurant.

Le Café des Arts
(HR)S   *90 92 08 50   30 Boulevard Victor Hugo   Cl. 28/1-3/3   All CC.*

All things to all travellers – bar, café, bistro, hotel and restaurant. The remarkable thing is that M. Caritoux does a good job of all of these at Les Arts. The 17 rooms are not large but more than adequate at 160-270f. There is a garage and a terrace for summer eating.

The emphasis is on small, light meals but you can enjoy boeuf à la camarguaise too. Menus at 70 and 80f during the week, three-course meals at 130 and 160f on week-ends.

Grand Hôtel de Provence
(H)S   *90 92 06 27   36 Boulevard Victor Hugo   Cl. 1/10-1/4   Visa, CB.*

You'll think you've got the wrong place – surely this grim, grey, massive old structure can't be a hotel? It is – and a very reasonable one, if you can ignore the outside.

Gilbert Tallet has a rather eccentric approach to hotel-keeping and you won't find the welcome mat out in any way. Once you're past all that though and installed in one of the 28 rooms which are only 150f and in the heart of Saint Rémy, you'll know you've got a bargain. The garden out in the back is delightful and the lounge is large, attractive and has TV. There is parking and a garage.

La France
(R)S-M   *90 92 11 56   2 Avenue Fauconnet   Cl. Mon; 11/11-31/1   Visa, CB.*

M. Devietti has a busy and popular restaurant here just out of the busy centre of Saint Rémy. It is next door but one to the Hôtel du Cheval Blanc and, understandably, most of their guests come here to eat – not just for the convenience but for the food.

It's an all-glassed-in building, a sort of fin-de-siècle brasserie, not posh just down to earth like most of Saint Rémy.

It's impossible to leave La France feeling either hungry or dissatisfied. There are lots of local dishes especially those which depend on what might be in season and what the hunters have bagged. The rabbit dishes are excellent and the civet de porcelet is outstanding. All appetites are catered for with a four-course meal at 70f, a five-course meal at 92f and a six-course meal at 130f.

L'Olivier
(R)S   *90 92 10 19   21 Boulevard Mirabeau   Cl. Tues   Visa, CB.*

Almost a brasserie atmosphere here, with a cheerful smile from the staff and good food at very reasonable prices. I had the oeufs Mimosa then the pintade, with a delicious little mixture of tomatoes and courgettes, plus a millefeuille for dessert, all for 65f. A really fancy four-course meal can be selected at 120f. The aïoli is known far and wide. The Domaine de Terres Blanches wines at around 50f are very good.

Le Canard sur la Table
(R)S-M   *90 92 61 05   53 Rue Carnot   Cl. Wed lunch   Visa, CB.*

Looking for a slightly more up-market restaurant in Saint Rémy is not too easy, for the whole town is geared to the casual. If that is your search, though, try this one.

The white walls emphasise the red table decorations and there are only seven tables so it is small and cosy. Menus at 90, 150 and 220f cover the range of almost anything you might want in the way of Provençal cooking. I can never resist the gambas à la marseillaise. The reasonably priced Côteaux d'Aix wines go excellently with them.

La Gousse d'Ail
(R)S-M   *90 92 16 87   57 Rue Carnot   Cl. Wed   All CC.*

Falling nicely in between the casual and the up-market, La Gousse d'Ail has been a favourite with the locals for many years.

The rosbif de taureau hardly needs translating. If you are a beef lover, you will appreciate the slightly different taste of the bull's meat. Different dishes appear every evening – an unusually ambitious undertaking but the quality doesn't suffer and there is a genuine attempt to find dishes that are a little out of the ordinary.

Map 2C   **SALON-DE-PROVENCE** 13300 (Bouches-du-Rhône) 35 km NW of Aix-en-Provence

---

This pleasant market town is mainly famous as the home of Nostradamus, the prophet of the 16th century who predicted the French Revolution and World War II, even identifying a 'Hister' as being responsible for starting it. The name was close, you must admit, for four hundred years earlier.

The Porte de l'Horloge, the main gateway with its chiselled date of 1630, takes you into the old town where Nostradamus' house has been restored. The seer was born in Saint Rémy but lived here for the last 19 years of his life. Open 10-12 and 3-7 every day from May to September except Tuesday.

The other sight in Salon is the massive Château de l'Empéri, a towering, glowering fortress which dominates the town. It was built from the 10th to the 13th centuries, originally as the residence of the Archbishops of Arles. In subsequent years many famous personages lived here – Roi René, Cathérine de Medicis, King Francis I, Louis XIII, Louis XIV and Cardinal Mazarin.

Today the château is a museum and displays eight centuries of art, architecture and history. Costumes, weapons, paintings, uniforms, documents, manuscripts and about thirty full-size models, many mounted on horse-back, illustrate French military history from Louis XIV to the First World War. *Open 10-12 and 2.30-6.30 every day except Tuesdays and Jan 1, May 1 and Dec 25.*

In July and August, the château holds a drama festival. Of most interest to the visitor is the historical re-enactment of an incident in 1564. With France wracked by religious wars, plague and famine, Cathérine de Medici took her son, King Charles IX, on a journey across the country to consult Nostradamus and learn from him the future of the country. The event is reconstructed by more than 400 actors in full costume – knights and nobles, farmers and hunters, soldiers and villagers. Known as 'The Renaissance of Nostradamus', the pageant lasts four days.

For shopping purposes, the Cours Victor Hugo has modern boutiques and stalls on the pavement which sell everything from strings of garlic to black lace underwear.

There are plenty of places to stay and to eat. The prestigious Abbaye de Sainte Croix, just east of Salon on the D16, is one of my favourites from the past but now that it costs 1,000f a night, I have to think twice about including it here.

Abbaye de Sainte Croix
(HR)L   *90 58 24 55   Val de Cuech   Cl. 31/10-1/3; R also cl. Mon lunch   All CC.*

All right, I've thought about it and just can't leave it out. It is a superb place to stay and to eat. It is expensive but there is no question that the value is there.

The Abbaye is about 5 kilometres east of Salon on the other side of the autoroute. Snug and secure in its fifty acres of wooded park, the 12th-century abbey has been converted into one of the finest hotels in Europe with a panoramic view from its terraces of the whole region.

The 5 apartments are spacious at 1040-1625f, the 19 rooms are smallish as they were once monks' cells and they are 520-920f. All are furnished with antiques in exquisite taste. Most have terraces or private gardens.

There is a large pool, ten tennis courts and horse-back riding can be organised.

The restaurant is now presided over by Pascal Morel and the cooking is classical Provençal. There are frequent original touches such as the filets de rouget à la vanille and the pigeons en cocotte à l'ail. Menus range from 195f, through 330 and 450 to 480f (well, I did say it could be expensive!). Dining out on the terrace in the summer is an experience to remember.

Hôtel de la Poste
(HR)S   *90 56 01 94   Cours Carnot   Visa, CB.*

A very convenient location if you want to be right in the heart of Salon. The Hôtel de la Poste is at the beginning of the Cours Victor Hugo and in front of the Tour de l'Horloge. The public rooms are small but have TV. The 27 bedrooms are not large either but priced fairly at 100-220f.

Grand Hôtel d'Angleterre
(H)S   *90 56 01 10   Cours Carnot   All CC.*

A pleasing Provençal building, right in town, below the huge clock tower. The 26 rooms are 240-290f and very good value now that the entire hotel has been renovated. All have bath or shower and colour TV. There is no restaurant, but a garage is a welcome feature.

Hôtel du Midi
(H)S   *90 53 34 67   518 Allée de Craponne   Open all year   All CC.*

Located on the main road going south out of Salon, the modern Hôtel du Midi is contemporary but a good bet for reasonably sized and well-equipped rooms. There are 27 of them at 150-240f. Not much else here – just good and reasonable rooms.

Domaine Roquerousse
(HR)M   *90 59 50 11   Route d'Avignon   Cl. Christmas   All CC.*

An ancient manor-house, 4 km out of Salon on the road to Avignon, set in a vast wooded park which is put to good use by hunting parties at the week-ends.

The results of la chasse appear on the table for dinner at very reasonable prices, considering the charm and distinction of the setting. Menus starting at 72f feature all manner of game in due season; the 105f version is particularly generous in its presentation of well-cooked venison as well as partridge, pheasant and pigeon.

Accommodation is in ten comfortable and well-equipped bungalows, set peacefully (except for those week-ends) in the grounds. 220-350f seems a bargain for such style. An annexe is being built, so enquire about alternative accommodation.

➤Mas du Soleil
(HR)M   *90 56 06 53   38 Chemin Saint-Comé   Open all year   All CC.*

Any previous visitor to Salon who has done any homework at all on places to eat will be familiar with the name of Francis Robin. His 'Restaurant Robin' at 1 Boulevard Georges Clémenceau has been one of the top eateries for twenty years and Francis himself has been 'Jeune Restaurateur de France', 'Mâitre Cuisinier de France' and holder of numerous other titles. Credit, too, to his wife Christianne – between them they have created some superb dishes and done so at prices reasonable enough to put many another restaurant to shame.

Now Francis and Christianne have opened a hotel right in Salon and, as might be expected, it is a winner. They offer comfort, quiet and excellent service in a decor which is modern but following the Provençal style; there are 10 rooms, all air-conditioned, at 480f, and two apartments at 700f. There is a garage.

The food is naturally of paramount interest though. From his Restaurant Robin, Francis has brought some specialities like civet de homard and cuisse de canard aux fruits et aux petits oignons.

Salon: Domaine de Roquerousse

Occasionally, he gives these an extra touch, like the addition of Banyuls (a sweetish wine) to the lobster. Many dishes are new and no doubt further new ones will continue to appear. Menus are 180, 220 and 380f.

Arrowed for all-round excellence at affordable prices.

Hôtel Roi René
(H)S   *90 53 20 22   561 Allée de Craponne   Visa, CB.*

Thirty simple rooms, pleasantly furnished in pastel colours and starkly modern but very functional. Just south of Salon yet still convenient for the town. Parking but no restaurant. The rooms are 155-250f.

La Table du Roy
(R)S   *90 56 31 98   35 Rue Moulin d'Isnard   Visa, CB.*

Between the château and the Nostradamus Museum, this is the place to get a good meal at very modest prices. Menus are 75, 90, 125 and 220f. A typical 90f meal might consist of escargots à l'ail or tarte des aubergines avec un coulis de tomates and then medallions de la morue à la champagne, concluding with cheese or patisseries. The 220f menu offers feuilleté de homard but whatever you choose, you will be satisfied.

Brasserie St Michel
(R)S   *90 56 19 89   Place des Centuries   Visa, CB.*

Brasseries are often good places to get a simple but adequate meal at low cost. Menus are 70f to 152f and encompass almost any taste. There is a long à la carte list if you want only one course. The terrines are excellent and their canard à l'orange is one of the best I have tasted.

Map 4D   **SANARY-SUR-MER** 83110 (Var) 12 km W of Toulon

Such a pleasant port was obviously used by both the Greeks and the Romans although the name stems from the 17th century and is an abbreviation of Saint Nazaire. His bust can be seen in the modern church.

Aldous Huxley came here to write in the 1920s and during the following decade, many other personalities from the arts could be seen in the Sanary cafés, including Thomas Mann, Franz Werfel, Norman Douglas, Arnold Zweig and Heinrich Mann. When France was occupied in 1940, many intellectuals from Sanary were taken to the internment camp at Les Milles near Aix.

Today it is as a beach resort that Sanary is best-known. Eight kilometres of coast stretch beneath the pine forests and the flowered gardens. Swimming, boating, sailing, canoeing, kayaking, diving, sail-boarding, para-gliding and any other aqua-sport you can think of is available and this strip of the coast has the advantage that it is (like Sanary's neighbours, Six-Fours and La Seyne) less well-known than the more prestigious parts of the Côte d'Azur. Consequently the beaches are less crowded and everything is cheaper. I'm not saying they don't get very busy in the peak months of July and August but they are less crowded than Nice and Cannes.

The long expanse of narrow but sandy beach runs from Sanary and into the adjacent Six-Fours. The Plage de Bonnegrace is known as 'Brutal Beach' and its popularity means that both Sanary and Six-Fours claim it. Even off-season, the beaches are an attraction and the pleasure port is well-frequented.

From January to May, the town of Sanary recognises this and has music and drama performances with big names such as the major ballet companies and operas, currently *La Bohème*.

Festivals

The Feast of Saint Nazaire celebrates the local patron saint at the end of July and also in July is the Feast of Saint Peter the Fisherman.

Eight kilometres off the coast from Sanary is the 230 acre Ile des Embiez owned, like the Ile de Bendor off nearby Bandol, by the pastis millionaire Paul Ricard. It has a large marina and seaport for pleasure and fishing and the Fondation Oceanographique Ricard is a notable aquarium, with most of the Mediterranean fish in their natural habitat. The Fondation is directed by Dr Alain Bombard who has contributed a vast amount of knowledge concerning the Mediterranean including spending weeks alone in an inflatable rubber boat using himself as a guinea-pig to establish how much sea water it is safe to drink. *Open 9-12 and 2-6 every day.*

A tiny open train with a bright red roof is a good way to see the island which prohibits traffic. You can therefore wander everywhere or rent bicycles. The other visit worth making is to the art museum with over 200 works on show. There are vineyards scattered round the island totalling about 20 acres which produce a fine A.O.C Provence.

Ile des Embiez is only a ten minute boat ride and boats leave about every 45 minutes from the port of Le Brusc, just east of Sanary and Six-Fours.

Grand Hôtel des Bains
(HR)S-M   *94 74 13 47   Avenue Estiennes d'Orves   R cl. 1/10-1/4   All CC.*

An impressive building in a commanding position looking out at the Mediterranean and the Ile des Embiez. It is in a flower-filled, floodlit park and still only minutes from the Mairie and the centre of town.

If it were sited anywhere else along the Riviera it would cost double, but seminars help to keep the price down (not intrusive – just 20 in the groups) and Sanary is generally good value.

The 30 rooms are modern and furnished in restful pastel colours. Some have a shower and face inland, others have a bathroom and face the sea, and the others have a bathroom, face the sea and have a balcony. Prices for these three categories run from 350-410f per person for demi-pension or 420-470f for full pension. There is a bar and parking.

Le Castel
(HR)M   *94 29 82 98   Route de Bandol   R cl. Sun p.m. from Oct-May   All CC.*

This is really a restaurant and it is as a restaurant that it has been well-known for many years. Accommodation is available too though and the six rooms have been increased to nine. They are 295-345f but M. Palacios prefers that, in season, you take demi-pension at 305-330f. Seafood features largely on the menu but other dishes are offered also and everything is well-prepared and presented.

L'Aricot
(R)S-M   *94 74 10 33   La Gorguette   Cl. Mon p.m. and Tue o.o.s.   All CC.*

Seafood dominates here in a restaurant of high quality where langoustines, salmon, rascasse and loup will all be found on the reasonable menu starting at 160f. You eat on a terrace shaded by large umbrellas looking out at a tiny port which opens on to the Bay of Bandol, west of Sanary.

Sanary has a number of ethnic restaurants if you are seeking a change from seafood and Provençal cooking. There is the Restaurant Vietnamien, the Restaurant Indonésien, Les Délices d'Asie, Le Corfou, and El Gaucho. For snacks and quick meals, the area around the Mairie has several crêperies, pizzerias and salad bars.

Helios Hôtel
(HR)M   *94 74 93 00   Ile des Embiez   May be cl. Dec and Jan   All CC.*

When you are on an island, the temptation to stay is great. On the Ile des Embiez, the temptation is there but the choice is limited – in fact, it's limited to one hotel and that's the Helios.

Its big business is seminars but with 50 apartments and 117 rooms, it is possible to avoid being disturbed and there is no question that a great array of recreational facilities is on hand. Tennis courts, practice golf, a pool, canoes, kayaks, scuba diving, fishing and a discotheque make sure that you can keep entertained.

The rooms are spacious and all have individually controlled air-conditioning and many have balconies. Some of the apartments are outside the hotel.

Buffets are a popular feature and you have a choice of various styles – country, fish, exotic. Bouillabaisse, aïoli and other specialities are on the various menus which are served in the 'Gardens of Helios', a terrace-restaurant resplendent with flowers and with a view over the pleasure port and marina.

Considering that anyone on an island is a captive audience, the prices are reasonable – 350-380f for demi-pension and 470-500f for full pension and these include wine and coffee.

Map 2B   **SAUMANE-DE-VAUCLUSE** 84800 (Vaucluse) 12 km S of
Carpentras

The village coat-of-arms carries an eagle wearing a golden crown and
a star with eight rays projecting from it. The significance of this is that
it is exactly the same coat-of-arms as that of the de Sade family.

The principal feature of Saumane is its castle, built in the 12th
century and re-built in the 14th and 15th centuries. This re-building
made it an even more formidable fortress than it had been before and
increased the thickness of the walls to more than six feet while
massive casements were added to accommodate huge cannons.

It was Baudet de Sade who bought the castle in the 18th century
though and he was the uncle of the wicked marquis who is the first
member of the family to come to mind when that name is mentioned.
The marquis spent much of his childhood here and was strongly
impressed by the subterranean passages and dungeons deep
underground.

The castle is open to visits today although it must be said that it
now conveys a rather more benign impression. It is more like a
residential château and less of the stern fortress that it once was.

Festivals

The village has a country fête and aiöli at the beginning of July and a
religious fête in the middle of August.

M. Robert Beaumet
(C)S   *90 20 32 97   Quartier Marculy   Open all year.*

There are several hotels in nearby Fontaine-de-Vaucluse so it can
hardly be expected that Saumane with only about 500 people should
try to compete. There is, however, M. Beaumet's fine chambre d'hôte
– an old stone Provençal house on a hill with a view of the old village
only a couple of hundred metres away.

There are three rooms, all with shower and private toilet. A lounge,
a large living room and a fully equipped kitchen are all accessible to
guests. Price is 170f for two people with breakfast included.

Map 2D   **SAUSSET-LES-PINS** 13960 (Bouches-du-Rhône) 31 km W of
Marseille

The strip of coastline west of the sprawling port of Marseille is one of
the lesser-visited areas of all the Provence sea-front. Between
Marseille and Martigues (to the west), there is only a short section of
coast road. Otherwise, there are rocky and sandy coves which are
largely deserted because they are difficult of access except on foot.
The short stretch of coastal road that does exist connects Carry-le-
Rouet and this former fishing village of Sausset-les-Pins.

As its name implies, the village is surrounded by pine forests. The
D9 gives an easy approach to the Mediterranean which makes Sausset

popular but not too crowded in summer. Every water sport is available and out of season the big event occurs in March when large numbers of 'oursins' (sea-urchins) are caught. As at nearby Carry-le-Rouet in February, the two principal specialities in the local restaurants of Sausset for three or four weeks become 'oursinade', a fish soup made from a purée of oursins, and omelettes made with fresh oursins.

The remarkably high population here – about 5,000 – comes from holiday homes and this means that Sausset is not particularly well-endowed with hotels. The best is –

Hôtel La Plage
(HR)S   *42 45 06 31   19 Avenue Siméon-Gouin   H open all year; R cl. Sun p.m.; Mon   All CC.*

A nice location right on the port. The 11 rooms all have TV, mini-bar and are large and airy. Almost all have views over the port. There is a garden, a terrace and a pool. La Plage holds seminars but not, fortunately, in summer. The restaurant has a good selection of seafood but other dishes too. The menu is 160f.

Les Girelles
(R)M   *42 45 26 16   Rue Frédéric Mistral   Cl. Sun p.m. o.o.s; Mon; Feb   All CC.*

Located at the entrance to the newer part of the port, Les Girelles has had a reputation for good food established by the Boudara sisters, Joelle and Antoinette. The terrace is very pleasant for summer eating and the service matches the care with which the dishes are prepared. Sauté de homard rôti en cognac is my favourite here and you might start with a gratin des huitres, sauce saffran. Menus start at 175f and go up over 300f if you want a really sophisticated and expansive meal.

Map 2B   **SEGURET** 84110 (Vaucluse) 9 km SW of Vaison-la-Romaine, 21 km N of Carpentras

---

The Dentelles de Montmirail are a small but fascinating range of sharp-toothed limestone peaks, a spur of the Ventoux mountains. The same geological disturbance which thrust up the Alps stood these strata on their very end and the erosion of milllons of years has carved them into spectacular pinnacles.

On a nearby hillside lies Séguret, a shining example of what man can do to preserve nature for the village has become a conservatory of the traditional way of life in this part of Provence. In 1950, the village population was under a hundred. In 1955, Les Amis de Séguret was formed, dedicated to the restoration of monuments and buildings of value and to the re-establishment of folklore and local culture. They have, in fact, done such a superb job that Les Amis de Séguret are now accused of making the village so attractive that it can be quite crowded in the summer months. Shame on such critics!

The earlier years of Séguret can be seen today in the 12th-century church and the 15th-century fountain. Much of the village is cobbled pedestrian-only alleys which make it easy to explore on foot. Be sure to see the Place du Midi where three enormous plane trees have intertwined their branches to form a vast canopy over the square in a unique sight. Adjacent is the ancient stone lavoir where the villagers washed their clothes until very recently and the huge stone arch which is an entrance to the village.

Festivals

The month of August is the time to be in Séguret. The date varies but the Provençal spectacle is one of the most dazzling in Vaucluse. A drama and folklore festival is combined with processions in honour of Our Lady of Grace and a wine festival named for the local saint, Saint Vincent. There is a 'bravade' – a mock military parade in full uniforms with muskets and 'farandoles', lines of swaying dancers. These converge on the Cellier des Vignerons where wine-tasting begins. A wine cask is carried to the Place des Arceaux where it is opened and its contents tasted.

As this happy festival has been re-created with the resurgence of Séguret, some of it may be present-day pageantry but most of it is based on earlier tradition. Les Chevaliers du Gouste-Séguret were a mediaeval brotherhood whose customs and history have been incorporated into the August jollifications. One of the chapels in which they worshipped is that of Sainte Thècle, now restored and used for exhibitions.

Lots of craftsmen are at work in the village including at the Atelier de Fabrication des Santons, the small exquisitely detailed and dressed dolls in traditional Provençal costumes. See also the Atelier Artistique International de Séguret where 500 artists in 50 countries form an organisation which exhibits works in shows all over the world. In the summer, there will probably be a show in progress here in Séguret.

Craftsmen of a different type will also be at work in Séguret during your visit for the village is not yet finished! Restoration continues, taking away some of the grimness of the harsh mediaeval days. If you feel like a stroll in the wilderness, the ruins of the Prebayon nunnery built around AD 800 adjoin a pretty little stream and an old bridge.

The local Côtes-du-Rhône wines are extremely drinkable and inexpensive, while never achieving great fame. Séguret is ideally placed among several vineyards where tasting is invited. Some of the best are:

Cave Coopérative de Roaix-Séguret
Domaine du Petit Quinquin
Château de la Diffre
Domaine de Cabasse
Domaine de Sommier

One unfortunate aspect of Séguret's success in bringing the charms of its past into the accessible present is that low-priced accommodation is hard to find. Nevertheless the places that are available are good value and these are:

Auberge de Cabasse
(HR)M   *90 46 91 12   H cl. Jan-Mar   R cl. Mon (except July and Aug); Dec-Mar
Visa, MC, EC.*

On the Route de Sablet just out of town, the 10 rooms here are very
nicely furnished and equipped and priced at 300f for a single and 450f
for a double. There is a garden and parking.

The dining facilities outshine the hotel and locals come here to eat –
and eat very well. The menu at 140f is gastronomic and could contain
the mignonins de veau aux olives which is delicious. Another of the
Auberge's specialities is aumônière de truite saumonée Florentine. A
fine selection from the neighbouring vineyards is available.

La Table du Comtat
(HR)M   *90 46 91 49   Cl. Tues p.m.; Wed o.o.s.; Feb; Easter and Christmas   All CC.*

This is really a restaurant with rooms – but no ordinary restaurant.
Franck Gomez was voted one of the Maîtres Cuisiniers de France last
year and even in a region as well-supplied with restaurants as Vaison-
la-Romaine (about ten kilometres away), the existence of a place with
the eminence of La Table du Comtat is a real draw.

Pave de loup rôti à la moelle de boeuf (beef marrow) is one of
Franck's specialities and his filet mignon d'agneau is an example of
his ingenuity at finding new variations on a familiar ingredient.
Making maximum use of Provençal flavours is another of Franck's
talents and the result is cooking that is so good you almost won't
notice the fabulous view!

Naturally, the prices are not cheap but 210, 275 and 450f are not
unreasonable for menus demonstrating such quality as this. The eight
rooms are good sized, fully equipped and very well furnished. They
range from 450-600f.

Mme Jacqueline Montjean
(C)L   *90 46 11 55   Domaine Saint Just   Cl. 15/10-15.4.*

The maximum of three stars here for a chambre d'hôte – and
deservedly so. Mme Montjean is a welcoming and solicitous hostess
and will go out of her way to make you satisfied and comfortable. It is
a fine old stone building with five rooms and there is a beautiful view.
There is a large lounge and a separate dining room. The rooms are all
on the second floor and all have private wash-basin and toilet. Priced
at 220f including breakfast.

Map 2B   **SERIGNAN DU COMTAT** 84830 (Vaucluse) 6 km N of Orange

(M) *Wed*

A fairly ordinary little village but famous because of the man whose
statue you see at the side of the Mairie.

He is Jean-Henri Fabré who lived the last thirty-six years of his life here in Sérignan. Self-taught, Fabré spent his whole life studying insects and most of his knowledge came simply from observation of what he saw in the fields and gardens near his home.

His family were unable to have him properly educated but with scholarships and sheer determination, he obtained diplomas in science and mathematics. He also wrote songs, composed poetry and painted with far above average talent. His ten volume work *Souvenirs Entomologiques* earned him the ribbon of the Legion of Honour but he was fired from his teaching position at the University of Aix because he allowed girls to attend his botany classes and his lectures on the fertilisation of plants were considered pornographic.

A friend of Charles Darwin and John Stuart Mill, Fabré is revered in France but less well-known abroad; you can see his house, l'Harmas, on the D976 going towards Orange. His study and his superb water-colours are on display and you can wander round the gardens which are still much as Fabré left them.

Hostellerie du Vieux Château
(HR)M   *90 70 05 62   Open all year   Visa, CB, EC.*

A long, red-roofed stone farm-house, carefully restored and with a welcoming look to it. Indeed, Jean-Pierre and Anne-Marie Truchot are very welcoming.

The six rooms are 360-800f and are large and comfortably furnished. The Hostellerie is incredibly quiet and peaceful.

The restaurant is rightfully very popular. The cooking is partly Bourguignonne and partly Provençal and between the two you will have a hard time making a choice. All the produce is local and fresh. Menus are 140-350f.

Map 4D   **LA SEYNE-SUR-MER** 83500 (Var) 6 km W of Toulon

 Every day

A lesser-known beach area where lovers of sea and sand can indulge in any known water-sport and at a lower cost than most of the 'name' resorts.

It lies inside the bay of Toulon and therefore enjoys protection from movement of wind and tide to a great degree. La Seyne is proud to remind you that it sits on forty hills and dominates 20 kilometres of coastline, much of which is beach.

The name of the town derives from 'sagno', the pinkish coloured swampy land which formed the coastal area here in ancient times. Fishing has, of course, always been the principal occupation and strong rivalry has existed for centurles between La Seyne and neighbouring Six-Fours.

La Seyne was destroyed during the siege of Toulon but was re-built and then grew significantly when the advent of steel warships placed greater demands on Toulon than it was able to provide. Additional shipyards were built at La Seyne and workers were brought from Piedmont in Italy which explains the number of Italian-style old houses you will see here.

The Musée Balaguier is a good place to learn something of La Seyne's history. It is on the Corniche Bonaparte, the eastern part of La Seyne juts out into the bay the furthest at this point. The tower in which the museum is built was constructed in 1636 and its eight cannon have protected the entrance to the bay of Toulon since. In 1793, occupied by English and Spanish forces, the Tower of Balaguier was captured by a unit commanded by a young artillery officer, Napoleon Bonaparte.

The museum is mainly concerned with marine affairs particularly concerning the Mediterranean but also dealing with the history of the Marseille slave ships and the prison in Toulon. There are models, video films and, in July, concerts. *Tours are available in English. Entry is 10f and it is open all year round except Monday and Tuesday from 10-12 and 2-6 (3-7 in July and August).*

The small 'tourist train' is good fun and shuttles along the Corniche, leaving every hour. The ride is 20f. One end is in front of the Hôtel de Ville and the other end is Les Sablettes (which is also the road which goes over the narrow neck of land and on to the 'island' of Saint Mandrier).

George Sand and Sacha Guitry are two of the famous people who have lived here and the brothers Lumière, who are credited with the invention of cinematography, made their first films here.

A flea market is held on the first and third Sunday of every month while the daily market among the plane trees of the Cours Louis Blanc (a few streets in from the port) is very picturesque.

Festivals

There is a local fête at the beginning of July and a Fête de la Mer on August 15.

Rives d'Or
(H)S-M   *94 94 72 75   Corniche Georges Pompidou   Open all year   All CC.*

A popular and inexpensive place looking out across the bay of Lazaret. There is a balcony with a panoramic view and the 25 rooms have bath or shower and TV. Some have a fully equipped kitchenette. Prices are 200-300f.

Hôtel Lamy
(HR)S-M   *94 94 87 87   Plage les Sablettes   Cl. Wed Visa   CB.*

A three-storey, smart white building on the beach. Every one of the 16 rooms opens on to a balcony with a seaview. Only eight of the rooms have a private bath or shower though, so remember this when booking. Rooms are 185-350f.

Hôtel Moderne
(H)S-M   *94 94 86 68*   *Rue León Blum*   *Open all year*   *All CC.*

Rooms are 165-320f in this hotel which lives up to its name. There are 26 rooms, 23 have bath or shower, 19 have private toilets and 20 are sound-proofed – so take your pick.

La Rascasse
(R)S-M   *94 87 29 08*   *Plage les Sablettes*   *Cl. Thurs*   *All CC.*

It's next door to the Hôtel Lamy so many of their guests eat here. The cheerful decor gains further advantage from the large and colourful paintings on the walls. Paella and bouillabaisse are two of their specialities but they need to be ordered in advance. Every day though, you can enjoy the fish soup, the grilled fish and the couscous and you will want to do so on the terrace with a view of the sea.
Menus at 80, 100, 120 and 160f and there is an extensive à la carte.

L'Aubergade
(R)M   *94 94 81 95*   *Rue Faidherbe*   *Cl. Sun, Mon*   *Visa, CB.*

Long one of the favourite restaurants in Le Seyne even though its prices are a little higher than the other restaurants around. 'Around' in this case means just west of the port.
Loup aux poivrous, poulet aux crevetes and ragout de coquilles St Jacques are just three of the dishes that will tempt you and you can't go wrong with any of them. Menus are 110, 155 and 185f.

Map 4D   **SIX-FOURS-LES-PLAGES** 83140 (Var) 12 km W of Toulon

The town is not named after an unlikely poker hand but the 'six forts' which surround it and provided defence against enemy ships entering the port of Toulon.
There are traces of the earlier Greek, Roman and Phoenician civilisations and several tourist sights of historical interest. La Chapelle de Pépiole was built in the 6th century and its architecture has numerous similarities to Middle Eastern buildings. It was enlarged in the 11th century and served for some time as a Benedictine monastery. Visible from afar, the Collegiale St Pierre is on top of a 700 foot hill. Greek and Roman remains were used to build, in the 5th century, a church which was enlarged several times. The Gothic nave has six chapels which contain works of art. *Open 2-6 every Saturday and Sunday.*
A pilgrimage destination still, the Church of Notre Dame du Mai was built in 1653 and towers more than a thousand feet at the top of Cap Scie, the southernmost point of the entire coast. It has a considerable number of relics and displays which relate the history of its pilgrimages, costumes, vehicles, natural disasters through the years, family dramas and other items of local interest.

Pointe Negre is on a small finger of land jutting out into the sea from the middle of Six Fours and has an ancient fort constructed during the Napoleonic era.

Despite these historical sites, it is as a modern beach resort that Six Fours strikes the visitor. It stretches along the coast, miles of narrow but sandy beaches of which the best is the two mile long Plage de Bonnegrace, known to surfboarders and sailplaners as 'Brutal Beach'.

Most of the hotels and restaurants are along the coastal strip and as one of the lesser well-known beach areas, Six Fours is less crowded than its more prestigious competitors.

Festivals

There is the Festival des Playes on July 14 and the local Fête du Brusc also in July. Another local fête is that of Six Fours on August 15 and there is the Pilgrimage to La Chapelle de Pépiole on September 8.

Ile Rose
(HR) *94 07 10 56   Plage de Bonnegrace   Cl. 15/11-15/12   All CC.*

This long-popular hotel and restaurant is now in the process of introducing a new system of seven-nights booking. This will still work out at only 300-350f per night on a demi-pension basis, which is what they have charged up to now for single night booking, but the Lamagna family tell me that, as the great majority of their customers come for a week at a time, the new method should be advantageous to all. We shall see. Its central position on the best beach in Six Fours makes it a favourite with all beach lovers and every conceivable water sport is there.

Hôtel du Parc
(HR)S *94 34 00 15   112 Rue Marius Blondil   Cl. Sun o.o.s.; 6/10-3/4   Visa, CB, EC.*

A smart but inexpensive little hotel with a welcome signalled by the candy-striped umbrellas on the patio. The 18 rooms are simple but only 200-320f, or you can take the demi-pension at 240-275f. There is a garden and parking. The restaurant serves Provençal food with a few variations, and menus are 90 and 135f.

Le Clos des Pins
(HR)S *94 25 43 68   101 bis Rue de la République   R cl. Sat; Sun   All CC.*

Only 200-300f for the 34 rooms, which are simple but adequate. Demi-pension is available too at 200-240f. There is a garage and parking and a pleasant garden. Menus are 70 and 100f and the fare, like the rooms, is simple but satisfying.

Map 2B   **SUZE-LA-ROUSSE** (Vaucluse) 17 km N of Orange

(**M**) *Fri*

The massive 12th-century fortress became a formidable mediaeval château and now it is the University of Wine. Sadder fates have befallen many other castles though and the one here at Suze-la-Rousse survives due to the vast amounts of money spent restoring it.

The castle is open to the public and it has a fine library and bookshop which include books in English. Anything and everything relating to the culture, growth, treatment and production of wine is covered. Courses are given on all phases of wine-making and wine-selling and there could hardly be a more pleasant place to study.

As the courses are residential and the accommodation palatial, Suze is not an hotel area but Sainte Cécile-les-Vignes, Rasteau, Sérignan-du-Comtat and Séguret all have good accommodation and are less than half an hour's drive to the east.

Map 2C   **LES TAILLADES** 84300 (Vaucluse) 6 km E of Cavaillon

The Lubéron is a land of mystery and strange sights. Few sights are stranger than the village of Les Taillades.

The name derives from 'hewers of stone' and the principal occupation for centuries here has been quarrying. The extraordinary feature is that the quarrying has not resulted in a huge hole in the ground. The rock that has been quarried has come from a large hill so that the work has all been done above ground level. This wouldn't be particularly strange if it were not for the fact that the village has been built on top of the quarry.

The result is a baffling amalgam of an ancient village, a quarry and a hill, made even more puzzling by the intricate way in which cut rock, uncut rock and man-made structures are all blended in together.

There is no appearance of a hill any more because the sheer cliffs of cut surfaces rise perpendicularly with grottoes, ledges, platforms for shrines and other orifices chopped out of the rock. The road to the village at the top is for pedestrians only. It is not arduous but winds like a snake, giving views of abandoned cottages, long forgotten stone walls and vegetation growing in profusion.

At the start of this climb is a statue of a 'Mourvelous', a mythical creature probably like a griffin but so old and battered that it's difficult to tell. The local belief is that it has a connection with Monsieur de Saint Véran, bishop of Cavaillon, who rid the district of a dragon and then turned his attention to other threatening monsters.

In the summer, performances of plays and concerts are put on in a large open-air chamber left by the sheer walls of the quarry. Otherwise, this is not a living village – no shops, no traffic, no people – just a handful of houses, some of which are occupied, though you'd never know it.

Les Taillades is without doubt one of the most bizarre villages you are ever likely to see.

Just outside this peculiar place and on the Canal de Carpentras is an absolutely gigantic water-wheel with paddles wider than any other water-wheel. The votive feast on August 15 puts on water games along the canal.

Michele Pastorel

(C)   *90 71 41 31   Chemin du Cabedan Vieux   Cl. Sept 16-March 23.*

Mme Pastorel has three rooms in a restored stone-built house (stone from the quarry, of course). There is a large lounge and a living room. Two of the rooms have bathrooms and private toilets, the other has toilet and wash-basin only. All are 180f. If you wish, a simple but tasty three-course meal can be had at 70f.

Map 2C   **TARASCON** 13150 (Bouches-du-Rhône) 18 km N of Arles, 26 km E of Nimes, 96 km NW of Marseille

---

 Tues

On the banks of the Rhône at Tarascon stands one of the most splendid castles you are ever likely to see. It was begun in the 13th century but most of the construction you will see today was done in the 15th century. It is particularly remarkable that it has suffered very little damage from either man or the elements since then. This is therefore the best-preserved 15th-century castle in France and, as you come from the west, you see it on a rock rising straight out of the Rhône; its reflection shines on the surface of the water on still days.

It was Charles I of Anjou who built the first fortress on the remains of an old Roman castle, Louis II of Anjou who began the magnificent structure that you see today and his son, King René, who completed it. From the 16th century until recently, it was used as a prison and on the walls of several of the rooms can be seen inscribed the names of English sailors captured in sea battles during the latter part of the 18th century. Some of these are in rhyme such as this one:

Here is 3 Davids in one mess
Prisoners we are in distress
By the French we was caught
And to this prison we was brought

The inner courtyard is theatrically elegant, with a loggia from which the royal family could watch the dancers, troubadors and jugglers. A spiral staircase leads up to the royal apartments on the upper floors. The rooms are spacious and lofty and those on the west side have a fine view of the ruined castle of Beaucaire just opposite across the Rhône.

From the battlements which surround the entire top of the castle, you can look across the roof-tops of the town of Tarascon and over the vineyards to the mountains of Provence. From these battlements prisoners taken during the Revolution were flung into the Rhône.

The castle is open 9-5 in April and May; 9-6 June to September and 10-4 in other months. Closed Tuesdays except July and August.

Festivals

If you are in Tarascon during the last week-end in June, you will watch the Fête de la Tarasque – and thereby hangs a long (and scaly) tail. The Tarasque may be the creature that gave Tarascon its name (or it may be the other way around). This fabled monster is the subject of much speculation and the various drawings, paintings and effigies do little to clarify its true appearance. The dummy monster carried by the townsfolk confuses the mystery even further.

One description says the Tarasque is 'bigger than a cow, longer than a horse, with the face and head of a lion, teeth like swords, a horse's mane, six paws like those of a bear, the tail of a serpent and the shell of a tortoise'. It adds that, 'A dozen lions could not kill it.'

One legend tells that Martha, sister of Mary Magdalen, found that the Tarasque was marauding the banks of the Rhône and gobbling up women and children. No knight could vanquish it but Martha tamed it and it followed her around like a dog ever after. Churches all over Provence have carved stone representations of the Tarasque – in Avignon, Marseille, L'Isle sur la Sorgue, Bollène, Apt, Arles and many others. One possibility is that the original Tarasque was in fact a gigantic crocodile brought back by Roman legionaires, perhaps to be used in the arena.

Alphonse Daudet, the Provençal writer, created a famous character called Tartarin, a bragging Walter Mitty-like adventurer who hunted tigers and climbed Alpine peaks. Daudet said that he had originally called the character Barbarin but a real Barbarin in Tarascon had threatened him if he did not change it. Daudet thought that by changing the name to Tartarin he would avoid any further similarity to a real person. The idea backfired because the whole town objected and for some time Daudet dared not visit Tarascon.

It has now relented and the buffoon figure of Tartarin is even portrayed in the annual Fête de la Tarasque in which he is accompanied by his faithful companions, Bézuquet, the pharmacist, Commandant Bravida and the armourer, Costecalde. The house where Tartarin is described in the trilogy as having lived is, in fact, a real one. It can be visited at 55b Boulevard Itam where there are souvenirs of Daudet and model scenes from the books.

The house is open every day 9.30-12.15 and 1.45-7.00 in summer and 9-12 and 1.30-5 in winter.

The Church of Saint Martha is opposite the castle and has 12th to 14th century origins. The collection of religious pictures is considered exceptional. Worth a look too are the Hôtel de Ville on Rue des Halles which dates back to 1648 and has an exceptionally beautiful façade and original panelling; Rue Arc de Boquy which is completely covered; the Cloister of the Cordeliers (rope-makers) which was built in 1450 and is today used mainly for exhibitions of the work of local painters; and the Condamine Gate, one of the three gates in the original ramparts of the city and built in 1379.

Festivals

There are several fêtes in addition to those already mentioned:
Flower Festival – Pentecost week-end
Fireworks Display, Fête de Saint Jean – Saturday before the Fête de la Tarasque
Bastille Day – July 14, numerous festivities including fireworks
Feast of Saint Martha – July 29
There is running of the bulls and other non-sanguine sport involving the animal at various times throughout the summer.

Les Mazets des Roches
(HR)M   *90 91 34 89   Route de Fontvieille   H cl. end Oct to Easter; R cl. Thurs except July and Aug   All CC.*

A red-roofed, two-storey building nestling delightfully among the pines on the Route de Fontvieille where Stéphane Baldaccioni has 24 pleasant and sizeable rooms at 380-650f. In season, demi-pension is offered at 385-475f.

There is a pool and two tennis courts. Check for seminars. The restaurant looks out over the pool and menus start at 130f.

Le Saint Jean
(HR)S   *90 91 13 87   24 Boulevard Victor Hugo   H cl. 15/12-15/1; R cl. Fri, Sat lunch   All CC.*

Only 12 rooms here but they are good value at 220-270f. Demi-pension is also a good bet at 220-250f. There is parking and TV and the food is good local fare with menus from 80-230f.

The 80f menu could start with soupe de moules and a good choice for the main course would be the coquelet Provençal. With cheese or dessert, this is a good, inexpensive meal.

Map 2B   **LE THOR** 84250 (Vaucluse) 14 km W of Fontaine-de-Vaucluse, 16 km E of Avignon

 Sat

This small little-known town was named Torus because a bull unearthed a statue of the Virgin Mary on the banks of the river Sorgue. The town is still entered through the old rampart gate which is capped by an iron belfry. Its 12th-century church is notable for its magnificent portico and its general impression of severe grandeur. A very unusual feature is that it has not been enlarged or modified since its completion in 1202.

The two-storey château was built about the same time but it lies in ruins today. The adjacent ruins of two chapels and a monastery make a romantic grouping on top of a hill called Thouzon. In the side of the hill was found a huge grotto with fantastic stalagmites and stalactites which is now open to visitors (but wear a sweater or jacket, it's extremely cold).

There are several markets featuring local produce. The most colourful are the asparagus market every Saturday in April and May and the grape market every day from August 1 to October 31.

Festivals

In August too is the local fair on the 15th which usually features a play or an operetta. The first Sunday in May is the occasion of a religious and a village fête focusing around the hill of Thouzon. There is an annual flea market in July.

This kind of area of Vaucluse is ideal for chambre d'hôte accommodation and there are several around Le Thor.

Mme Thérèse de Mazieux
(C)M   *90 33 85 90   Quartier du Mejean (on Route de Sain)   Open all year.*

This is an old restored farm-house with many of the amenities of a small hotel. There is a lounge with TV, a living room, parking, a garage and garden. Three of the rooms have bathrooms, though all have to share one toilet. The fourth room has private bath and toilet. The price is 170f for a double.

Serge André
(C)M   *90 33 72 44   La Colonelle   Open all year.*

An old farm in the country just outside Le Thor has been converted into this enjoyable guest house, with dining room, terrace and garden. Of the four rooms, one has only a wash-basin and costs 190f; the other three have private toilets and cost 220f.

Map 4D   **TOULON** 83000 (Var) 64 km E of Marseille

 Tues to Sat

The headquarters of the French Navy in the Mediterranean is not a likely tourist spot. Most people would not choose to come here for sightseeing or beaches or hotels or restaurants – and not even for history, although Toulon has plenty of it; but just in case ...

The perfect, sheltered port is ideal for modern warships but wasn't of much interest to the Romans and it was not until the 15th century that it became a naval base. Napoleon was promoted for the part he played in repulsing the English fleet when it attacked Toulon.

When the Germans moved into the South of France to commandeer the Vichy fleet of over sixty ships in 1942, the French scuttled all of them. Heavy bombing by the Allied air armadas in 1943 and 1944 did considerable damage and then the Germans blew up most of the harbour when retreating before the Allied invasion in August 1944.

The old town is still quite pleasant and much of it escaped destruction. Toulon is proud of its 18 fountains – they range from the Fontaine de la Pigno in Rue Paul Landrin, built in 1740, to the magnificent Fontaine de la Fédération in the Place de la Liberté and built in 1889 and include the headless and armless statue in the Place de la Pucelle and the vegetation-covered Fontaine des 3 Dauphins of 1779.

The Naval Museum is on the Quai de Stalingrad and on the site of the old arsenal. There are some fine ship models here and other naval devices while three fortifications remain as lures to shutter-clickers. The Tour Royale out on the southern tip of the peninsula was built by Louis XII in 1514. Its walls are fourteen feet thick and its guns cover the whole port. *Open every day except Monday from 10-12 and 3-6.*

Fort St Louis was built in 1692, just east of the Tour Royale, as additional protection. It is not open to the public but remains photogenic.

In 1845, the dangers of attack by land were a major cause of concern now that the sea fortifications were believed to be impregnable. The Tour Beaumont was built about three kilometres inland and at a height of 530 metres. It was part of a fortification system around Mont Faron which has since been taken over by the Musée Memorial du Débarquement en Provence August 1944.

As its name suggests, this commemorates the Allied landings which General Eisenhower and General de Gaulle both designated as a turning point in WW II. The museum contains two exhibition halls and a gallery with souvenirs, mementoes, photographs, weapons and uniforms. There is a diorama, a cinema showing films of the landings and a terrace with a panoramic view and the salient points identified. *Open 9.30-11.30 and 2.30-4.30 every day except Monday.*

The Musée d'Art et d'Archéologie (also called the Musée d'Histoire Naturelle) is on the Boulevard du Maréchal Leclerc and covers Greek, Egyptian, Roman, Gallic, Near East and Far East archaeology and has paintings from the 13th century to the present. *Open 9.30-12 and 2-6 every day.*

On the Cours Lafayette, the Musée du Vieux Toulon shows the history of the town and the region. *Open every day from 10-12 and 3-6 except Monday and Wednesday.*

Festivals

There is plenty going on in Toulon all the year round. The principal event is the music festival in July while the same month sees the Festival of Saint Pierre, the patron saint of fishermen. The Commercial Fair in October attracts a lot of visitors and in November the annual film festival of films relating to sea exploration is held.

In addition, lots of concerts, rugby matches, antique fairs, stamp fairs and similar events keep the social calendar humming. The Opera House is beautifully decorated though winter is the season. Circus performers put on a show in the old town in the summer.

As Toulon is not considered a tourist destination, its hotels are quite inexpensive.

Les Trois Dauphins
(H)S   *94 92 65 79   Place des Trois Dauphins   Open all year   All CC.*

This may not be one of the best-known hotels in Toulon but in value for money it has to be near the top of the list. The 13 rooms are priced at 70-140f. They are quite adequate, all have TV and look out on to the square containing the famous fountain. English is spoken.

Hôtel d'Europe
(H)S-M   *94 92 37 44   7b Rue de Chabannes   Open all year   All CC.*

Right in the centre of town and near the railway stations. 27 rooms at 125-310f have TV, and the decor is modern and very pleasing. Air-conditioning, sound-proofing, bath and enclosed parking is included in the price of the rooms at the upper end of the range. There is a caféteria opposite. English is spoken.

Grand Hôtel du Dauphiné
(HR)S-M   *94 92 20 28   10 Rue Berthelot   Open all year   All CC.*

In the pedestrian zone, devoid of traffic noise but the rooms are sound-proofed in case you object to the sound of pedestrians. Only a few minutes walk to the port and the Opera House. The 57 rooms cost 170-305f. There is a bar and a TV lounge and the only snag is that parking is 50 metres away. Meals are OK at about 100f.

La Corniche
(HR)M   *94 41 35 12   17 Littoral Frédéric Mistral   Open all year   All CC.*

In case you feel like spending a bit more money and having a fair amount of luxury, you can do both here although with Toulon's more than reasonable prices, you are still not being extravagant. The 22 rooms are 320-520f, are air-conditioned and have TV. Many of the rooms look out over the port of Le Mourillon on the south-east edge of town, the decor is rustic, there is a garden, a bar and a garage.
   The restaurant is renowned for Patrick Suère's gastronomy so you had better check the menu prices as you might consider them a bit high relative to the hotel prices. There is no doubt though that the food is good and the servings are very generous. Raviolis de langouste is one of the specialities. Menus are 160-220f.

Madeleine
(R)S-M   *94 92 67 85   7 Rue des Tombades   Cl. Tues p.m.; Wed   All CC.*

Rustic decor in one of the most popular restaurants in Toulon. The cooking too has a rustic touch with homey dishes like cassoulet and coq au vin. The range of styles is wide though and excellent use is made of spices and flavours from many parts of France. Menus from 110f up and very good value. The wines are well chosen and not too expensive.

L'Atalante
(R)S   *94 03 05 71   Port de Toulon   Cl. Nov   All CC.*

> Right on the port and very popular. Fish specialities abound but there
> are meat and chicken dishes too. Menus are 90f and 130f and there are
> different plats du jour every day.

Cafétéria du Centre
(R)S   *94 92 68 57   29 Rue Gimelli   Open every day   All CC.*

> It's not often that caféterias are recommended in this guide but this
> one is the type that it's good to know about when you need an
> inexpensive meal without any fuss and at any hour.
>   It is just off the Place Liberté and it's air-conditioned. The six rooms
> can accommodate 400 people – and often do. There are 14 dishes
> offered every day at 22.50f and complete menus at 39f and 50f with
> wine included.

Map 3C   **TRETS** 13530 (Bouches-du-Rhône) 18 km SE of Aix

> A truly ancient village, mediaeval, authentic yet built on a site
> occupied previously by the Romans and before them by the Celtic-
> Ligurians.
>   The village is typical, with its narrow, winding streets, its vaulted
> passages and cobbled stairways. Most of it dates from the 13th
> century, as does the château where the ramparts and the fortified
> gates are still to be seen.
>   The Church of Sainte Marie is also old, dating from the 12th century
> but the Gothic chapels were added around the 15th century.
>   Trets boasts two gastronomic specialities. One of these is the
> 'rocambole' which is sometimes described as a shallot and sometimes
> as a giant garlic. The other is a civet which is sometimes made from
> sanglier (wild boar) and sometimes from marcassin (young wild boar).

Festivals

> The Ramado, a Provençal feast dating from the time of Mistral, is
> celebrated around the time of Pentecost. There are fireworks on the
> Feast of St Jean and there is the same fête that you will encounter in
> many parts of Provence – that of Saint Eloi, the patron saint of
> blacksmiths who miraculously restored a leg to a horse. This is on the
> first Sunday after July 14. It is accompanied by Provençal folklore
> singing and dancing.

Vallée de l'Arc
(HR)S   *42 61 46 33   1 Avenue Jean Jaurès   Open all year   Visa, CB.*

> 20 rooms in this modest establishment costing only 200f. Menus start
> at 65f and are good, healthy fare. There is a garage.

L'Oustaou du Vin
(R)M   *42 61 51 51   Cl. Wed; Sun p.m.; Feb   All CC.*

It is strange that a town of 6,000 people does not have more good places to stay but at least it has restaurants. L'Oustaou is an old inn with genuinely good food. The salade à l'homard et aux asperges is very popular and so is the langoustines avec coquilles Saint Jacques – this is called a 'gateau' but don't let that put you off. There are several other dishes which are all imaginative and enjoyable and you will be amazed at the menu prices of only 75, 130 and 170f.

Map 2B   **LA TOUR D'AIGUES** 84240 (Vaucluse) 26 km NE of Aix-en-Provence, 27 km SW of Manosque, 41 km SE of Apt

---

(M) *Tues*

If the château here were still intact, there would be few finer in Europe. You may have had similar thoughts about other such buildings but the sentiment seems truer in the case of La Tour d'Aigues than anywhere else. Alas, the château stands in ruins – but they are ruins that touch your heart.

The beautiful yellow stones of the triumphal arch are almost intact – but then you see beyond it the violated mass of the old keep and this just emphasises the vandalism that destroyed one of the most magnificent châteaux of the Renaissance period.

An ancient fortress had existed on the site when Louis Nicholas de Bouliers erected a really grandiose edifice in 1560 using the foundations, the moats and part of the walls. The origins of the earlier building are uncertain – it is mentioned as already standing in archives dated 1039.

When Catharine de Medici came here to stay in 1579, the castle looked like new. Two centuries later, during the Revolution, it was pillaged and destroyed and then set on fire, burning for five days. Amazingly enough, the ruins are still breathtaking, for they are the façades of the buildings and together with walls and towers look like an abandoned movie set. At the entrance, you will see drawings of how La Tour d'Aigues looked in its heyday and you can use your imagination to bridge the gap. The enormous moat looks wide enough and deep enough for a good-sized ship.

Today the remaining buildings surround a courtyard which is used for concerts, festivals and plays. Among this year's performances are *King Lear* and *Les Misérables*. Underground is a Musée des Faiences, a Musée de l'Histoire and caves where you can taste and buy wine.

The site is open every day 9.30-11.30 and 3-6 except Tuesday afternoon, Saturday morning and Sunday morning.

The village is rather scruffy, with not much to see, but La Tour d'Aigues is one of the most unusual sites in Provence and well worth a detour.

Les Fenouillets
(HR)S-M   *90 07 48 22   Quartier Revol   Cl. 16/2-12/3   All CC.*

On the edge of the village and near the château, Les Fenouillets is a popular stop for both food and lodging. The ten rooms are priced at 210-320f. All have TV and there is a garden and parking. Many come here just to eat, which is a good recommendation in itself; in summer, dining spreads outside and in the garden.

Cooking is from the south-west of France and features duck and grilled meats. Menus are 100f and up. There is a good selection of Lubéron wines.

Map 2B   **VACQUEYRAS** 84190 (Vaucluse) 12 km N of Carpentras

---

Located on the D7 going north out of Carpentras, Vacqueyras is another of those little villages whose name you recognise only because you have seen it on a wine-label.

That's not a bad reason though – especially when the wine is as good as it is here, the rich, red, earthy Côtes-du-Rhônes prevailing. The fame of the nearby Châteauneuf-du-Pape overshadows most of the others, while even the more modest Gigondas appears on most lists that don't include Vacqueyras. It's inexpensive – you can buy a three year old for as little as 30f – but if you like strong, gutsy reds, you will enjoy Vacqueyras. None of the names have become memorable but the wines of 'La Font de Papier' are worth keeping an eye open for.

There are several 'wine roads' running through this area and one of them is 'La Route Lavande'. It covers 70 kilometres on its way between Beaumes-de-Venise and Bollène. As well as passing Vacqueyras, it gives plenty of other opportunities for wine-tasting (and sight-seeing) in charming small villages, including Gigondas, Sablet, Rasteau and Cairanne.

In the village square is a bust of Rambaud de Vacqueyras, one of the most famous of the Provence troubadors. He exceeded his duties and was found in bed with Beatrice, the wife of William, Prince of Orange. It is said that the wit and talent of the young poet impressed William to the extent that he did not have him executed. William did, however, wisely take Rambaud with him to the Fourth Crusade, and the troubador was killed in a battle with the Turks at the age of 27.

Hôtel Le Pradet
(H)S-M   *90 65 81 00   Route de Vaison   Open all year   All CC.*

A simple village hotel with twenty rooms, inexpensively priced at 190-300f. The rooms are quite adequate and all have TV. There is parking and no restaurant but the hotel will probably advise you to eat at the following ...

Restaurant des Dentelles
(R)S-M *90 65 86 21   Open all year.*

>   Any restaurant with over 200 seats and located in a tiny village like
>   Vacqueyras – well, you know it must be good. This one is, with menus
>   at 75 and 85f, local produce, well-prepared and plenty of it.

M. Claude Chabran
(C)M *90 65 84 51   Domaine de l'Oustau des Lecques*

>   This is another chambre d'hôte that gives real value for money and
>   provides a pleasing alternative to hotel accommodation. The five
>   rooms all have private toilets and there is TV. The setting in a domaine
>   surrounded by vineyards and just on the edge of the village is hard to
>   beat. So too is the price of 200f for a room occupied by two people
>   and a table d'hôte meal offered at 90f per person. The demi-pension at
>   330f for two people is an equally good bet.

Map 2B   **VAISON-LA-ROMAINE** 84110 (Vaucluse) 47 km NE of Avignon

Ⓜ *Tues*

>   Approach this old Roman town along the D938 from Carpentras and
>   Malaucène if you can. The ruins of the 12th-century castle stand stark
>   against the skyline in dramatic outline.
>   Vaison-la-Romaine consists of two towns. The Voconces, a Gaullish
>   tribe, were the original inhabitants and they built a settlement up on
>   the high ground north of the river Ouvèze. They prospered under the
>   Romans centuries later but the city was devastated by the Visigoths
>   and the Ostrogoths when they invaded France. The 'haute ville' to
>   which the inhabitants withdrew for defence against these barbarians
>   is on the south side of the river and is capped by the castle you see
>   when approaching.
>   The Roman sights here are deserving of more time than many other
>   larger and better-known towns in the south of France. Vaison was a
>   residential town, popular with retired Legion officers and wealthy
>   merchants and politicians and the excavation work, which is still
>   continuing, is yielding information which makes comparisons with
>   Pompeii inevitable.
>   There are two Roman areas, Quartier de Puymin and Quartier de la
>   Villasse but they are separated only by the road and the Tourist
>   Bureau. A small entry fee procures a guide (including English
>   language) but everything is quite visible from the surrounding streets.
>   The lay-out of the streets and houses is clearly distinguishable. The
>   Maison de la Buste en Argent is named for the silver head on display –
>   it was made of one of the villa's early owners. Maison des Messii is a
>   mosaic-tiled villa in which the various rooms and their functions are
>   obvious and Maison du Dauphin is nearby.
>   The amphitheatre seated 7,000 people and is still in use – every year

during the Festival. The museum has many artefacts discovered during the excavations and these lend an air of reality to the site as they include many everyday items such as door-knobs, water faucets, mirrors and water pipes in addition to statues and other decorative pieces. Reconstructions of panels and walls help to get the feel of the town as a place where people really lived. The Tourist Bureau is worth a visit too. It contains a great deal of information on the town and the adjacent area as well as a fine display of local wines for sale at 15f a bottle.

The ruins and the museum are open 9-7 from June to September; 9-6 in March, April, May, October and November; and 9-5 in December, January and February.

Immediately to the west of the Roman ruins in the Quartier de la Villasse is the Cathedral of Notre Dame de Nazareth. Pierre of Mirabel, one of the most powerful of the bishops of Vaison, commenced the construction of the cathedral in the 11th century on the foundations of a Gallic-Roman temple; the edifice is still a subject of learned controversy though current belief is that the early basilica dates from Merovingian times, early in the 6th century.

Near the main apse, a number of Chapter Houses and Romanesque columns have been found along with a sarcophagus. The remains of a paleolithic temple have also been uncovered and this has been associated with a Christian community which existed here in the 3rd century.

A short road leads from the cathedral to the Chapel of Saint Quenin, named after an early bishop of Vaison and now patron saint of the town. Like the cathedral, the origins of the chapel are wreathed in the mists of history. Several architectural features are not yet properly explained, the most perplexing being the apse, which is triangular. One suggestion is that this was once a temple of Diana – another that it was a Christianised re-build of a Roman original – and a third that it was once a Carolingian sanctuary.

The Roman remains alone ought to be enough attraction for any town, but in Vaison there's more. The Haute Ville is a perched mediaeval village. The 12th-century castle is now closed but it is a joy to ramble around the narrow streets of the village and view the old buildings while thanking the Counts of Toulouse for their foresight in renovating the town in the 14th century so that it would still be here for you to see today.

In the busy modern part of Vaison, the Tuesday market paralyses traffic and forces detours. On the north side of the Place Montfort, cafés and restaurants are lined up and all have extensive outdoor seating for use in the summer months. Three-course menus go for 69f up.

There are several 'wine routes' which thread their way through the vineyards and villages of Vaucluse and two of these terminate (or start) in Vaison. La Route Dorée (the Golden Road) covers 110 km as it goes to Avignon via Puymeras, Malaucene, Beaumes-de-Venise, Châteauneuf-du-Pape and Sorgues. The Red Road (La Route Rousse) is only 60 km and goes to Bollène passing through Nyon, Buisson, Tulette and Rochegude. Opportunities for wine tasting occur all the way along both these routes and you will want to stop at many of these charming villages.

Hotel accommodation is not easy to come by in the season so book well ahead or be prepared to have to go driving around the neighbouring countryside. If you can book ahead, the best are:

Le Beffroi Rue de l'Eveche
(HR)M   *90 36 04 71   Haute Ville   H cl. 15/3-15/1   All CC.*

A 16th-century building and plenty of mediaeval charm to go with it. It is next to the old belfry (hence the name) and the 21 rooms are delightfully unconformist. There are wooden beams, slightly creaky stairs and the floors are not always flat.

Room prices are 380-520f, justified by the charm and spaciousness. As you might expect in a mediaeval hilltop village, parking is difficult.

Food in the restaurant is of a very high quality. A la carte selections may be the best approach and you may expect to pay 100-200f.

➤Hôtel les Auric
(H)S-M   *90 36 03 15   Route d'Avignon   Cl. early Nov to mid March   Visa.*

Although this hotel is just out of town, 2 km on the road to Avignon, it is good enough to rate high on the list of choices of all the places to stay in the district. It is a delightful old stone structure and there are 14 sound-proofed rooms. Some with wood-beamed stone walls, ceilings, furnished with antiques.

Prices range from 240-290f – really exceptional value. Be sure to ask for a bathroom if you specifically want one though as two of the rooms have a shower only.

There is a large pool, private parking, a bar, a lounge and a terrace. M. Robert Jardin and his staff work hard to make your stay pleasant. Arrowed for good value.

Hôtel Burrhus
(HR)S-M   *90 36 00 11   Place Montfort   Cl. 1/11-12/12   All CC.*

The shady terrace overlooks the Place Montfort, right in the heart of town, next to the Quartier Puymin with its Roman ruins and amphitheatre; this is a convenient and pleasant place to stay.

The light blue shutters against the sand-coloured walls are an attractive exterior and the public rooms are cosily furnished with big fireplaces and stuffed heads on the walls as a reminder of the hunting facilities in the region. There is a shaded terrace on the first floor, with views out on to the Place.

The 14 rooms are very comfortable, all different and some with one or two stone walls. The pricing at 180-240f with toilet and shower and 280-320f with bath and shower is very good value, especially as the service throughout is very attentive and there is a garage (30f).

Until now, there has not been a restaurant as the management felt that the numerous establishments on the Place Montfort provided an adequate choice of eating facilities. However, a restaurant will be open

Vaison la Romaine: Hôtel les Auric

by the time this appears in print and it is proposed to offer a menu at 100f consisting of three courses and using all Provençal produce.

By the way, the unusual name of the hotel derives from Maurice Burrhus, a former resident of Vaison and namesake of the tutor to the Emperor Nero. It was Maurice who provided the financing for the excavation of the Roman ruins and the reconstruction of the amphitheatre.

Hôtel du Théâtre Romain
HR)S-M   *90 36 05 87   Rue Abbé Sautel   R cl. Sun p.m. o.o.s   CB, Visa.*

Right in the centre of town and next door to the Roman ruins, the 21 rooms here are priced at 120-225f, which is very reasonable. There is a bar, a terrace and parking but no garage. For a budget stay and convenient to all the sights in the Roman town, this may be hard to beat especially in summer when the region is swarming with tourists.

The restaurant serves Provençal food and a popular favourite is the lapin Provençal. The menu at 70f satisfies most diners but for 100f you can eat well off the à la carte list.

A L'Escargot d'Or
(HR)S-M   *90 36 02 88   Cl. Tues. o.o.s.; Jan, Feb   All CC.*

The Flumel brothers run a busy and popular hotel and restaurant next to the Pont Neuf which crosses the river Ouvèze as you head for the haute ville, the mediaeval part of town, or south towards Carpentras.

It's not the fanciest place and none of the 20 rooms have baths – just showers – but they're reasonably sized and priced at 220-315f.

The buildings stand in their own grounds which lends an air of tranquillity and you can fish in the river.

There is a large dining room though in the season most guests prefer to eat outside on the terrace. There are menus at 80, 110 and 150f and the local wines start at an astonishing 30f a bottle! The specialities are fish, grills and game.

Le Colibri
(R)S-M   *90 36 09 18   32 Cours Taulignan   Cl. Mon; Tues lunch   All CC.*

You may be looking for something different to eat after several Provençal-cooked meals and, if so, you can't do better than Le Colibri.

Mme Colibri calls on her Antilles background and her husband helps bring you such specialities as blaff antillais, stuffed crab and the tasty colombo de poulet.

The spices of the Isles will introduce you to a host of food flavours you may not recognise and the prices are very reasonable. Menus are 75, 95, 110 and 130f; I find the 110f meal the best. Wines are a modest 52f and up.

Le Bateleur
(R)M   *90 36 28 04   1 Place Theo Aubanel   Cl. Sun and Mon and all Oct   Visa, EC, MC.*

This is a cosy little place, with only 8 tables, and next to the Roman bridge. The lace curtains add to the quaintness but there's nothing quaint about the food.

There is only one menu and it's a modest 108f. This offers a choice of 8 starters, a dozen main courses and 10 desserts. It's a fussy eater who can't find satisfaction here!

The pintadeau braised with cèpes is my choice here (breast of guinea-fowl) but if you would rather choose from the à la carte menu, there are selections at 55f and up.

Restaurant du Vieux Vaison

(R)S-M   *90 36 19 45   Rue Gaston Gevaudan   Cl. Wed except July and Aug; Jan 15; Feb 15   All CC.*

If you're up in the old mediaeval village when the hunger pangs strike, you must give some consideration to eating here. Don't be put off because it serves pizza – it is a restaurant too and the terrace has a really spectacular view of the river and the Roman town.

Menus are 76, 98 and 160f and wines are a sensible 45f up. The 98f menu is highly recommendable and you might have this consisting of a first course of moules cassoulette then civet de porcelet (wild boar and one of the local specialities) plus a choice of desserts, the cakes being particularly good.

You'll also enjoy a tour of the restaurant which is a mediaeval building with some amusingly ancient features.

Brasserie du Siècle

(R)S-M   *90 36 00 19   Place Montfort   All CC.*

It's often helpful to know a place where you can get a light meal at any hour. This is such a place. It's handily located too – on the main square. There is a large terrace and though the regional cuisine is featured there are plenty of other choices such as home-made pastas, couscous or moussaka.

Map 4C   **VALENSOLE** 04210 (Alpes de Haute-Provence) 15 km W of Riez

---

The vast plateau of Valensole lies between the Durance river and Lac St Croix. It is in an unusually isolated position for it is not surrounded by numerous small villages as are so many Provence towns.

This is almond country. Most of the almonds you will eat in the south of France come from this plateau. Many are picked by hand but the birds often get them first. The jays and the magpies love almonds and sweep down in flocks while the nuts are still green. When the nuts are ripe, the birds crack open the shells.

Lavender covers the hillsides and many a photographer has shown the church of Valensole and belltower as brown shapes against an all-lavender background.

Hostellerie de la Fuste

(HR)M-L   *92 72 05 95   H cl. 15/11-15/12   R cl. Sun p.m.; Mon   All CC.*

Despite Valensole's rather remote position, you will find here one of the most renowned hostelleries in Provence. It is an old farm-house building surrounded by orchards and in a park full of flowers and hundred-year-old plane trees. The building is 17th century and the 11 rooms are furnished in comparable manner with antique furniture and tapestries. There is a pool and the atmosphere is peaceful and very relaxing.

The cooking is traditional but done with great flair and style using imagination and originality. The gigontin d'agneau is an example and, of course, truffles and game are always on the menu when in season.

The prices here are not cheap. Rooms are 500-1100f and a meal will cost 300-400f. The standards of both the hotel and the restaurant justify these prices but the off-the-beaten-track location of the hostellerie raises the only question mark.

Map 2A   **VALREAS** 84600 (Vaucluse) 29 km NE of Bollène

 Wed

Every reference you will see to Valréas describes it as 'the enclave of the Popes'. It is, in fact, in a tiny area which is part of Vaucluse but completely surrounded by the neighbouring departement of Drome. The background to this is that, in 1317, Pope John XXII bought Valréas while he was intent on increasing his power around Avignon, at that time the seat of the Papacy. But when the limits of the departements were established in the late 18th century, the people of Valréas were allowed to decide which one they wanted to be in. They chose to be part of Vaucluse.

It's a pleasant little town with vineyards all around. The Château de Simiane is 17th century. *Open for guided tours 10-12 and 3-7 in summer and 10-12 and 3-6 other months. The 12th-century church of Notre Dame de Nazareth and the adjacent Chapelle des Pénitents Blanc are open similar hours.*

Festivals

Valréas' big night is June 23 when nearly 400 locals in splendid, multi-coloured costumes and unusual hats march through the town by torchlight and to the accompaniment of a large band. This is the ceremony of the enthroning of 'Petit Saint Jean', a four-year-old child with golden curls who receives the homage of the town. He is presented with a ewe lamb and the fleur-de-lis flag which is brought over from Quebec specially for the occasion. Some locals condemn it as too theatrical and no-one knows the origins of many of the features of the spectacle but it is a sight to see.

Valréas hasn't finished with festivals though – at the beginning of August, the 'Corso de la Lavande' (the Lavender Festival) goes on for three days and two nights. Should you not be here on either of these occasions, at least try to see the weekly market. It is held every Wednesday and it is one of the most colourful and picturesque of all the markets in Provence.

L'Hostellerie du Lubéron
(HR)S-M   *90 77 27 19*   *Cl. Sun p.m.; Mon*   *Visa, CB.*

The 16 rooms in this old but recently renovated auberge are 260f making this a very good choice for an overnight stop. Breakfast is 40f and the dining room has fine views over the Durance valley.

Shellfish are the speciality and menus start at 135f. Since the hostellerie re-opened (after enlargement) it has become popular.

Map 2B   **VEDENE** 84270 (Vaucluse) 5 km NE of Avignon

Virtually on the northern outskirts of Avignon, Védène has managed to preserve a modicum of independence. Unfortunately, some of its buildings such as the Chapel of Sainte Anne, have been over-restored and with a noticeable lack of sympathy and taste. The Church of St Thomas has not suffered as badly and is, unusually, in the design of the Maltese Cross.

Festivals

It is in Védène, however, that the Provençal fête is alive and not only well but thriving. Two folklore groups, la Reneissenco and Lei Pastoureu put on performances in July at the local fête and also at the horse fair and the antiques fair. There is a festival at the Château des Hirondelles and another group known as Seden put on the traditional Feast of the Kings with food and wine for all.

Védène's proximity to Avignon has helped promote the popularity of restaurants here.

Hôtel de la Poste
(H)S-M   *90 31 05 48   51 Rue Notre Dame   Open all year   All CC.*

Its situation in the village near the autoroute exit makes this hotel a popular overnight stop. The price range is 90-180f and there are 13 rooms. There is parking and a garage but no restaurant, though there are several very close by.

Restaurant L'Affiche
(R)S-M   *90 23 46 15   98 Rue Pelican   Cl. Mon   Visa, CB, MC.*

The shaded terrace is a great crowd puller but then so is the food. The soupe de poissons is expertly done and the crab farci, Creole-style, is one of my favourites. Menus start at 67f and several local wines are inexpensively featured.

Le Flory
(R)S-M   *90 31 07 76   Route d'Entraigues   Cl. Wed; Sun o.o.s.   All CC.*

A big and very popular place, sprawling over a large shaded park and a terrace. There is a pool and a play area for children. The cooking is partly local Provence-style and partly south-west France. Menus start at 54f (lunch) or 79f (dinner) but the à la carte choice is always a good alternative and still won't cost more than 100-120f.

Map 2B   **VELLERON** 84740 (Vaucluse) 11 km S of Carpentras,
          15 km W of Avignon

Ⓜ *Wed*

The 13th-century Château des Crillons has managed to keep some of
its crumbling façade and its neighbouring Château Cambis is
struggling to keep up.

Festivals

Velleron has a lot of festivals throughout the year and begins with one
on May Day. There is a Grand Aiöli on Bastille Day (July 14) and this is
co-ordinated with neighbouring L'Isle-sur-la-Sorgue's river festival.
There is the Feast of St Michael on the second Sunday in September
and 'Provençal Days' on the first Sunday in October with a folk-
dancing group.

La Grangette
(HR)M   *90 20 00 77   Quartier Cambuisson, Route de Carpentras   Open every day*
All CC.

Despite its proximity to bigger places, Velleron has a popular and
always busy hotel and restaurant in La Grangette. The 15 rooms are
very attractively furnished and fully equipped and are 440-680f plus
55f for breakfast. The park surrounding gives a calm country
atmosphere and the pool and tennis court are additional advantages if
you are feeling energetic.

Seminars are occasionally held but these are a common hazard of
many country hotels. Menus are 160, 210 and 425f but the cooking is
good and the portions large.

Map 2B   **VENASQUE** 84210 (Vaucluse) 12 km SE of Carpentras,
          32 km N of Cavaillon

In this part of Provence, the perched village is less common than in
the Var but this makes Venasque all the more notable. While being a
perfect example of the perched village, it is only 310 metres altitude
and easily accessible by a good road.

It sits up on top of a large rock, a village of 650 people, with a wall
leading to three round towers at one end and a church at the other.
Between these is a maze of narrow, twisting streets, not over-restored
but then not neglected either so that the result is a delightful village to
stroll around and take photographs to your heart's content.

From the 5th to the 10th century, the bishops of Carpentras would
take refuge at Venasque whenever one of the frequent Barbarian
invasions occurred. Carpentras was then the bishopric of Venaissin
which was the name for this large area of Provence and it was from
the name Venaissin that the village was named Venasque.
Neighbouring villages resented the prominence bestowed on
Venasque due to the residence of the bishops there and – perhaps out

of jealousy rather than reason – called the inhabitants of Venasque 'teto-bout', suggesting that their drinking habits were excessive.

The 13th-century church has next to it a 6th-century baptistry with elegant marble columns. The building is believed to have even earlier origins and have been a temple to Venus and there is some speculation that this contributed to the modern name of Venasque. Whatever the reality, the church is very well equipped to instruct the visitor and you will note the references to Saint Siffrein, bishop of Carpentras, who died in 570. His body is believed to be buried underneath the baptistry but has never been located, which is why he is referred to by some recent historians as 'the mysterious Saint Siffrein'.

You may be in Venasque when one of the occasional pilgrimages is made to the nearby chapel of Notre Dame de Vie. It was built in the 6th century and re-built in the 11th. During the 18th century some of the old buildings were reconstructed as a convent and today it is occupied by the Carmelites.

The village of Venasque is a very pleasant place to stay and it makes a good base from which to explore the neighbouring countryside. It is perhaps a better choice in this regard than Fontaine and, relative to its size, offers several establishments which can be recommended.

Auberge de la Fontaine
(HR)L   *90 66 02 96   Place de la Fontaine   Cl. Wed, 15/11-15/12   All CC.*

A very popular and well-known hotel and restaurant. It has only five rooms so booking is imperative. Christian and Ingrid Soehlke do a really good job here and especially in maintaining the atmosphere of this 18th-century building

The rooms might be better described as apartments and are completely equipped with TV, kitchen, dining area and air-conditioning.

At 700f a room they are a little expensive but there is no question that they are value for money, as they offer so much more than the usual hotel room.

The two delightful dining rooms are on the first floor and you can dine by candlelight, enjoying the food that is dictated by the best products that the local market has to offer that day. Game is always offered when in season. A meal will cost 200f per person up.

➤ La Maison des Volets Bleus
(C)L   *90 66 03 04   Cl. 12/11-14.3.*

It is a very rare occasion when it is possible to recommend a chambre d'hôte as being in the same quality and value category as a 700f-a-night hotel but this is the case with the aptly-named Maison des Volets Bleus – and even then it is no reflection on the other establishment. La Maison is right in the heart of the old town and was once just another house. It has been transformed by Martine Maret and her husband and now Martine runs it with efficiency, style and careful attention to her guests' needs.

There are six rooms and all are different and beautifully furnished.

All have TV and bathroom. It is not only like being in a home – it is a home. Prices are 260-330f a room including breakfast.

If desired (and I strongly suggest that you should desire), you can take dinner, which is served at 8.00. The charge is 100f per person and the produce and the cooking are Provençal. Lamb and trout are two of the carefully prepared and extremely tasty specialities of the region.

Martine speaks English. Parking is not immediate but there are several spots in the village only a couple of minutes away.

Arrowed for comfort, value and good cooking.

Hôtel des Remparts
(HR)H-S, R-S-M   *90 66 02 79   Cl. Wed o.o.s.; 1/1-8/3; 2/11-31/12   All CC.*

On Rue Haute in the old village, this hotel is literally chopped out of the massive ramparts. There are only five rooms separate from the main building. They are furnished a bit spartan but are clean and neat and all have showers; so, all in all, 195f is a fair price.

The terrace restaurant is very popular with visitors and locals alike and can seat nearly a hundred so you can tell that this is really a restaurant with rooms. Menus are 80, 100, 145 and 205f which caters to a range of appetites and wallets. Provençal cooking is featured and I can recommend the filets de rougets on the four-course 145f menu as being copious and succulent.

Parking is about 100 metres away by the huge walls.

Map 3C   **VENTABREN** 13122 (Bouches-du-Rhône) 12 km W of Aix-en-Provence

---

Most people visit Ventabren to see the Aqueduct of Roquefavour which is two kilometres south of the village. You might think it is Roman but it was in fact built in 1842 for the purpose of bringing water from the Durance river to Marseille. It is a really impressive structure, 1,250 feet long and 280 feet high. It is in three stages with twelve arches forming the base and fifteen arcades the upper section.

The village of Ventabren takes its name, which was formerly 'Vente-Bien', from its exposed position which makes it particularly susceptible to the winds. Its inhabitants insist that because of the winds, Ventabren has never been afflicted by the plague. Additional protection has come from the little chapel of Saint Honorat de Roquefavour, a Romanesque building once a hermitage but restored in the 19th century. The relics you will see around the entrance were deposited there to give thanks when the plague was decimating neighbouring villages but leaving Ventabren unscathed.

No less than three ruined castles are around the village – Château Blanc to the north-east, Château Noir to the south-east and the château of Reine Jeanne.

Festivals

There is a big sale of bric-à-brac in June and the Fête of Saint Jean during the same month. The Fête of Saint Denis is in October.

Hôtel Arquier
(HR)S-M   *42 24 20 45   Cl. Sun p.m.; Mon; Feb   Visa, CB.*

The massive aqueduct looms above the hotel which sits on a river
bank in woody land. The red and white awnings and the red-tiled roof
make it stand out against the stark stonework. The 16 rooms are quiet
and very cosy, at 140-300f. There is private parking.

You can fish in the river but you will probably settle for your fish
from a different source. The restaurant serves an exceptional
mousseline de brochet and the preparation of coquilles Saint Jacques
is unusual. Menus are 150, 200 and 270f.

Moulin de Roquefavour
(HR)S   *42 24 21 91   Route de la Fare les Oliviers   Open every day   All CC.*

Nearer to Ventabren than Roquefavour, this really was a mill in the
18th century and has been nicely converted, maintaining the rustic
atmosphere. It is on the river bank and you can fish.

There are only six rooms and only 180f. Menus are 80, 100, 145 and
195f and local fare features strongly.

André and Paulette Davin
(C)M   *42 28 84 56   Amound'Aut Les Béreoudes   Open all year.*

Continuing with good quality, low-priced accommodation in the
Ventabren area, the Davins have a very recommendable chambre
d'hôte. It is a very attractive Provence-style house with sloping red-tile
roofs and stands alone in a thick pine forest where peace and quiet are
guaranteed. There are two double rooms priced at 195f. They share a
toilet. You can use the living room of the Davins (it has a TV). There is
a terrace and with all those pine trees it is shaded all around the
house.

Map 3B   VIENS 84750 (Vaucluse) 14 km E of Apt

This small and quiet village was once teeming with prehistoric
monsters. Remains have been found of more than 200 species from
giant rhinoceros and pterodactyls to monster bears and colossal
turtles.

Viens was one of the areas in Provence where the Saracens
established themselves. Their motive was to mine the high-grade iron
ore for the manufacture of swords and daggers while the waterfalls
feeding the Calavon river provided the power for their water-wheels.

Today it has little commerce and few tourists although its ancient,
narrow streets are typical of more developed perched villages. The old
church has a lavoir (for washing clothes) on one side and a massive
fortified tower built into it on the other.

Le Petit Jardin
(R)S-M   *90 75 20 05   Rue du Faubourg   Cl. Mon   All CC.*

Muguette and René Bride have made a very popular little restaurant here opposite the church and seating is now increased to over 100 with a very nice garden and terrace. There is one menu at 125f which might start with feuilleté forestière then the excellent blanquette de veau grand-mère and cheese and dessert.

Marc Rose
(C)   *90 75 27 83   Rue du Ravelin   Cl. Jan and Feb and Xmas.*

In an area where only small villages are to be found, M. Rose's chambre d'hôte can be a welcome sight as it's a long way to the nearest hotel. Simple is the keyword but that keeps the prices down and 136f is hard to beat. There are four rooms. Two have a wash-basin only with a toilet common to all rooms. One has a wash-basin and shower and the other has a shower and a bath. There is a large lounge which goes out on to a terrace. Meals are 60-120f.

Map 2B   VIOLES 84150 (Vaucluse) 25 km N of Avignon

 Wed

Surrounded by vineyards, Violes has little to offer other than wine. But then what else does it need?

Violes may be almost unique in not having a Co-operative Vinicole. Asked why, the locals shrug. Why do they need one? they reply, but the truer answer would seem to be that these are all family vineyards which have been handed down through many generations and there is a lot of jealousy and fierce competition between them. A co-operative would mean the risk that many of the tricks of the trade might leak out.

So you can enjoy yourself wine-tasting but you will have to go to each of the vineyards – not that it means much travelling for they are all grouped around the village. The names to look for include:

Domaine des Richards	Vignoble de la Tuilerie
Vignoble Merlot	Domaine de la Damase
Lou Moulin d'Oli	Domaine de Maguelone
Domaine du Martinet	Domaine de l'Espigouette
Vignoble Gleize	Château Malijay

Festivals

Every year on July 1st, Violes puts on a wine festival. After a Provence mass, the priest blesses a wine bottle which is paraded through the streets with all the reverence that other parades bestow on a sacred statue. There is an honour guard of mounted men and songs and dances by Provence folk-lore groups. Free tasting of the wines is, of course, an integral part of the ceremony.

This is the kind of area that people like to stay in after a day's sampling and there is a good choice.

Mas de Bouvau
(HR)S-M   *90 70 94 08   Cl. Mon all year; Sun in season; plus R only – Dec 20-30 and Aug 24-Sept 8   Visa, CB.*

Really a restaurant with rooms which often means good value in both. The five rooms all have TV and the garden is pleasant. Room prices are 260-330f with parking.

The restaurant specialises in dishes cooked in local wines which is not surprising. Lapin aux Côtes du Rhône and foie gras de canard au Beaumes de Venise are two of these and the pricing is not unreasonable – 110f for the menu.

Château le Martinet
(HR)S-M   *90 70 94 98   Cl. Wed o.o.s.   Visa, CB.*

Also a restaurant with rooms – eight in this case. They are all well-equipped. The park-like surroundings are peaceful with a pool and an enclosed area for children. Rooms are 200-400f.

There is a large terrace and a garden for outdoor dining and menus start at 105f. You can spend more but you will find you don't need to – the beef cooked in Gigondas wine is delicious and the quail with shrimps equally good. Other dishes including salmon cooked in champagne may cost a little more but you will eat very well here.

Roland Gourjon
(C)   *90 70 92 40   Cl. Nov through Feb   No CC.*

Completing a range of places to stay in Violes, this chambre d'hôte is deservedly popular. It is on the edge of the village and has been built out of an old farm-house. There is a large lounge and a living room, parking, television and a garden.

The five rooms all have access to bathrooms and toilets. They are priced at 130-150f.

Map 2B   **VISAN** 84820 (Vaucluse) 9 km S of Valréas, 26 km N of Orange

 Fri

There is really only one time of year to be in Visan and that is around Bastille Day, 14 July. One of the great ceremonies of the wine country takes place when the procession leaves from the Cave Co-operative and heads for the Chapel of Notre Dame des Vignes in the heart of the vineyards.

The procession consists of members of the Confrerie of St Vincent, a wine brotherhood dating back to 1475 and which is remarkable today in that it extends an equal welcome to women as well as men. At the head are the 'king', the 'queen' and the 'lieutenant at arms'.

They and the members following wear elaborate uniforms of black, white and red, carry banners and one member holds high a vine stock. Trumpets play as they all march to the chapel.

A Provençal mass is said and the priest blesses the vine stock to assure a good vintage the next year. The procession returns to the village where the girls burn the vine stock in the middle of the square. New members are initiated into the confraternity then everyone goes to a great champagne feast accompanied by folk singing and dancing. A set number of thousands of bottles of wine are put into the cellars and an equal number are taken out for consumption.

Many Provençal villages have wine festivals accompanied by parades but the one here in Visan has an authenticity about it which has clear roots in mediaeval days when man, the vine and nature were in very close harmony. The pageantry in Visan has obvious purpose and meaning and is not just pomp. Wine is not just a beverage but a vital element of the soil and life.

The rest of the year, Visan does not offer the visitor very much, although there is the almost inevitable 12th-century castle, now in ruins, on top of the hill.

Hôtel du Midi
(HR)S   *90 41 90 05   Avenue des Alliés   Cl. Sun o.o.s. plus all Jan and Feb All CC.*

This is a tried and trusted establishment, really a restaurant with rooms and in the village. There are eight rooms, 125-200f, nothing fancy but nice and cosy.

Almost 200 people fill the restaurant in summer with the terrace and the garden being the first choices for seating. Menus are from 59-150f and the cooking is hearty Provençal with the sauté de veau Provençal being popular. A few variations such as poulet à l'espagnol turn up on the menu from time to time, depending on what comes from the local market. The local Côtes du Rhône wines are inexpensive.

Les Troubadours
(R)S-M   *90 41 92 55   Cl. Mon; Tues; also beginning Nov to end March and always the last week in September   All CC.*

Located right at the top of the village and near the château ruins. It's a strange building and all credit due to the Lyonnaise couple who have developed it into a popular restaurant.

The cooking is naturally Lyonnaise with some delicous dishes including pigeon with Roquefort cheese and rabbit braised in sauce, butter, eggs and cream.

Menus are 120, 180 and 230f and an enjoyable meal is certain.

Wines and spirits by John Doxat

Bonne cuisine et bons vins, c'est le paradis sur terre.
(Good cooking and good wines, that is earthly paradise.)

King Henri IV

OUTLINE OF FRENCH WINE REGIONS

Bordeaux

Divided into a score of districts, and sub-divided into very
many *communes* (parishes). The big district names are
Médoc, St Emilion, Pomerol, Graves and Sauternes. Prices
for the great reds (châteaux Pétrus, Mouton-Rothschild,
etc.) or the finest sweet whites (especially the miraculous
Yquem) have become stratospheric. Yet château in itself
means little and the classification of various rankings of
châteaux is not easily understood. Some tiny vineyards
are entitled to be called château, which has led to disputes
about what have been dubbed 'phantom châteaux'.
Visitors are advised, unless wine-wise, to stick to the
simpler designations.

Bourgogne (Burgundy)

Topographically a large region, stretching from Chablis
(on the east end of the Loire), noted for its steely dry
whites, to Lyons. It is particularly associated with fairly
powerful red wines and very dry whites, which tend to
acidity except for the costlier styles. Almost to Bordeaux
excesses, the prices for really top Burgundies have gone
through the roof. For value, stick to simpler local wines.

Technically Burgundies, but often separately listed, are
the Beaujolais wines. The young red Beaujolais (not
necessarily the over-publicised *nouveau*) are delicious,
mildly chilled. There are several rather neglected
Beaujolais wines (Moulin-à-Vent, Morgon, St Amour, for
instance) that improve for several years: they represent
good value as a rule. The Maçonnais and Chalonnais also
produce sound Burgundies (red and white) that are usually
priced within reason.

Rhône

Continuation south of Burgundy. The Rhône is particularly
associated with very robust reds, notably Châteauneuf-du-
Pape; also Tavel, to my mind the finest of all still *rosé*

wines. Lirac *rosé* is nearly as good. Hermitage and Gigondas are names to respect for reds, whites and *rosés*. Rhône has well earned its modern reputation – no longer Burgundy's poorer brother. From the extreme south comes the newly 'smart' dessert *vin doux naturel*, ultra-sweet Muscat des Beaumes-de-Venise, once despised by British wine-drinkers. There are fashions in wine just like anything else.

Alsace
Producer of attractive, light white wines, mostly medium-dry, widely used as carafe wines in middle-range French restaurants. Alsace wines are not greatly appreciated overseas and thus remain comparatively inexpensive for their quality; they are well placed to compete with popular German varieties. Alsace wines are designated by grape – principally Sylvaner for lightest styles, the widespread and reliable Riesling for a large part of the total, and Gerwürtztraminer for slightly fruitier wines.

Loire
Prolific producer of very reliable, if rarely great, white wines, notably Muscadet, Sancerre, Anjou (its *rosé* is famous), Vouvray (sparkling and semi-sparkling), and Saumur (particularly its 'champagne styles'). Touraine makes excellent whites and also reds of some distinction Bourgueil and Chinon. It used to be widely believed – a rumour put out by rivals? – that Loire wines 'did not travel': nonsense. They are a successful export.

Champagne
So important is Champagne that, alone of French wines, it carries no AC: its name is sufficient guarantee. (It shares this distinction with the brandies Cognac and Armagnac.) Vintage Champagnes from the *grandes marques* – a limited number of 'great brands' – tend to be as expensive in France as in Britain. You can find unknown brands of high quality (often off-shoots of *grandes marques*) at attractive prices, especially in the Champagne country itself. However, you need information to discover these, and there are true Champagnes for the home market that are *doux* (sweet) or *demi-sec* (medium sweet) that are pleasing to few non-French tastes. Champagne is very closely controlled as to region, quantities, grape types, and is made only by secondary fermentation in the bottle. From 1993, it is prohibited (under EEC law) to state that other wines are made by the 'champagne method' – even if they are.

Minor regions, very briefly

Jura – Virtually unknown outside France. Try local speciality wines such as *vin jaune* if in the region.

Jurançon – Remote area; sound, unimportant white wines, sweet styles being, the better.

Cahors – Noted for its powerful *vin de pays* 'black wine', darkest red made.

Gaillac – Little known; once celebrated for dessert wines.

Savoy – Good enough table wines for local consumption. Best product of the region is delicious Chambéry vermouth: as an aperitif, do try the well distributed Chambéryzette, a unique vermouth with a hint of wild strawberries.

Bergerac – Attractive basic reds; also sweet Monbazillac, relished in France but not easily obtained outside: aged examples can be superb.

Provence – Large wine region of immense antiquity. Many and varied *vins de pays* of little distinction, usually on the sweet side, inexpensive and totally drinkable.

Midi – Stretches from Marseilles to the Spanish border. Outstandingly prolific contributor to the 'EEC wine lake' and producer of some 80 per cent of French *vins de table*, white and red. Sweet whites dominate, and there is major production of *vins doux naturels* (fortified sugary wines).

Corsica – Roughish wines of more antiquity than breeding, but by all means drink local reds – and try the wine-based aperitif Cap Corse – if visiting this remarkable island.

Paris – Yes, there is a vineyard – in Montmartre! Don't ask for a bottle: the tiny production is sold by auction, for charity, to rich collectors of curiosities.

HINTS ON SPIRITS

The great French spirit is brandy. Cognac, commercially the leader, must come from the closely controlled region of that name. Of various quality designations, the commonest is VSOP (very special old pale): it will be a cognac worth drinking neat. Remember, *champagne* in a cognac connotation has absolutely no connection with the wine. It is a topographical term, *grande champagne* being the most prestigious cognac area: *fine champagne* is a blend of brandy from the two top cognac sub-divisions.

Armagnac has become better known lately outside

France, and rightly so. As a brandy it has a much longer history than cognac: some connoisseurs rate old armagnac (the quality designations are roughly similar) above cognac.

Be cautious of French brandy without a cognac or armagnac title, regardless of how many meaningless 'stars' the label carries or even the magic word 'Napoleon' (which has no legal significance).

Little appreciated in Britain is the splendid 'apple brandy', Calvados, mainly associated with Normandy but also made in Brittany and the Marne. The best is *Calvados du Pays d'Auge*. Do taste well-aged Calvados, but avoid any suspiciously cheap.

Contrary to popular belief, true Calvados is not distilled from cider – but an inferior imitation is: French cider (cidre) is excellent.

Though most French proprietary aperitifs, like Dubonnet, are fairly low in alcohol, the extremely popular Pernod/Ricard *pastis*-style brands are highly spirituous. *Eau-de-vie* is the generic term for all spirits, but colloquially tends to refer to local, often rough, distillates. Exceptions are the better *alcools blancs* (white spirits), which are not inexpensive, made from fresh fruits and not sweetened as *crèmes* are.

Bringing Back Those Bottles

When thinking of what to bring back from France in the way of alcoholic beverages, apart from considerations of weight and bulk conditioned by your mode of travel, there are a few other matters to bear in mind. Within the theoretically unlimited import for personal consumption of products which have paid any national taxes in the country of origin ('duty free' is a separate subject), there are manifest practical as well as some semi-official restrictions.

In wine to choose sensibly is not inevitably to go for the least expensive. Unless you envisage having to entertain a lot of relatives, beware the very cheapest of French table wines! Though France produces many of the world's greatest, her prolific vineyards also make wines to which no British supermarket would allocate shelf-space. Quality does count along with value. Primarily what you are saving by purchasing in France is the comparatively high excise duties imposed in Britain against the minimal ones in France. However, the British tax is just the same on a bottle of the most ordinary *vin ordinaire* as on the rarest of vintage claret. When it comes to the latter, buying fine vintage wines in France does not automatically mean obtaining a bargain, unless you are an expert. There are not that many specialist wine merchants in France, a commerce in which Britain excels.

To summarise: it is undoubtedly sound, middle range wines that are the most sensible buy.

If you like those famous liqueurs, such as Bénédictine, Chartreuse, the versatile Cointreau, which are so expensive in Britain, shop around for them: prices seem to vary markedly.

I have briefly dealt elsewhere with French spirits. If you are buying Scotch whisky, gin or vodka, you may find unfamiliar names and labels offering apparent bargains. None will harm you but some may have low, even unpleasant, taste characteristics. It is worth paying a trifle more for well-known brands, especially de-luxe styles. Though they are little sold in Britain, former French colonies distill several excellent types of rum (*rhum*).

I deem it a good idea to make an outline list of intended purchases, after deciding what you can carry and how. much you wish to spend. As to wines, do you want mainly red, or only white, or what proportion of both types? Can you afford champagne? Best to buy that in visiting the region where you should have the opportunity to taste and possibly find a bargain. What about other sparklers? What do you require in dessert wines, vermouths, liqueurs, spirits? Does your list work out at more cases (12 bottles) than you can easily transport? A conspicuously overloaded vehicle may be stopped by police as a traffic hazard. Now you have a list of sorts. What about cost? For essential comparisons, I would put against each item the maximum (per bottle) I would be prepared to pay in Britain. Certainly carry a pocket calculator so, as you examine potential purchases, you can easily work out what you are saving.

Condensed glossary
of French wine and ancillary terms

Alsace – See Wine Regions.

Abricotine – Generic apricot liqueur: look for known brands.

Alcool blanc – Spirit distilled from various fruits (not wine); not fruit-flavoured cordials.

Aligoté – Light dry Burgundy.

Anis – Aniseed, much flavoured in Pernod-type aperitifs.

Anjou – See Loire (Wine Regions).

Aperitif – Literally 'opener': any drink taken as an appetiser.

Appellation (d'origine) Contrôlée – or A.C. See Introduction to French wines.

Armagnac – See Hints on Spirits.

Barsac – Very sweet Sauternes of varying quality.

Basserau – A bit of an oddity: sparkling red Burgundy.

Beaumes-de-Venise – Well-known *vin doux naturel*; see Provence (Minor Regions).

Beaune – Famed red Burgundy; costly.

Bergerac – Sound red wine from south-west France.

Blanc de Blancs – White wine from white grapes alone. Sometimes confers extra quality but by no means always. White wine made from black grapes (the skins removed before fermentation) is *Blanc de Noirs* – Carries no special quality connotation in itself.

Bordeaux – See Wine Regions.

Bourgeuil – Reliable red Loire wine.

Bourgogne – Burgundy; see Wine Regions.

Brut – Very dry; description particularly applicable to best sparkling wines.

Brut Sauvage – Dry to the point of displeasing acidness to most palates; very rare though a few good wines carry the description.

Cabernet – Noble grape, especially Cabernet-Sauvignon for excellent, if not absolutely top grade, red wines.

Cacao – Cocoa; basis of a popular *crème*.

Calvados – See Hints on Spirits.

Cassis – Blackcurrant; notably in *crème de cassis* (see Kir).

Cave – Cellar.

Cépage – Indicates grape variety; e.g. *Cépage* Cabernet-Sauvignon.

Chablis – See Burgundy (Wine Regions). Fine Chablis are expensive.

Chai – Ground-level storehouse, wholly employed in Cognac and sometimes in Bordeaux and other districts.

Champagne – See Wine Regions. Also specially note *Méthode Traditionelle* below.

Château(x) – See Introduction to French wines (Bordeaux).

Châteaneuf-du-Pape – Best known of powerful Rhône red wines.

Chenin-blanc – Grape variety associated with many fine Loire wines.

Clairet – Unimportant Bordeaux wine, its distinction being probable origin of English word Claret.

Clos – Mainly a Burgundian term for vineyard formerly (rarely now) enclosed by a wall.

Cognac – See Hints on Spirits.

Corbières – Usually a sound south of France red wine.

Côte – Indicates vineyard on a hillside; no quality connotation necessarily.

Côteau(x) – Much the same as above.

Crème – Many sweet, sometimes sickly, mildly alcoholic cordials with many local specialities. Nearer to true liqueurs are top makes of *crème de menthe* and *crème de Grand Marnier* (q.v.). See also Cassis.

Crémant – Sparkling wine with strong but rather brief effervescence.

Cru – Literally 'growth'; somewhat complicated and occasionally misleading term: e.g. *grand cru* may be only grower's estimation; *cru classé* just means the wine is officially recognised, but *grand cru classé* is most likely to be something special.

Cuve close – Literally 'sealed vat'. Describes production of sparkling wines by bulk as opposed to individual bottle fermentation. Can produce satisfactory wines and certainly much superior to cheap carbonated styles.

Cuvée – Should mean unblended wine from single vat, but *cuvée spéciale* may not be particularly special: only taste will tell.

Demi-sec – Linguistically misleading, as it does not mean 'half-dry' but 'medium sweet'.

Domaine – Broadly, Burgundian equivalent to Bordeaux *château*.

Doux – Very sweet.

Eau-de-vie – Generic term for all distilled spirits but usually only applied in practice to roughish *marc* (q.v.) and the like.

Entre-deux-Mers – Undistinguished but fairly popular white Bordeaux.

Frappé – Drink served with crushed ice; viz. *crème de menthe frappé*.

Fleurie – One of several superior Beaujolais wines.

Glacé – Drink chilled by immersion of bottle in ice or in refrigerator, as distinct from *frappé* above.

Goût – Taste; also colloquial term in some regions for local *eau-de-vie* (q.v.).

Grand Marnier – Distinguished orange-flavoured liqueur. See also *crème*.

Haut – 'High'. It indicates upper part of wine district, not necessarily the best, though Haut-Médoc produces much better wines than other areas.

Hermitage – Several excellent Rhône red wines carry this title.

Izarra – Ancient Armagnac-based liqueur much favoured by its Basque originators.

Juliénas – Notable Beaujolais wine.

Kir – Well-chilled dry white wine (should be *Bourgogne Aligoté*) plus teaspoon of *crème de cassis* (q.v.). Made with champagne (or good dry sparkling wine) it is Kir Royale.

Liqueur – From old *liqueur de dessert*, denoting post-prandial digestive. Always very sweet. 'Liqueur' has become misused as indication of superior quality: to speak of 'liqueur cognac' is contradictory – yet some very fine true liqueurs are based on cognac!

Litre – 1.7 pints; 5 litres equals 1.1 gallons.

Loire – See Wine Regions.

Méthode Traditionelle – Most widely used description of superior sparkling wine made as is champagne, by fermentation in bottle, now that any labelling association such as 'champagne method' is banned.

Marc – Mostly coarse distillations from wine residue with strong local popularity. A few *marcs* ('mar') – *de Champagne*, *de Bourgogne* especially – have achieved a certain cult status.

Marque – Brand or company name.

Meurseult – Splendid white Burgundy for those who can afford it.

Minervoise – Respectable southern red wine: can be good value as are many such.

Mise – As in *mise en bouteilles au château* ('château-bottled', or ... *dans nos caves* ('in our cellars') and variations.

Montrachet – Very fine white Burgundy.

Moulin-à-Vent – One of the rather special Beaujolais wines.

Muscadet – Arguably the most popular light dry Loire white wines.

Muscat – Though used for some dry whites, this grape is mainly associated with succulent dessert-style wines.

Nouveau – New wine, for drinking fresh; particularly associated with now tiring vogue for *Beaujolais Nouveau*.

Pastis – General term for powerful anis/liquorice aperitifs originally evolved to replace banned *absinthe* and particularly associated with Marseilles area through great firm of Ricard.

Pétillant – Gently, naturally effervescent.

Pineau – Unfermented grape juice lightly fortified with grape spirit; attractive aperitif widely made in France and under-appreciated abroad.

Pouilly-Fuissé – Dry white Burgundy (Macon); sometimes over-valued.

Pouilly-Fumé – Easily confused with above; a very dry fine Loire white.

Porto – Port wine: usually lighter in France than the type preferred in Britain and popular, chilled, as an aperitif.

Primeur – More or less the same as *nouveau*, but more often used for fine vintage wine sold *en primeur* for laying down to mature.

Rosé – 'Pink wine', best made by allowing temporary contact of juice and black grapes during fermentation; also by mixing red and white wine.

Sauvignon – Notable white grape; see also *Cabernet*.

Sec – 'Dry', but a wine so marked will be sweetish, even very sweet. *Extra Sec* may actually mean on the dry side.

Sirop – Syrup; e.g. sugar-syrup used in mixed drinks, also some flavoured proprietory non-alcoholic cordials.

Supérieur(e) – Much the same as *Haut* (q.v.) except in VDQS. See Introduction.

VQRPD. – See Introduction to French wines.

Vin de Xeres – Sherry ('vin de 'ereth').

Glossary of cooking terms and dishes

(It would take another book to list comprehensively French cooking terms and dishes, but here are the ones most likely to be encountered.)

Aigre-doux	bittersweet
Aiguillette	thin slice (*aiguille* – needle)
Aile	wing
Aiolli	garlic mayonnaise
Allemande (à l')	German style, i.e.: with sausages and sauerkraut
Amuse-gueules	appetisers
Anglaise (à l')	plain boiled. *Crème Anglaise* – egg and cream sauce
Andouille	large uncooked sausage, served cold after boiling
Andouillettes	ditto but made from smaller intestines, usually served hot after grilling
Anis	aniseed
Argenteuil	with asparagus
Assiette Anglaise	plate of cold meats
Baba au rhum	yeast-based sponge macerated in rum
Baguette	long, thin loaf
Ballotine	boned, stuffed and rolled meat or poultry, usually cold
Béarnaise	sauce made from egg yolks, butter, tarragon, wine, shallots
Beurre blanc	sauce from Nantes, with butter, reduction of shallot-flavoured vinegar or wine
Béchamel	white sauce flavoured with infusion of herbs
Beignets	fritters
Bercy	sauce with white wine and shallots
Beurre noir	browned butter
Bigarade	with oranges
Billy By	mussel soup
Bisque	creamy shellfish soup
Blanquette	stew with thick, white creamy sauce, usually veal
Boeuf à la mode	braised beef
Bombe	ice-cream mould
Bonne femme	with root vegetables
Bordelais	Bordeaux-style, with red or white wine, marrowbone fat
Bouchée	mouthful, e.g. vol-au-vent
Boudin	sausage, white or black
Bourride	thick fish-soup
Braisé	braised

Brandade (de morue	dried salt-cod pounded into a mousse
Broche	spit
Brochette	skewer
Brouillade	stew, using oil
Brouillé	scrambled
Brûlé	burnt, e.g. *crème brûlée*
Campagne	country style
Cannelle	cinnamon
Carbonnade	braised in beer
Cardinal	red-coloured sauce, e.g. with lobster, or in *pâtisserie* with redcurrant
Cassolette or *cassoulette*	small pan
Cassoulet	rich stew with goose, pork and haricot beans
Cervelas	pork garlic sausage
Cervelles	brains
Chantilly	whipped sweetened cream
Charcuterie	cold pork-butcher's meats
Charlotte	mould, as dessert lined with sponge-fingers, as savoury lined with vegetable
Chasseur	with mushrooms, shallots, wine
Chausson	pastry turnover
Chemise	covering, i.e. pastry
Chiffonade	thinly-cut, e.g. lettuce
Choron	tomato Béarnaise
Choucroute	Alsatian stew with sauerkraut and sausages
Civet	stew
Clafoutis	batter dessert, usually with cherries
Clamart	with peas
Cocotte	covered casserole
Cocque (à la)	e.g. *oeufs* – boiled eggs
Compôte	cooked fruit
Concassé	e.g. *tomates concassées* – skinned, chopped, juice extracted
Confit	preserved
Confiture	jam
Consommé	clear soup
Cou	neck
Coulis	juice, purée (of vegetables or fruit)

Court-bouillon	aromatic liquor for cooking meat, fish, vegetables	Galette	Breton pancake, flat cake
Couscous	N. African dish with millet, chicken, vegetable variations	Garbure	thick country soup
		Garni	garnished, usually with vegetables
Crapaudine	involving fowl, particularly pigeon, trussed	Gaufre	waffle
Crécy	with carrots	Gelée	aspic
Crème pâtissière	thick custard filling	Gésier	gizzard
		Gibier	game
		Gigot	leg
Crêpe	pancake	Glacé	iced
Crépinette	little flat sausage, encased in caul	Gougère	choux pastry, large base
		Goujons	fried strips, usually of fish
Croque-Monsieur	toasted cheese-and-ham sandwich	Graine	seed
		Gratin	baked dish of vegetables cooked in cream and eggs
Croustade	pastry or baked bread shell		
Croûte	pastry crust	Gratinée	browned under grill
Croûton	cube of fried or toasted bread	Grecque (à la)	cold vegetables served in oil
Cru	raw	Grenadin	nugget of meat, usually of veal
Crudités	raw vegetables	Grenouilles	frogs; cuisses de grenouille – frogs' legs
Demi-glace	basic brown sauce	Grillé	grilled
Doria	with cucumber	Gros sel	coarse salt
Émincé	thinly sliced	Hachis	minced or chopped
Étuvé	stewed, e.g. vegetables in butter	Haricot	slow cooked stew
		Hochepot	hotpot
Entremets	sweets	Hollandaise	sauce with egg, butter, lemon
		Hongroise	Hungarian, i.e. spiced with paprika
Farci	stuffed		
Fines herbes	parsley, thyme, bayleaf	Hors-d'oeuvre	assorted starters
Feuilleté	leaves of flaky pastry	Huile	oil
Flamande	Flemish style, with beer		
Flambé	flamed in spirit	Île flottante	floating island – soft meringue on egg-custard sauce
Flamiche	flan		
Florentine	with spinach	Indienne	Indian, i.e. with hot spices
Flûte	thinnest bread loaf		
Foie gras	goose liver	Jambon	ham
Fondu	melted	Jardinière	from the garden, i.e. with vegetables
Fond (d'artichaut)	heart (of artichoke)		
		Jarret	shin, e.g. jarret de veau
Forestière	with mushrooms, bacon and potatoes	Julienne	matchstick vegetables
		Jus	natural juice
Four (au)	baked in the oven		
Fourré	stuffed, usually sweets	Lait	milk
Fricandeau	veal, usually topside	Langue	tongue
Frais, fraîche	fresh and cool	Lard	bacon
Frangipane	almond-cream pâtisserie	Longe	loin
Fricadelle	Swedish meat ball		
Fricassé	(usually of veal) in creamy sauce	Macédoine	diced fruits or vegetables
		Madeleine	small sponge cake
Frit	fried	Magret	breast (of duck)
Frites	chips	Maïs	sweetcorn
Friture	assorted small fish, fried in batter	Maître d'hôtel	sauce with butter, lemon, parsley
Froid	cold	Marchand de vin	sauce with red wine, shallots
Fumé	smoked		
		Marengo	sauce with tomatoes, olive oil white wine
Galantine	loaf-shaped chopped meat, fish or vegetable, set in natural jelly		

Marinière	seamens' style e.g. *moules marinière* (mussels in white wine)
Marmite	deep casserole
Matelote	fish stew, e.g. of eel
Médaillon	round slice
Melange	mixture
Meunière	sauce with butter, lemon
Miel	honey
Mille-feuille	flaky pastry, (lit. 1,000 leaves)
Mirepoix	cubed carrot, onion etc. used for sauces
Moëlle	beef marrow
Mornay	cheese sauce
Mouclade	mussel stew
Mousseline	Hollandaise sauce, lightened with egg whites
Moutarde	mustard
Nage (à la)	poached in flavoured liquor (fish)
Nature	plain
Navarin (d'agneau)	stew of lamb with spring vegetables
Noisette	nut-brown, burned butter
Noix de veau	nut (leg) of veal
Normande	Normandy style, i.e. with cream, apple, cider, Calvados
Nouilles	noodles
Onglet	beef cut from flank
Os	bone
Paillettes	straws (of pastry)
Panaché	mixed
Panade	flour crust
Papillote (en)	cooked in paper case
Parmentier	with potatoes
Pâté	paste, of meat or fish
Pâte	pastry
Pâté brisée	rich short-crust pastry
Pâtisserie	pastries
Paupiettes	paper-thinslice
Pavé	thick slice
Paysan	country style
Périgueux	with truffles
Persillade	chopped parsley and garlic topping
Petits fours	tiny cakes, sweetmeats
Petit pain	bread roll
Piperade	peppers, onions, tomatoes in scrambled egg
Poché	poached
Poêlé	fried
Poitrine	breast
Poivre	pepper
Pommade	paste
Potage	thick soup

Pot-au-four	broth with meat and vegetables
Potée	country soup with cabbage
Pralines	caramelised almonds
Primeurs	young veg
Printanier (printanière)	garnished with early vegetables
Profiteroles	choux paslry balls
Provençale	with garlic, tomatoes, olive oil, peppers
Pureé	mashed and sieved
Quenelle	pounded fish or meat bound with egg, poached
Queue	tail
Quiche	pastry flan, e.g. *quiche Lorraine* – egg, bacon, cream
Râble	saddle, e.g. *râble de lièvre*
Ragoût	stew
Ramequin	little pot
Râpé	grated
Ratatouille	Provençale stew of onions, garlic, peppers, tomatoes
Ravigote	highly seasoned white sauce
Rémoulade	mayonnaise with gherkins, capers, herbs and shallots
Rillettes	potted shredded meat, usually fat pork or goose
Riz	rice
Robert	sauce with mustard, vinegar, onion
Roquefort	ewe's milk blue cheese
Rossini	garnished with foie gras and truffle
Rôti	roast
Rouelle	nugget
Rouille	hot garlicky sauce for *soupe de poisson*
Roulade	roll
Roux	sauce base – flour and butter
Sabayon	sweet fluffy sauce, with eggs and wine
Safran	saffron
Sagou	sago
St-Germain	with peas
Salade niçoise	with tunny, anchovies, tomatoes, beans, black olives
Salé	salted
Salmis	dish of game or fowl, with red wine
Sang	blood
Santé	lit. healthy, i.e. with spinach and potato
Salpicon	meat, fowl, vegetables, chopped fine, bound with sauce and used as fillings

Saucisse	fresh sausage	*Thé*	tea
Saucisson	dried sausage	*Tiède*	luke warm
Sauté	cooked in fat in open pan	*Timbale*	steamed mould
Sauvage	wild	*Tisane*	infusion
Savarin	ring of yeast-sponge, soaked in syrup and liquor	*Tourte*	pie
		Tranche	thick slice
Sel	salt	*Truffes*	truffles
Selle	saddle	*Tuile*	tile, i.e. thin biscuit
Selon	according to, e.g. *selon grosseur* (according to size)	*Vacherin*	meringue confection
		Vallée d'Auge	with cream, apple, Calvados
Smitane	with sour cream, white wine, onion	*Vapeur (au)*	steamed
		Velouté	white sauce, bouillon-flavoured
Soissons	with dried white beans		
Sorbet	water ice	*Véronique*	with grapes
Soubise	with creamed onions	*Vert(e)*	green, e.g. *sauce verte*, with herbs
Soufflé	puffed, i.e. mixed with egg white and baked		
		Vessie	pig's bladder
Sucre	sugar (*sucré* – sugared)	*Vichysoise*	chilled creamy leek and potato soup
Suprême	fillet of poultry breast or fish		
		Vierge	prime olive oil
Tartare	raw minced beef, flavoured with onions etc. and bound with raw egg	*Vinaigre*	vinegar (lit. bitter wine)
		Vinaigrette	wine vinegar and oil dressing
		Volaille	poultry
Tartare (sauce)	mayonnaise with capers, herbs, onions	*Vol-au-vent*	puff-pastry case
Tarte Tatin	upside down apple pie	*Xérès*	sherry
Terrine	pottery dish/baked minced, chopped meat, veg., chicken, fish or fruit		
		Yaourt	yoghurt

FISH – Les Poissons, SHELLFISH – Les Coquillages

Alose	shad	*Daurade*	sea bream
Anchois	anchovy	*Écrevisse*	crayfish
Anguille	eel	*Éperlan*	smelt
Araignée de mer	spider crab	*Espadon*	swordfish
		Étrille	baby crab
Bar	sea bass	*Favouille*	spider crab
Barbue	brill	*Flétan*	halibut
Baudroie	monkfish, anglerfish	*Fruits de mer*	seafood
Belon	oyster – flat shelled	*Grondin*	red gurnet
Bigorneau	winkle	*Hareng*	herring
Blanchaille	whitebait	*Homard*	lobster
Brochet	pike	*Huître*	oyster
Cabillaud	cod	*Julienne*	ling
Calamar	squid	*Laitance*	soft herring-roe
Carpe	carp	*Lamproie*	lamprey
Carrelet	plaice	*Langouste*	spring lobster, or crawfish
Chapon de mer	scorpion fish	*Langoustine*	Dublin Bay prawn
Claire	oyster	*Lieu*	ling
Coquille St-Jacques	scallop	*Limand*	lemon sole
		Lotte de mer	monkfish
Crabe	crab	*Loup de mer*	sea bass
Crevette grise	shrimp	*Maquereau*	mackerel
Crevette rose	prawn	*Merlan*	whiting

Morue	salt cod		*St-Pierre*	John Dory
Moule	mussel		*Sandre*	zander
Mulet	grey mullet		*Saumon*	salmon
Ombre	grayling		*Saumonette*	rock salmon
Oursin	sea urchin		*Seiche*	squid
Palourde	clam		*Sole*	sole
Pétoncle	small scallop		*Soupion*	inkfish
Plie	plaice		*Thon*	tunny
Portugaise	oyster		*Tortue*	turtle
Poulpe	octopus		*Torteau*	large crab
Praire	oyster		*Truite*	trout
Raie	skate		*Turbot*	turbot
Rascasse	scorpion-fish		*Turbotin*	chicken turbot
Rouget	red mullet			

FRUITS – Les Fruits, VEGETABLES – Les Légumes, NUTS – Les Noix

HERBS – Les Herbes, SPICES – Les Épices

Ail	garlic		*Courgette*	courgette
Algue	seaweed		*Cresson*	watercress
Amande	almond		*Échalote*	shallot
Ananas	pineapple		*Endive*	chicory
Aneth	dill		*Épinard*	spinach
Abricot	apricot		*Escarole*	salad leaves
Arachide	peanut		*Estragon*	tarragon
Artichaut	globe artichoke		*Fenouil*	fennel
Asperge	asparagus		*Fève*	broad bean
Avocat	avocado		*Flageolet*	dried bean
Banane	banana		*Fraise*	strawberry
Basilic	basil		*Framboise*	raspberry
Betterave	beetroot		*Genièvre*	juniper
Blette	Swiss chard		*Gingembre*	ginger
Brugnon	nectarine		*Girofle*	clove
Cassis	blackcurrant		*Girolle*	edible fungus
Céléri	celery		*Grenade*	pomegranate
Céléri-rave	celeriac		*Griotte*	bitter red cherry
Cêpe	edible fungus		*Groseille*	gooseberry
Cerfeuil	chervil		*Groseille noire*	blackcurrant
Cerise	cherry		*Groseille rouge*	redcurrant
Champignon	mushroom		*Haricot*	dried white bean
Chanterelle	edible fungus		*Haricot vert*	French bean
Châtaigne	chestnut		*Laitue*	lettuce
Chicorée	endive		*Mandarine*	tangerine, mandarin
Chou	cabbage		*Mangetout*	sugar pea
Chou-fleur	cauliflower		*Marron*	chestnut
Choux de Bruxelles	Brussels sprouts		*Menthe*	mint
			Mirabelle	tiny gold plum
Ciboulette	chive		*Morille*	dark brown crinkly edioble fungus
Citron	lemon			
Citron vert	lime		*Mûre*	blackberry
Coing	quince		*Muscade*	nutmeg
Concombre	cucumber		*Myrtille*	bilberry, blueberry
Coriandre	coriander		*Navet*	turnip
Cornichon	gherkin		*Noisette*	hazelnut
Courge	pumpkin		*Oignon*	onion

Oseille	sorrel	Pomme	apple
Palmier	palm	Pomme de terre	potato
Pamplemousse	grapefruit	Prune	plum
Panais	parsnip	Pruneau	prune
Passe-Pierre	seaweed	Quetsch	small dark plum
Pastèque	water melon	Radis	radish
Peche	peach	Raifort	horseradish
Persil	parsley	Raisin	grape
Petit pois	pea	Reine Claude	greengage
Piment doux	sweet pepper	Romarin	rosemary
Pissenlit	dandelion	Safran	saffron
Pistache	pistachio	Salsifis	salsify
Pleurote	edible fungi	Thym	thyme
Poire	pear	Tilleul	lime blossom
Poireau	leek	Tomate	tomato
Poivre	pepper	Topinambour	Jerusalem artichoke
Poivron	green, red and yellow peppers	Truffe	truffle

MEAT – Les Viandes

Le Boeuf	Beef	Le Porc	Pork
Charolais	is the best	Jambon	ham
Chateaubriand	double fillet steak	Jambon cru	raw smoked ham
Contrefilet	sirloin	Porcelet	suckling pig
Entrecôte	rib steak		
Faux Filet	sirloin steak	Le Veau	Veal
Filet	fillet	Escalope	thin slice cut from fillet
L'Agneau	Lamb	Les Abats	Offal
Pré-Salé	is the best	Foie	liver
Carré	neck cutlets	Foie gras	goose liver
Côte	chump chop	Cervelles	brains
Epaule	shoulder	Langue	tongue
Gigot	leg	Ris	sweetbreads
		Rognons	kidneys
		Tripes	tripe

POULTRY – Volaille, GAME – Gibier

Abatis	giblets	Lièvre	hare
Bécasse	woodcock	Oie	goose
Bécassine	snipe	Perdreau	partridge
Caille	quail	Pigeon	pigeon
Canard	duck	Pintade	guineafowl
Caneton	duckling	Pluvier	plover
Chapon	capon	Poularde	chicken (boiling)
Chevreuil	roe deer	Poulet	chicken (roasting)
Dinde	young hen turkey	Poussin	spring chicken
Dindon	turkey	Sanglier	wild boar
Dindonneau	young turkey	Sarcelle	teal
Faisan	pheasant	Venaison	venison
Grive	thrush		